THE REFORM DECADE IN CHINA

THE REFORM DECADE IN CHINA

THE REFORM DECADE
IN CHINA

From Hope to Dismay

Edited by

MARTA DASSÙ and
TONY SAICH

KEGAN PAUL INTERNATIONAL
London and New York
IN ASSOCIATION WITH
CENTRO STUDI DI POLITICA
INTERNAZIONALE (CeSPI)
Rome

First published in 1992 by
Kegan Paul International Ltd
PO Box 256, London WC1B 3SW, England

Distributed by John Wiley & Sons Ltd
Southern Cross Trading Estate
1 Oldlands Way, Bognor Regis,
West Sussex, PO22 9SA, England

Routledge Chapman & Hall Inc
29 West 35th Street
New York, NY 10001, USA

© Centro Studi de Politica Internazionale 1992

Phototypeset by Intype, London
Printed in Great Britain by
TJ Press (Padstow) Ltd

British Library Cataloguing in Publication Data
The reform decade in China: from hope to dismay
1. China. Political events
I. Dassù, Marta II. Saich, Tony
951.058

ISBN 0–7103–0417–X

Library of Congress Cataloging-in-Publication Data
The Reform decade in China: from hope to dismay / edited by Marta
Dassù and Tony Saich.
240pp. 243cm.
Includes bibliographical reference and index.
ISBN 0–7103–417–X
1. China – Politics and government – 1976– I. Dassù, Marta.
II. Saich, Tony.
DS7798.26.R32 1990
951.05′7 – dc20   90–38456
CIP

CONTENTS

ACKNOWLEDGEMENTS

This book began with a discussion between Marta Dassù and Tony Saich, in Rome, over the possibility of producing the first book for the Italian public analysing the ten years of reform in the PRC. Realising that such a project did not exist in the English language, it was decided to publish the book simultaneously in both languages. That was the easy part. Next came the trials and tribulations of finding contributors who could bring the idea to fruition. We were particularly interested in putting together an international set of authors who would analyse the events of the last ten years in terms of the effects on her or his fields of expertise. We were very lucky that such a distinguished set of scholars agreed to participate in the project.

In addition, a number of individuals and organisations provided the necessary support to ensure that the project promoted by the Centre for International Politics (CeSPI), Rome, did not go off the rails.

Firstly, we would like to thank the University of Bologna, and in particular Professor Gianni Sofri, and the Feltrinelli Foundation, and in particular Francesca Gori, who co-sponsored with CeSPI a meeting entitled 'China Since Mao: From Reform to Tiananmen' held in Bologna in November 1989 at which the first drafts of the chapters were presented. Secondly, The Royal Institute of International Affairs, London, co-sponsored a second meeting in February 1990 at which some of the authors were able to discuss the chapters between themselves and a number of British China specialists. The organisation of these two meetings would not have been possible without the help of Vittoria Antonelli (CeSPI), Luisa Pece (Bologna), Marisa Di Gioia (Feltrinelli Foundation), and Gabrielle Galligan (RIIA).

However, the project still needed a publisher and here we were particularly lucky to be helped by Kegan Paul International. In particular, we would like to thank Kaori O'Connor and Peter Hopkins for their enthusiasm and help in guiding us through the publication process. Last but not least, we should thank the staff of CeSPI, and particularly Vittoria Antonelli. If not for their help, we would still be sticking pieces of paper together and trying to type chapters onto disks.

Marta Dassù,

Tony Saich

Rome
June 1990

NOTES ON CONTRIBUTORS

Marie-Claire Bergère is Professor at the National Institute for Oriental Languages and Civilisation (Paris) and Director of studies at the école des hautes études en sciences sociales. She is the author of many books and articles on modern China's development including *L'age d'Or de la bourgeoisie chinoise* and most recently *La République Populaire de Chine de 1949 à nos jours*.

Roberto Bertinelli is a China analyst for the *Banca Toscana*, Rome. He has written widely on Chinese economic legislation and development. His most recent publication is *Economia e Politica nella Cina Contemporanea*.

Yves Chevrier is the co-Director of the Centre Chine of the école des hautes études en sciences sociales, Paris. He is co-editor of *Dictionnaire Biografique du Mouvement Ouvrier Internationale – la Chine*. He researches the intellectual history of late Qing and early Republican China as well as the reforms and society of post-Mao China.

Marta Dassù is Director of the Centre for the Study of International Politics (CeSPI). A specialist in international relations, she is the editor of *La frontiera difficile. Evoluzione e prospettive delle relazioni tra URSS e Cina*.

Kathleen Hartford is an Associate Professor of political science at the University of Massachusetts in Boston and a Research Fellow at the Fairbank Center, Harvard University. Her manuscript *Dilemmas of Socialist Reform: Rural Development and Food Policy in China, 1978–1989* will be published by the Harvard Council on East Asian Studies.

Tony Saich is Professor with reference to contemporary Chinese politics and organisation at the Sinologisch Instituut, Leiden and a Senior Research Fellow at the International Institute of Social History, Amsterdam. Apart from publishing on contemporary China, he has published *The Origins of the First United Front in China: The Role of Sneevliet (Alias Maring)*.

Gerald Segal is a Research Fellow at the Royal Institute of International Affairs, London, Reader in International Relations at Bristol University, and editor of *The Pacific Review*. His most recent publication is *Rethinking the Pacific* and he is the editor of *Chinese Politics and Foreign Policy Reform* and co-editor with Akihiko Tanaka of *Chinese Reforms in Crisis*.

Su Shaozhi is a Visiting Research Fellow at the Bradley Institute for Democracy and Public Values, Milwaukee. He was until 1987 the Director of the Institute of Marxism-Leninism and Mao Zedong Thought, the Chinese Academy of Social Sciences. He is a researcher at the Academy and a Professor of its graduate school. A collection of his earlier essays has been published in *Democratization and Reform* and his most recent publication in English is *Understanding Democratic Reform in China*.

ABBREVIATIONS

ASEAN	Association of Southeast Asian Nations
CCP	Chinese Communist Party
FBIS	Foreign Broadcast Information Service
FDI	Foreign Direct Investment
FEA	Foreign Economic Affairs
JPRS	Joint Publications Research Service
MMT	Million Metric Tons
NEP	New Economic Policy
NPC	National People's Congress
NSC	National Security Council
PLA	People's Liberation Army
SEZ	Special Economic Zone
SWB:FE	Summary of World Broadcasts: the Far East
UPM	Unified Purchase and Marketing

Romanisation. The system of romanisation for Chinese characters used throughout this book is *Hanyu pinyin*.

1

INTRODUCTION

Marta Dassù

In May–June 1989, China experienced its most serious domestic crisis since 1976, the year of Mao Zedong's death. This crisis, which flared with the student demonstrations in Beijing and was apparently extinguished with the intervention of the army, caught many observers by surprise. Almost overnight, the image of Deng Xiaoping's China was turned upside down: from a leader in domestic reforms in the Communist world, to a stubborn opposer of the kind of liberalisation underway in the Soviet Union and of the democratic revolution in Eastern Europe; from a country finally open to the rest of the world, to a country once again turned in on itself; from a 'pragmatic' regime, to an ideological regime, the ultimate stronghold of Marxism–Leninism with its struggle against 'bourgeois liberalisation'.

The drastic and sudden change in the foreign perception of China was not only the result of the turnaround in 1989 and the temporary defeat of those in the CCP most determined to push ahead with the reform programme but also was due to errors in evaluating the developments of the previous ten years. These were often considered in an oversimplified manner: a typical example is the view held by some American observers of China as an almost 'capitalist' country, well on the way towards a market economy.

This is one of the reasons why the events of May–June 1989 spur the need for more serious thought about the period following Mao Zedong's death – a period that, especially since the end of 1978 (i.e., after the new economic policy was launched by the Third Plenum of the Eleventh Central Committee), can be defined as the 'decade of reforms'. As indicated by the title

1

of this book and as will be seen subsequently, the Chinese 'NEP' initially aroused great hopes and met with considerable success. But as of 1985, a series of setbacks frustrated initial expectations. Moreover, since the leadership centred around Deng Xiaoping had based its political legitimacy on promises of economic prosperity, the partial failure of the reforms coincided with a serious crisis of confidence in the CCP so clearly expressed in the Tiananmen protests. Thus, the May–June crisis cannot be considered as an isolated event, merely triggered by the open conflict between the students' requests and the rigidity of the regime. To understand its origins, a review of the economic and political choices pursued throughout the decade of reforms and their consequences for society, is required; this is the purpose of the chapters in this book.

1 What did the reforms entail and why did they partially fail?
Most recent studies agree on one point: the Chinese economic reforms – introduced in an experimental, piecemeal fashion lacking a consistent grand design – were aimed exclusively at furthering economic modernisation through the introduction of selected features of a market economy. Unlike Gorbachev's efforts in the Soviet Union, Deng Xiaoping's 'pragmatic' strategy never really aimed for political liberalisation, other than in so far as it was necessary for the construction of a 'socialist market economy'.

The achievements of the new Chinese economic policy, in particular the decollectivisation of agriculture, were very encouraging from 1979 to 1984, resulting in a remarkable increase in the growth rate of the Chinese economy and average per capita income. In fact, in the early stages, the economic reforms enjoyed widespread social consensus. However, in the mid-1980s a number of strong destabilising factors arose (spiralling inflation, increased unemployment, growing budget and trade deficits, etc.) that the Chinese leadership were unable to control. Political conflict within the party leadership concerning management of the reforms, opposition by the bureaucracy, the confusion between political and administrative powers, lack of a coherent strategy, and the social repercussions of the reforms: all these factors made consistent decision-making difficult. The

2

oscillations in the government position on price liberalisation in the second half of the 1980s are highly indicative.

The essays by Hartford and Chevrier accurately retrace the parabola of Chinese reforms in agriculture and industry. Both conclude that the new economic policy was already suffering from the effects of a structural crisis in the second half of the 1980s, manifested by a decline in the production of grain in the rural economy and by the loss of control over the economic cycle and the increase in inflationary pressures in the urban economy. Moreover, neither agricultural decollectivisation nor the first steps of industrial reform actually led to the establishment of a market economy, nor were the foundations for gradual modernisation laid. For example, in the mid-1980s the government substantially reduced its investments in agriculture, with the hope that these would be taken up by private and collective enterprise. However, such new investments were not forthcoming on anything like the scale imagined because of uncertainty about the future of the reforms. The outcome? A marked decline in the medium-term development prospects for Chinese agriculture. Thus, in the course of a decade, China came up against the typical difficulties of a 'halfway reform' bearing the combined defects of a centrally planned economy and a market economy.

The study of the social repercussions of the reform – conducted by the authors – makes the disequilibria and difficulties even more evident. In broad terms, the consensus that existed at the beginning of the 1980s gradually faded in the second half of the decade. The social groups that benefited from the reforms were later penalised by the austerity programme introduced in September 1988. Further, a segment of the population (in particular, the urban wage-earners) not only never enjoyed the benefits promised by the reform but later was stricken by inflation and unemployment. Similarly, in the countryside many, especially those in the poorly endowed regions, did not partake of the new found rural wealth.

The stalemate in economic policy eventually aggravated the divisions within the CCP leadership. As pointed out by Tony Saich in his essay, from 1988 onwards, the conflict within the top ranks of the party concerning management of the economy became more acute and public.

2   After having retraced the course of the economic reforms, the question remains *why* the post-Mao period gradually entered into a new political crisis culminating in the events of Tiananmen. Recent studies tend to give two different explanations. The first mainly attributes the crisis in 1989 to the contradiction between the rigidity of the political system and the rapid social and economic changes taking place in the country; in short, to the predictable failure of a strategy of economic modernisation in the absence of political reforms. Thus, China fell victim, with due specificities, to the same vicious cycle to which all attempts at reform undertaken by socialist countries from the 1950s onwards succumbed. In the case of China, this vicious circle is summed up by Tony Saich as follows: the inevitable conflict, in the absence of genuine political liberalisation, between the 'revolution from above' (the strategy of economic modernisation promoted by Deng Xiaoping) and the 'revolution from below', that is, the social pressure naturally produced by the economic reforms. This idea is partially shared by Yves Chevrier, who feels that Deng Xiaoping's crucial error was that he did not grasp the opportunity to introduce political reforms in either 1986–7 or 1989. Drawing the extreme political consequences of this kind of approach, the essay by Su Shaozhi, one of the best known Chinese Marxist intellectuals and a major supporter of democratic reform, emphasises that only the abolition of the CCP's political monopoly can pave the way for modern development in China.

The second explanation sees the difficulties with the economic reform and the crisis in Tiananmen as stemming from a situation more analogous to that of developing countries and, in any case, closer to the specific Chinese 'tradition', than that of Soviet-type Socialist regimes. This is the fundamental point made by Marie-Claire Bergère, who believes that the epilogue to the 'Chinese Spring' reveals a problem of lack of modernisation rather than one of lack of liberalisation. Ten years after the introduction of Deng Xiaoping's modernisation plans, typical elements of underdevelopment were still widespread: the lack of a modern state structure, of an autonomous society and of institutionalised dialogue between the state and society.

No definite answer to this debate on the linkage between political reform and economic reform, or in other words, between democracy and modernisation, has yet been found or is it likely to be found in the near future. It is one of the questions that divided the Chinese 'reformers' themselves, as indicated by the discussions in 1988–9 on 'neo-authoritarianism'. This theory posed the possibility (defended by the 'pragmatic' wing of the CCP but contested by the democratic intellectuals) of working towards an authoritarian modernisation of China, following the example of the newly industrialised countries in the Asian area of the Pacific.

The complexity of the Chinese situation is determined precisely by the existence of both dimensions: by the dilemmas generated by all attempts at reform in Socialist centrally planned economic systems (despite its specificities, even the Maoist system was largely based on the 'historical' Soviet model) and those typical of attempts at economic growth in developing countries that, like China, are still prevalently agricultural and heavily overpopulated. Thus, both explanations mentioned above are tenable and are supported by convincing arguments. One of the objectives of this book is to compare them and, in some way, to try to combine them, in the belief that a unidimensional answer would not have the same validity.

3   After the crisis in Tiananmen, China's political prospects are uncertain. The feeling of uncertainty about the future, which is at least partly prompted by the unsolved problem of the succession to Deng Xiaoping, also dominates the conclusions to this volume. As Marie-Claire Bergère writes, the chances that a democratic regime can emerge remain very low. But there are numerous alternatives: the restoration of the power of the party, warlordism, or liberalised Communism.

On the whole, the essays published tend towards pessimism, particularly the two essays on the economy. According to Kathleen Hartford, the austerity programme adopted in autumn 1988 in an attempt to curb inflation 'has had a deleterious impact on the wellbeing of rural society, in terms of employment, income and consumption'. Given the growing contradiction between the pressures arising from the agricultural reform and the interests of urban society, the Chinese Communist regime has once again decided – in keeping with an approach that has prevailed from the 1950s to the present – to give priority to the latter and, more generally, to the traditional industrial sectors. For example, the increase in food subsidies to urban consumers has, above all, penalised state investment in agriculture, while the credit squeeze has mainly affected the rural enterprises (more than the state-owned companies), thus accentuating the already serious problem of unemployment in the rural areas. Furthermore, the decision to impose new controls in the countryside (in an attempt to curb the decline in grain production) marks a turnaround in the approach underlying the reforms of the 1980s, and has drawn protest and opposition from the farmers. It is felt that the Communist regime may well find itself up against a 'crisis of legitimation' in rural China, that would potentially be much more serious than the urban crisis of 1988–9.

The prospects for the industrial economy are not much better notwithstanding the signals of recovery that emerged in late 1990. According to Chevrier, the austerity measures introduced in 1988 have produced an economic depression in 1989–90 that has not solved – only frozen – the existing structural economic disequilibria. With the accent back on central planning, the economy has moved from 'overheated' and uncontrolled growth to a temporary stagnation. But, given the loss of any real regulatory capacity by the state, it is likely that this period of adjustment will be supplanted (as occurred in 1980–1) by a new inflationary cycle. On the other hand, the fragmentation of economic controls and social disintegration will reinforce the ability to oppose central measures in defence of the economic reforms at the local and provincial levels. Furthermore, China will be forced to balance the costs of the domestic crisis with a policy of indebtedness on international financial markets. Essentially, the 'open door' policy of the last fifteen years will be confirmed and relaunched, albeit under less favourable political conditions.

Economic performance will not be the only factor in determining China's future; domestic political developments will have a decisive impact. In this light, the only definite implications of the 1989 crisis have been the temporary defeat of the 'reformist' wing of the CCP; the collapse in Deng Xiaoping's prestige and his ability to keep the leadership coalition formed at the end of the 1970s united; the recovery of the PLA's political weight, which had gradually diminished during the last decade; the accentuation of society's lack of confidence in the regime; and the growth of regionalism. However, insufficient information is available (on the scope of the new compromises in the CCP leadership, on the state of relations between the party and the army, on trends in society) to be able to see beyond the immediate succession struggle to what kind of a China will emerge. What seems obvious to the authors of this volume is that China is still in a transitory political phase tending towards instability and marked by paralysis of the political system. In this setting, the succession to Deng Xiaoping could act as a catalyst for a new internal crisis.

4 Domestic trends will also affect China's international role. However, as pointed out by Gerald Segal in his essay, the link between domestic choices and foreign policy – the most successful sector in the post-Mao period – is less rigid than commonly believed. Even at times of greatest preoccupation with internal affairs, China has maintained its international openness begun in the 1970s. This relative separation has been confirmed after the events in Tiananmen. In spite of new ideological attacks on 'foreign interference' (seen as one of the direct causes of the 1989 movement) and the greater restrictions on political and cultural contacts with the West, the Chinese Communist regime has clearly tried to safeguard foreign economic and trade relations. For their part, while Western countries soon abandoned the sanctions taken against Beijing in summer 1989, Asian countries, on the whole, did not significantly alter their relations with China. Detente with the Soviet Union has been consolidated, despite Chinese polemics about the international consequences of Gorbachev's 'new thinking' such as the 'counter-revolution' in Eastern Europe and the Soviet disengagement from old allies in the Third World. Essentially, China has managed, after the events in Tiananmen, to defend its major diplomatic success of the 1980s: the establishment of 'normal' and co-operative relations with both the United States and the USSR and the more advantageous and secure international position long aspired to by the Chinese leadership.

As Segal suggests, it is highly unlikely that any CCP faction considers relative international isolation as a feasible option for the country. It is, however, difficult to predict what kind of role China will play or be able to play in the international system. According to Segal, serious consideration must be given to the hypothesis of China as a potentially unstable factor within the international system, especially in the Asian–Pacific region. This hypothesis is supported by the persistence of nationalist impulses and China's behaviour as a still partially 'revisionist' power, more interested in changing than willing to accept the existing hierarchy and constraints of the international system.

Some general data on China's potential and limits as an international power may provide a helpful introduction to this kind of analysis. One important fact is that the normalisation of relations with the USA and the Soviet Union has eliminated the perception of acute threat from the one or the other that conditioned the orientation of Chinese foreign policy for almost forty years. On the other hand, China's balanced position with respect to the USA and the USSR and the rise of multipolarism have weakened the country's former role as a decisive 'card' to play in managing relations between the superpowers. Thus, the decline of the 'strategic triangle', the nucleus of the international balance in the 1970s, has also led to the relative decline of China's strategic weight. Yet, China remains a regional power with a central role in the Asia–Pacific region. Given the growing importance of this area and China's geographic position on the crossroads of American, Soviet and Japanese interests, Beijing's regional role also acquires a global projection.[1]

While China thus remains an international 'power' on the political level, as confirmed by its status as a nuclear military power and its seat on the United Nations' Security Council, economically it is still a developing country. Its international economic integration, sanctioned by its entry into the major international economic organisations during the 1980s, has not much progressed, as Bertinelli shows in his essay, beyond the initial stages and appears to be mainly directed towards the Asia–Pacific region. Segal rightly points out that such shortcomings in the foreign policy instruments available to China have undoubtedly affected the country's ability to manage foreign policy. Also, given the transformations underway in the international system, this has confronted China with a number of new and difficult challenges. While most of these challenges are external (the economic and technological dynamism of the Pacific area, the growing importance of economic as opposed to military instruments in the management of international relations, the fall of the Communist regimes in Eastern Europe), their repercussions on domestic policy are evident and long lasting. Equally evident is the fact that the political choice made in June 1989 cannot provide convincing answers to these new international pressures.

NOTES

[1] See Michael B. Yahuda, 'The People's Republic of China at 40: Foreign Relations', *China Quarterly*, No. 119, September 1989.

2

THE REFORM DECADE IN CHINA: THE LIMITS TO REVOLUTION FROM ABOVE *

Tony Saich

The reforms launched under Deng Xiaoping's leadership in 1978 have led to enormous changes in virtually every facet of Chinese life. The countryside was decollectivised with households becoming the key economic units; in areas such as southern Jiangsu rural enterprise began to flourish; and in the cities collective and privately run businesses began to fill in the gaps left by the state sector. The relaxation of the party's grip on society also led to visible changes. China's urban population became more cosmopolitan and the younger generation traded in their Mao suits for denim jeans. China's arts and literature enjoyed a notable renaissance and intellectual debate became lively and critical. In the mid-1980s, China appeared to be a country on the move with a relatively united leadership committed to the pursuit of economic growth.

Thus, the scale of the breakdown in the Chinese political system that occurred during April to June 1989 came as a shock to many. Yet, in the latter half of the decade, flaws in Deng Xiaoping's 'revolution from above' became increasingly apparent. Citizen frustration mounted and, as the system came under stress, leadership stability fell apart. As a civil society began to emerge, citizens began to think in terms of a political agenda set independent of party guidance. Many 'loyal intellectuals' were beginning to lose faith in the party's capacity to reform itself and began to question the parameters of debate defined by the party. Running parallel with this process, disillusionment with the economic reforms was beginning to set in. However, the lack of institutional reform meant that demands from below had no chance of finding adequate expression and consequently political activity became increasingly anti-systemic.

Faced by these problems, the party leadership failed to provide an adequate response. At the heart of the reform programme there was a fundamental dilemma. Deng, and indeed most senior leaders, subordinated political reform to the needs of economic development. Deciding exactly how much reform this meant in practice divided the leadership. Orthodox party members were unwilling to deal with the political consequences of the economic reform programme and continually resisted any significant dilution of party control. Hu Yaobang, latterly Zhao Ziyang, and on occasions Deng Xiaoping, recognised that a major shake-up of the party's organisational structure and a re-think of its role were necessary. Without this, the economic reforms would slide into stagnation. Political reform and the speed and extent of economic reform became key issues dividing the leadership. Deng's ambivalence on the issues, at one moment encouraging faster reform and the next throwing his weight behind those who urged caution added to the uncertainty. In relation to these issues, this chapter covers the legacy inherited by Deng Xiaoping and his supporters, their programme for change, the breakdown of the reforms and its consequences for the future.

DENG XIAOPING'S INHERITANCE: ECONOMIC STAGNATION AND POLITICAL PARALYSIS

In the mid-1970s, Chinese state and society was still trying to come to terms with the enormous upheavals created by the Cultural Revolution launched by Mao Zedong in 1966. Mao had sought to destroy the old party–state system and rebuild it from the bottom up, staffing it with people who would be loyal to his own visions of the future society. Such an attempt to overcome bureucratic resistance stands in stark contrast to Deng Xiaoping's attempts to reform the system from the top down. Indeed, the chaos and disorder that arose in the Cultural Revolution goes much of the way to explaining the fear which Deng Xiaoping and his supporters have of political activity that takes place outside of the party's and its agencies' direct control. Like Mao Zedong, although not to anything like the same extent, Deng has relied on his own prestige to push through his plans. In both cases this has had the effect of undermining further the party's prestige as an institution and preventing the process of

11

institutionalisation of the political system. The lack of institutionalisation has meant that the fate of the reform programme
has depended on the disposition at any given moment of influential individuals.

The failure of Mao's radical economic experiments in the
Great Leap Forward (1958–60), left him politically sidelined and
the Cultural Revolution represented his last chance to remove
his political opponents, replace them by loyal supporters and
to ensure that his ideas formed the basis for policy after his
death. While it proved relatively easy to mobilise forces to attack
the old, construction of the new eluded him and posed fresh
problems.

Mao summoned the students to attack the existing institutions but, after meeting his aim of singling out 'those in
authority taking the capitalist road', they divided and became
increasingly unruly. Even Mao very quickly became aware of
the need to bring the situation under control and to rebuild
some kind of party and state structure. Yet, the Red Guards
could not be wished away as easily as they had been created.
Many groups opposed the recreation of a system which they
felt was essentially similar to that which they had been trying
to destroy. Even among those groups that supported the return
of a modified party–state system there was considerable disagreement about precisely what form it should take.

With the 'masses' divided and the party–state structure in
disarray, the process of restoring order fell to the PLA. Mao
had already ensured army support through the appointment of
his loyal supporter, Lin Biao, as Defence Minister. The result
was military Maoism. Mao, with his infallible capability to map
out the correct road to Socialism, provided the system with its
legitimacy, while the PLA provided the institutional continuity
and necessary force to deal with 'class enemies'. For a while, it
appeared as if Mao wished to extend the PLA's supposed tradition of plain living and unquestioning loyalty to society as a
whole.

Not all in the PLA were happy about its new role. Local PLA
commanders were often faced with the difficult task of deciding
who were the revolutionary forces. Often they chose to side
with the old, local bureaucrats whom they had known for years
rather than the more unruly 'revolutionary rebels'. This put
local commanders in conflict with their own central military

command. Not surprisingly, the student and other groups who had been promised a new system were disillusioned by these events. Mao had destroyed their faith in the party–state system and now his use of the military destroyed their faith in Mao as the invincible leader.

The convocation of the Ninth Party Congress in 1969 signalled the abandonment of the attempt to rebuild the system from the bottom up. Yet, the issue of the nature of the CCP had not been resolved and now there was the even more pressing issue of what to do about the increasing military influence in the Chinese political system. The latter problem proved easier to solve. The purge of Lin Biao and his military supporters at the centre decreased military influence and local army commanders were persuaded to return to their barracks in return for assurances that the forces of the left would not be allowed to attack them subsequently.

The question of what kind of party should rule China was resolved less easily and indeed today still remains the core political issue. As the influence of the radicals was curbed and military influence decreased, increasing numbers of officials who had been purged during the Cultural Revolution returned to senior positions. The best example was Deng Xiaoping who had been criticised as the 'Number Two Person in Authority Taking the Capitalist Road'.[1]

By the mid-1970s, the Chinese political and economic systems were beset by major problems. The political system was excessively dominated by a 'supreme leader', the institutions attacked in the Cultural Revolution possessed no legitimate authority in the eyes of many, the people who staffed the institutions were severely divided about the way forward thus paralysing decision-making, and many urban residents had become cynical about the whole political process. Not for the first time in a Communist system, it was the death of the 'supreme leader' (Mao Zedong in September 1976) that offered a window of opportunity for a radical break with the past. This possibility was aided further by the arrest in October of the Mao's closest supporters in his later years, the 'Gang of Four'. However, it still took a full two years before the radical break was fully realised.

While the economy might not have been in crisis, it was in bad shape with a major structural overhaul necessary. Current leaders denounce the decade 1966–76 as 'ten lost years' for the economy. However, this is a political judgement by the post-Mao leadership rather than an objective appraisal of economic performance. By 1975 the gross value of agricultural output was 35.7 per cent higher than in 1966. The growth in total output value of industrial and agricultural output was 9.6 per cent during the period 1966–70 and 7.8 per cent between 1970 and 1975. With the exception of labour productivity in state enterprises the growth figures were reasonable. While labour productivity rose 2.5 per cent between 1966 and 1970, it declined by 0.3 per cent in the subsequent period. In comparison with other developing countries, growth rates had not been too bad and were better than large nations such as India and Indonesia. Further, the distribution of income and the indicators covering the quality of life stood up quite well when compared to the rest of the developing world.

Yet these aggregate figures mask increasing problems and structural imbalances in the Chinese economy. Further, it is important to note that after a recovery in the early 1970s the growth rate showed a tendency to decline. By 1976, the decline did began to assume crisis proportions. In 1976, the average growth rate of the national income dropped 2.3 per cent and the growth of total production was, at 1.7 per cent, below the rate of population growth. In part, these poor results can be explained by the serious Tangshan earthquake of 1976. However, it is more plausible to explain the seriousness of the results in terms of the paralysis that gripped China's economic decision-making in the years prior to 1976.

This economic downturn was combined with a longer term dissatisfaction about stagnating living standards on the part of much of the population. The government's consistent over-concentration on accumulation at the expense of consumption meant rationing, queuing and hours spent on laborious household chores were the daily fare for most urban residents. The lack of consumer goods was offset by the fact that few had sufficient disposable income to buy them. In fact, in 1977, the average wage of state employees was 5.5 per cent lower than it had been in 1957; that of industrial workers was 8.4 per cent lower.[2] Given the 'anti-bureaucratic' rhetoric of the Maoist era, it is interesting to note that the average wage for government employees was almost the same in 1977 as it was in 1957. In the countryside, the attacks on private plots of land and free markets as 'tails of capitalism' had caused peasant resentment by undermining alternative sources of income. Although the collective functioned effectively in some regions, many peasants saw it as an alien entity that made unfair demands on the peasants' time without supplying just returns.

It seems no exaggeration to conclude that China's population had probably had enough of tightening their belts in return for the promise of a bright future. In the years 1974–6, there were increasing numbers of reports seeping out about peasant resistance and workers' strikes and go-slows. For example, in July 1974, a Central Committee circular called on workers to stop criticising the government's economic policy and making wage claims and to concentrate on increasing production and the criticism of Lin Biao and Confucius, a political campaign sponsored by the 'Gang of Four'.[3] Popular resentment reached its high point with the mass demonstrations in Tiananmen Square on 5 April 1976.

The chance to break out of this deteriorating economic system was frustrated by the deep divisions within the top party leadership that paralysed decision-making. In the couple of years before Mao's death, the Cultural Revolution left, in particular the group later denounced as the 'Gang of Four', clashed with those party and state cadres, such as Zhou Enlai and Deng Xiaoping, who favoured concentrating on economic growth, over the correct policies to be followed. In January 1975 at the Fourth National People's Congress (NPC), Zhou re-presented his 'Four Modernisations' policy programme[4] and it seemed that a coalition had been put together between the opposing groups within the leadership. However, it was a very fragile coalition and it fell apart shortly after the Congress.

Two main factors accelerated the collapse of this attempt at conciliation. Firstly, the ill health of the older generation of China's leaders brought the question of succession to the forefront of Chinese politics. Secondly, concrete economic plans had to be drawn up for the new Five Year Plan to be implemented beginning in 1976. This brought the differing approaches to development strategy into sharp focus. While Zhou, Deng and their supporters started convening meetings and conferences to draw up programmes for their growth-oriented policies, their opponents launched a series of theoretical campaigns directed against those whom they saw as 'whittling away' the gains of the Cultural Revolution.

Apart from the deadlock over policy direction, the question of what was the correct political structure to devise and implement policy had not been resolved. Although differences existed between Mao and his supporters on the question of the ideal form of the party, his thinking on organisational issues influenced the whole programme of party rebuilding until the late-1970s. As indicated above, Mao's attitude to organisation of any form was ambivalent. While he saw leadership as necessary to guide the revolution forward, he was suspicious of those who occupied leadership positions. He was constantly aware of the possibility of leaders becoming alienated from the masses and adopting bureaucratic postures. In the 1960s, this trend of thought led Mao to believe that the party itself provided a crucial basis for the emergence of a new class dedicated to serving themselves rather than the masses and socialism. If the party as an organisation had a tendency towards bureaucratism and if its top leaders could be seduced along the 'capitalist road' purely internal party mechanisms of control could not be relied upon. Leaders were exhorted to maintain close contacts with the 'masses', formalised through programmes such as those for cadre participation in manual labour. The 'masses', for their part, were expected to exercise supervision over the leadership and offer criticism. The internal party control mechanisms that had operated before the Cultural Revolution were abolished. They were replaced by a faith in a leadership committed to revolutionary values and in the ability of the 'masses' to point out problems as they arose.

However, this theoretical position does not mean that genuine participatory forms were actually developed. As Mao had already made clear back in the caves of Yan'an during the 1940s, he was unwilling to accept a plurality of views among the 'masses'. They were expected to display loyalty towards him. With the benefit of hindsight, it can be seen that the realities of Maoist experiments such as the Great Leap Forward and the Cultural Revolution diverged, over time, radically from the stated intent. Initially, both these movements seemed to open up new mechanisms for participation and the Cultural Revolution in particular, led to a relatively spontaneous mass participation that went far beyond experiences in other state-socialist systems. China's 'masses' had an unprecedented opportunity to attack their 'bureaucratic leaders', read classified materials and express their opinions openly. This experience and the lessons learned provided the basis for the emergence of critical ideas about the Chinese body politic in the 1970s ranging from the Li Yizhe poster of 1974 to the many posters of the Democracy Movement in 1978–9.[5]

Such a system of mass participation could not be regularised, indeed such institutionlised participation would have been an anathema to Mao at his most radical. Mass participation in the Great Leap Forward did not lead to the breakthrough in economic development that was expected but planning and coordination were rendered a virtual impossibility and widespread famine occurred. Mass participation in the Cultural Revolution led to the temporary destruction of the old party elite but proved incapable of providing a suitable organisational form that could oversee the process of modernisation. Legitimacy became a key problem, one that neither Mao, the 'Gang of Four', nor Hua Guofeng was able to solve.

Mao's ambivalence concerning questions of organisation meant that he could not provide his supporters with a clear idea of the precise organisational forms which he would prefer. Despite the attempts to separate the party as an organisation from the individuals in the party who were under attack, the effect was to undermine the party's prestige. This brought to the fore the question of legitimacy. With the discrediting of the party as a source of authority and legitimacy in the Chinese polity the tendency was to resort to the invocation of Mao's name.

The 'Gang of Four' sought to devise new organisational forms that would be able to combine more traditional Leninist concepts with those thrown up by the Cultural Revolution. But, according to the political scientist Gordon White, 'they failed to break with the structural and normative logic of Leninist (i.e. Stalinist) political economy by offering an alternative 'associationist' model of socialism which could have transferred real, not symbolic, power to the population'.[6] In fact they used hierarchical means to bring about democracy, and invoked obedience to encourage initiative.[7] The organisational forms experimented with failed to gain legitimacy. This fact, combined with the 'Gang of Four's' suspicion of the party and lack of support

17

within its top leadership, meant that they fell back all too readily on the invocation of Mao's name as a source of legitimacy.[8]

With the arrest of the 'Gang of Four', the challenge of coming to terms with this economic and political legacy first fell to Hua Guofeng, who adopted a policy of 'Maoism without Mao'. For the economy, Hua favoured the 'quick fix' approach, setting ambitious planning targets and using the selective import of high-level technology to transform the ailing situation. The basis for this transformation was to be the 1976–85 Ten Year Plan presented to the Fifth NPC (February–March 1978), a plan that owed much to Deng's alternative policy prognosis from 1975–6. The plan set forward a number of optimistic targets and bore resemblances to Mao's twelve-year plan of the mid-1950s that had preceded the Great Leap Forward. Indeed, the initial rhetoric began to mirror that which accompanied the Leap: references were made to the Leap's general line of of 'going all out, aiming high to achieve greater, faster, better and more economical results in building socialism'. Hua reversed the previous sectoral priority, placing the emphasis on heavy industrial development rather than agriculture. Some 120 large-scale projects were to be completed by 1985 and an almost 150 per cent increase in steel production was called for.[9] The Maoist obsession with grain production was retained with the call for an increase in production of over 40 per cent.

This initial strategy only served to compound the problems. The import of modern technology, the 'Great Leap Westward' as some have dubbed it, far outstripped both China's export capacity and the ability to absorb the imports. The trade deficit with 'capitalist' countries grew from US $1.2 billion in 1977 to $4.5 billion in 1979. There was the notorious case of the modern Wuhan steel plant that would have required more electricity to run it than could be generated to supply the needs of the entire city. Many of the large-scale projects could not be completed because of planning errors and a shortage of the necessary skilled personnel.

In the political realm, Hua also failed to address the problems of the Maoist legacy. Little attention was paid to politico-administrative reform. For the most part, such problems as were recognised were put down to the excesses of the 'Gang of Four', the 'bad work-style' to which officials had grown accustomed as a result of the Cultural Revolution, and the remaining influences of a 'feudal' way of thinking. No moves had been made to redefine party–society relations or to reduce the excessively leader-dominated system.

Hua and his supporters, who were later denounced as the 'Whateverists' retained certain ideas from the Cultural Revolution period along with the ambiguities.[10] Further, their attitude toward the party's role in society was designed to complement their optimistic proposals for economic development. Essentially, Hua and his supporters proposed the continuance of the party as a vehicle of mobilisation to conduct mass campaigns, both economic and political, to achieve the ambitious economic targets. They persisted with the Maoist ambiguity that while the party was to be in command, the masses were to monitor abuses by party officials. This view caused suspicion of the party to remain while failing to create organisations with legitimacy. It was too dependent on the more 'radical' aspects of Mao's legacy and the creation of a new personality cult around Hua to resist policy shifts to the new economic programme.

Hua Guofeng was never able to come to terms with the problem of leadership. He continued the Mao cult and set about creating one of his own. Politically, it would have been extremely difficult for Hua to have dismantled the excessively Mao-centred system as his own right to rule was based on the claim that he was Mao's hand-picked successor. The increasing emphasis from December 1978 onwards on the need to regularise procedures and the mounting criticism of 'feudal work-style' did not augur well for Hua's continued occupation of top party and state posts. Indeed, he gave up the premiership in July 1980 and his position as chair of the party in July 1981. The quaint poster that was widely distributed of the aged Mao handing the youthful Hua the piece of paper with the inscription 'With you in charge, I am at ease' written on it by Mao smacked far too much of the Emperor passing on the Mandate of Heaven to his chosen successor.

By the late-1970s, it was becoming clear to the group of veteran leaders around Deng Xiaoping, many of whom had been purged during the Cultural Revolution, that the economic and political problems required a major overhaul of the system to solve them. Hua's 'new' economic policy had not produced a major rise in standards of living. The political twists and turns

19

and the manipulation and mobilisation of the population to support the goals of the various factions increased the tendency towards a deep, bitter cynicism and apathy on the part of many. The claim that, despite changing its 'correct line' every couple of years, the party was the only body in society capable of mapping out the correct road to socialism was looking a little tenuous. Party leaders could no longer invoke such claims to ensure allegiance to a particular set of policy preferences.

THE THIRD PLENUM AND DENG'S INITIAL REFORM AGENDA

Deng Xiaoping's second political resurrection was completed in July 1977 and together with his supporters, he set about putting together a new programme that would place China on the path of self-sustaining economic growth. The criticism of Mao Zedong and the attempts by Deng and his supporters to dismantle the personality cult meant that Mao's name could no longer be invoked effectively to underpin legitimacy. As a result, Deng and his supporters chose the option of promising a bright economic future for all within a relatively short space of time. Future legitimacy would be linked closely to the party's ability to deliver the economic goods.

The political breakthrough for Deng came at the third plenum of the eleventh Central Committee held in December 1978. By this time, Deng had formed an alliance with pragmatic planners, in particular Chen Yun, accepting their views of an alternative approach to economic development. In this sense, the initial victory at the plenum was Chen Yun's rather than Deng's. However, later developments and the official history that ascribes the new line and its development almost exclusively to Deng has tended to obscure this fact. Deng's usurpation of full credit for the original reform programme and its subsequent radicalisation has angered Chen and he has become Deng's strongest opponent on the question of pace and extent of political reform. On a number of occasions, Chen has upbraided Deng for ignoring the opinions of others thus defying the principles of collective leadership which Chen claims were restored at the plenum.[11]

The plenum decided to concentrate on economic modernisation subordinating all other work to meeting this objective.

The rationale for policy adoption became essentially a pragmatic one summed up in the slogan, launched in May 1978, 'practice is the sole criterion for testing truth' and the corresponding policy line of 'correcting mistakes wherever they are discovered'. Despite the plenum's effective decision to forget about the past and to concentrate on the future, the new 'practice' slogan was used both at the plenum and subsequently to reverse a whole series of previous political judgments. These were used both to undermine the basis of legitimacy of Hua Guofeng and his supporters, and to establish the credibility of Deng's and Chen's policy positions. Essentially, Mao's increasing radicalism in his later years was denounced while previous attempts to moderate 'economic excesses' through a policy of economic liberalisation were praised.[12] To award themselves the mantle of popular legitimacy the Tiananmen Incident of 1976 was reassessed and proclaimed a revolutionary movement that had demonstrated support both for Zhou Enlai's and Deng's policy programme.

After the plenum, Deng and the more pragmatic economic planners such as Chen Yun and Bo Yibo began to criticise the ambitious economic plans identified with Hua Guofeng and warned of 'economic rashness'. The need to comply with 'objective economic laws' was repeatedly stressed. These warnings were reflected in the new economic policies presented to the Second Session of the Fifth NPC (June–July 1979): policies that Chen Yun had a greater role in drafting than Deng Xiaoping. The Ten Year Plan was postponed and abandoned at the Third Session (1980). In its place a three-year period of 're-adjusting, restructuring, consolidation and improvement of the national economy' was introduced. Economic priorities were re-ordered. Heavy industry was relegated to last place behind agriculture and light industry. The primary focus was to be on fixing targets for the agricultural sector. Rather than leading the economy, heavy industry would receive only such funds as were necessary for its adaptation to the needs of the other sectors.[13]

The third plenum ratified a policy intended to encourage growth in agricultural production by substantial increases in procurement prices and by modernising agriculture through investments by the brigades and teams.[14] Through 1979, specific measures were introduced to implement the policy of raising procurement prices. At the same time, policy was relaxed to let different regions make use of the 'law of comparative advantage'. Also, private plots of land and sideline production were stressed as playing an important role in agricultural growth. To allow the peasants to sell their products – for example, their above quota grain – private markets were again tolerated. This policy was firmly based on the collective and represented nothing radically new.[15]

As it developed, the reform programme had at its core the liberalisation of previous practices in both the economic and the political realm. In the economic sector, policy revolved around the promotion of market mechanisms to deal with the inefficiencies of allocation and distribution that occur with the central planning system. Awareness of the 'new technological revolution' increased the Chinese leaders' desire to make their system more flexible and thus more amenable to change. To take advantage of the market opportunities, more power of decision-making was to be given to the localities, and in particular to the units of production themselves. Production units were given greater autonomy to decide what to produce, how much to produce and where to sell it. At the core of this system was the ubiquitous contract that was expected to govern economic activity. Correspondingly, material incentives were seen as the major mechanism for causing people to work harder, and the socialist principle of 'to each according to his (her) work' was to be firmly applied. Egalitarianism was attacked as a dangerous notion that retarded economic growth. These reforms of the domestic economy were accompanied by an unprecedented opening to the outside world in the search for export markets and the necessary foreign investments, technology and higher quality consumer goods.

INITIAL SUGGESTIONS FOR POLITICAL REFORM AND THEIR CONSTRAINTS

The period 1978–80 was a high tide for suggestions for political reform with not just the Democracy Wall activists but also highly placed party members floating ideas on far-reaching reforms. Deng Xiaoping indicated his approval for political reform in August 1980 when he called for people's democracy to be developed to the fullest extent possible. According to Deng, it was necessary to ensure that the people as a whole really enjoyed the power of supervision over the state in a variety of effective ways. In particular, they were to 'supervise political power at the basic level, as well as in all enterprises and undertakings.'[16] The fact that this speech was republished in June 1987 indicated that, even at that time, Deng wanted to keep the question of political reform on the agenda despite the severe divisions that had become apparent within the party leadership towards the end of 1986 and early 1987.[17]

Although Deng's speech was not published officially the first time until 1983, it did set the tone for subsequent discussions about reform. In October 1980, veteran party official Liao Gailong offered the most elaborate programme. Liao indicated that democracy was not just a means but was also an end – 'our ultimate end' – and stated that people did not only want affluence but also 'freedom, extensive freedom, as well as a high degree of democracy'.[18] Liao made a number of practical suggestions to help make China a 'strong, modern, highly democratic and highly civilised socialist nation'. He proposed turning the NPC into something more than a 'rubber stamp' by reducing the number of delegates and splitting it into two chambers that would supervise the work of the State Council and act as a check on one another. Representatives to the first chamber were to be elected on a territiorial basis, whereas those in the second chamber were to be representatives of social groupings. Local government was to be strengthened at the expense of central government, an independent judiciary was to be set up free of party influence, and a freer role was to be given to the media.

Liao's plans were never realised and early promises of extensive reform were not combined with sufficient substantive change thus causing many intellectuals and students to become frustrated. Substantive change was ruled out by the refusal of senior party leaders to accept structural reform that would lead to a redistribution of power to other groups and organisations in society. Orthodox party members were offended by the attacks on the party–state system that were aired during the Democracy Movement of 1978–9, attacks that were sometimes repeated in the official media. Their view that too great a relaxation of political control would lead to loss of control was reinforced by the rise of Solidarity in Poland in 1980.

Thus, even as Liao Gailong and others were putting forward

blueprints for a new political structure, party leaders, including Deng Xiaoping were setting stringent limits to the extent of possible reform. The essentail question was how far control could be relaxed to ensure that ideas useful for economic modernisation would surface without party dominance being weakened. The adoption of the new development strategy made the need for reform of political structures all the more apparent. The shift to a more market-oriented, decentralised economy reliant on officials who could give expert technical advice was not readily served by a rigid, over-centralised political system dominated by the party and staffed by personnel who felt at home only when hiding behind administrative rules and regulations.

The experiences of the Hundred Flowers, the Great Leap Forward, the Cultural Revolution caused leaders such as Deng Xiaoping to be suspicious of participation that took place outside of direct party control. Thus, they tried to restore the effective leadership of the party while, at the same time, not negating the contributions that 'articulate social audiences' could make to the modernisation process.

In effect, this meant that change was to be brought about by a 'revolution from above'. The party was to define the limits of what was acceptable and it was anticipated that continued party control over the process of change would ensure stability and stop the possibility of degeneration into chaos. Deng, and other party leaders argued in rather tortuous fashion that the reforms of the party were, in fact, intended to strengthen party leadership and discipline rather than to weaken it. Thus, key groups of technicians and intellectuals were allowed greater freedom in their work and a more relaxed social environment in return for their policy input and their acceptance of the parameters of debate laid down by the party. Urban workers and peasants were offered the vision of a more rationally functioning economy that would put more goods on the shelves and that would lead to a consistent rise in living standards.

The notion of continued party leadership was enshrined in promotion of the slogan of adherence to the 'Four Basic Principles'. These principles were first put forward formally by Deng Xiaoping in March 1979 at a Central Theoretical Work Conference.[19] This was in response to both the Democracy Movement of the late-1970s and the criticisms raised by party intellectuals that were circulating internally. After initially using the movement in his political struggle against his opponents in the party leadership, he had no further use for the movement and wished to set limits to political activity that was not sanctioned by the party. Further, Deng had apparently been alarmed at the way in which critical ideas had been raised at the theoretical work conference by party intellectuals such as Li Honglin, Su Shaozhi and Yan Jiaqi.[20] By calling for adherence to the 'Four Basic Principles', Deng indicated that there were limits to the reforms and suggested a range of obligations for those engaged in discussions about political reform. Many critical intellectuals and students saw the promotion of the principles as an excuse to hold back on genuine political reform.

Secondly, political reform was to be subordinated to the needs of economic regeneration. Only such changes would be introduced as were necessary to make the wheels of economic modernisation turn more smoothly. As Deng Xiaoping reaffirmed in September 1986:

> The major problem is that the political structure does not meet the requirements of reform of economic structure. Therefore, without reforming the political structure, it will be impossible to safeguard the fruits of economic reform or to guarantee its continued advance.[21]

As the reforms progressed, this subordination of economic to political reform was questioned by a number of reform-minded intellectuals. They saw the increasing diversification of economic life and the resultant social differentiation as creating the need for genuine political reform to deal with the growing plurality in Chinese society. Such critics claimed that it was not mere 'subjective whim' that led to calls for overhauling China's outdated political structure.[22] Not only did the over-centralised political structure hamper the attempts to decentralise economic activity but also it could not accommodate the increasing number of people who were beginning to function on the margins of, or outside of, the old centralised system.

The fact that party leaders decided to tie their legitimacy to rule to their demonstrated economic competence meant that more freedom had to be given to those groups that could devise and implement the plans to bring about economic success. Such an approach contained problems. The promise, and initial delivery of economic success created strong expectations among China's population.

The party found itself faced by a population with rising expectations, sometimes quite unrealistic, that were increasingly hard to meet. To an extent, party leaders such as Deng Xiaoping only had themselves to blame. To justify and legitimise their policies, they filled the official media with accounts of rural and urban dwellers who had become very wealthy as a result of the reforms. A popular slogan was 'to get rich is glorious'. Failure to deliver would undermine regime legitimacy.

The erosion of mechanisms of political control and the decrease in the importance of ideology left the party exposed to criticism once it failed to meet the rising expectations. The reforms as launched were 'open-ended'.[23] This was useful in terms of maintaining flexibility of response but neither party members nor citizens were given a clear indication of the direction in which the reforms were taking them. With ideology eroded, there was nothing to bind society together other than economic success both at the system level and for the individual. As citizens became disillusioned with the reforms as they began to falter, the party had nothing to fall back on to defend its 'leading position' in society other than force.

Despite the constraints, a number of notable inititiatives were undertaken to reform the political system, including the adoption of new party and state constitutions as a part of the attempt to define more clearly the division between the party and governmental sectors, measures to trim the bureaucracy and to improve the quality of its officials and steps were taken to promote more effective citizen participation.[24] For example, measures were introduced to give more meaning to the electoral process. A new chapter in the electoral law (effective as of 1 January 1980) stated that electors, or electoral units, would have the power to supervise and recall their deputies; elections, within limits, were to become competitive with more candidates standing than places available; and party dominance of the electoral process was to be loosened by relaxing the regulations for nominating candidates. Apart from these procedural changes, the scope for elections was to be extended. In June 1979, Hua Guofeng announced that leading members should be 'elected by the masses not only in the rural people's communes but at the grassroots in enterprises and establishments such as factories, mines and stores'.[25] The principle of direct elections was to be extended to include people's congresses up to, and including, the county level.[26] The euphoria for elections even led to suggestions in the official press that direct elections at the county level could 'lay a solid and reliable foundation for direct provincial or even national elections'.[27]

OPPOSITION TO THE REFORM PROGRAMME

Although restructuring of the party and state apparatus continued throughout the first half of the 1980s, a major overhaul was resisted. In particular, the question of the party's dominant role was not tackled and many cadres balked at the idea of any curtailment in their power. At the political centre, opposition came from three major groups that were able to ally on occasions to frustrate far-reaching reforms. However, while these groups have been able to frustrate the progress of reforms, they have not been able to roll them back for a consistent period of time, not even after the violent suppression of the people's movement in 1989.

First, there are those who have attacked the reforms on primarily economic grounds and who represent the traditional central planning and economic apparatus. This group includes those such as Chen Yun, Li Xiannian and Bo Yibo. They are concerned about the destabilising effect of pushing the marketisation of the economy too far too fast. They have criticised the over-reliance on the market and are worried about the 'over-heating' of the economy caused in part by the rapid growth of the collective sector, particularly the rural industries. While Chen Yun is not opposed to an increased role for the market, indeed he has been one of its main proponents, he does view a too rapid introduction of market forces as causing the recurrent economic problems during the 1980s. Chen has consistently argued for the importance, and primacy, of planning within the economic system. This defence of the state sector is reflected in the periodic criticisms of private enterprise and the refusal to redefine property rights in order to protect the state's priviledged position in the economy. Chen was particulalry concenred about the fall in grain production that occurred in 1985 and the subsequent stagnation after four years of record harvests and was able to use this to put Zhao Ziyang and the more pragmatice reformers under pressure. Further, this group fear that current policies will deepen regional inequalities betwen China's poor hinterland and its more advanced coastal regions. Finally, they are concerned about the mushrooming of corruption that has sprung up as a result of the more liberalised policies and increased contacts with the West.[28] This group has substantial support within the ministries and apparatus associated with the old central planning system and particularly from those associated with the heavy industrial sector.

The concern about corruption has been echoed by a second group that includes Peng Zhen, Hu Qiaomu and Deng Liqun. They are worried about the consequences of liberalisation for the social fabric of China. These orthodox party leaders have consistently insisted that the party must reaffirm its leading role also in the realm of ideology. They argue that socialism has a moral spiritual goal as well as a material goal, and that these goals can only be defined by the party. These leaders feel that the party's role is to dictate the nation's ethical and moral values. In this respect, the party has taken over the traditional role of the state in China. At the Twelfth Party Congress (1982), Hu Yaobang, then General Secretary, announced a reversal in the listing of the party's tasks placing the building of spiritual civilisation before democratisation, thus making it a prerequisite for democratisation. This paved the way for subsequent campaigns against 'spiritual civilisation' and 'bourgeois liberalisation' in 1983, 1987 and 1989–90. Further, they see the 'open-door policy' as a source of problems within the party; a point they were able to get officially accepted in October 1983. An official decision on party consolidation, while stating that the 'open-door policy' had been entirely correct, noted that there had been an increase in the 'corrosive influence of decadent bourgeois ideology remnant feudal ideas'.[29] It is important to note that one year earlier at the Twelfth Party Congress when Hu Yaobang announced formally that a programme for the rectification of party-style and 'consolidation' of party organisations would be launched, he did not cite this as a reason for problems in the party.

Third, there are some senior military leaders who had been closely associated with Mao during the war years and who subsequently have provided a rallying point for those disaffected with the reform programme. Such military figures have

28

retained a 'leftist' ideology and have been concerned by the erosion of Mao's legacy and the tarnishing of his image. Some were disgruntled about the low priority which the military had been accorded within the modernisation programme, while others have opposed the shift to a less political and more pro-fessionalised army. Discontent surfaced among the rank-and-file peasant recruits when they saw the new possibilities for making money opening up in the rural areas which they had left behind. The impact of the responsibility system, in the form of providing outlets for making a decent living, caused China to introduce a conscription law in 1984.

Faced with this opposition, Deng Xiaoping was remarkably successful until the end of 1986 in limiting its influence. For example, in 1984–5, a shake up of party and military leadership resulted in a major weakening of these groups' influence in formal leadership bodies. Further in 1982, the Central Advisory Committee to the Central Committee was set up. The intention was that the Commission would function as a 'retirement home' for elderly officials. This was seen as a way to open up positions in the formal political system for a younger generation more in tune with the demands of the modern world. The Commission was explicitly referred to as a temporary organ but the failure to institutionalise retirement has meant the Commission has become a permanent feature of the political landscape. It has provided traditional party leaders with an institutional support base from which to launch their attacks on the reform pro-gramme. This tendency to express conservatve orthodoxy become more marked in late 1987 when Chen Yun took over the Chairmanship of the Commission after his 'retirement' from the Standing Committee of the Politburo.

The military's direct political influence was also reduced and many elderly officers were replaced by a younger generation more committed to the idea of a less political, more professional military. In December 1984, forty senior officers of the PLA general staff retired, the largest retirement ever; in January 1985 budget cutbacks were announced; and in April, Hu Yaobang announced that troop levels would be cut back by 25 per cent, some 1 million personnel. To weaken the PLA's political influ-ence, two other important measures were taken. First, in June 1985, a meeting of the Central Military Afairs Commission, chaired by Deng Xiaoping, announced a restructuring of the military regional command structure. Apart from reasons of efficiency, this had the effect of breaking up powerful regional ties of key military leaders.[30]

The second important step was the shake-up of the party leadership at the special party conference held in September 1985. This saw a sharp reduction in military representation in the Politburo. Of the ten resignations, six were military figures and no military appointees were among the six full new members of the Politburo. The military establishment resisted, however, one important change of personnel. Deng Xiaoping had tried to pass on his post as Chair of the Military Affairs Commission to General Secretary, Hu Yaobang. While senior military officers were willing to concede ultimately to Deng's authority, they were not prepared to accept his then protégé. This clearly reduced Hu's prestige and prevented him from forging an alliance with reformers in the military. It presaged later events when Deng was similarly unable to install his second chosen successor, Zhao Ziyang as head of the Commission. Given the fact that control of the military remains the key to power in China this was a serious blow to the pragmatic reformers and was a worrying sign that later developments confirmed.

By summer 1986, it was clear that political reform had become a severely divisive issue within the political leadership. During the spring and early summer, critical intellectuals began to raise ideas for radicalising the reforms yet by the end of the year their views had been rejected and Hu Yaobang who was thought to be sympathetic had been dismissed from his post as General Secretary. A summer 1986 Hong Kong newspaper report referred to a meeting at Beidaihe at which some leaders had expressed the view that, on the whole, the current political system was basically suited to the needs of economic development and that reform could lead to the negation of the party's leadership and the 'Four Basic Principles'. To counter the perceived 'liberal' tendencies of the time, these opponents suggested a strict set of obligations for those engaged in discussions about reform. Disagreements led to the postponement of an expected decision on political reform until the Thirteenth Party Congress (October 1987).[31] In fact, the Sixth Plenum of the Twelfth Party Congress (September 1986) instead of discussing political reform passed a resolution on the need to improve work in the ideological and cultural spheres. These are issues more closely identified with those seeking to limit the extent of political reform. The opponents of too radical reform continued to link wide-ranging changes with bourgeois contamination. In November 1986, (then) Politburo member Peng Zhen warned against those who yearned for bourgeois democracy 'as if the moonlight of capitalist society was brighter than our socialist sun.' The student demonstrations in late 1986, provided these opponents with their chance to launch a counter-attack and remove Hu Yaobang in January 1987.

However, the campaign against 'bourgeois liberalisation' launched after Hu's dismissal was short-lived and his replacement by Zhao Ziyang seemed to indicate that the attack by the orthodox party members had caused little more than a hiccup in the reform process. This appeared to be borne out at the Thirteenth Party Congress held in October 1987 at which Zhao delivered a speech that on balance favoured commitment to continued reform.[32] Further, personnel changes were made that seemed to strengthen those made at the September 1985 special conference. Orthodox party members Li Xiannian and Chen Yun stood down from the Standing Committee of the Politburo together with Deng Xiaoping.

However, the removal of Hu Yaobang had left its mark. The manner of his 'retirement', the launching of an old-style political campaign and the expulsion of three prominent, critical intellectuals from the party showed that the old guard still possessed the power to block what they did not like and that Deng Xiaoping was willing to throw his weight behind them on issues of political actions that took place outside of party control. Yet, the short duration of the campaign showed that they lacked the power to produce a decisive policy turnaround. Despite the greater vehemence of the campaign launched in June 1989, the phenomenon is apparent. In effect, this has meant while reform cannot be rolled back entirely neither can it be pursued properly. The continuous need for compromise leads to lack of consequent direction in the reform programme.

As discussed below, Hu's dismissal caused critical intellectuals and students to lose faith in Deng Xiaoping's top-down approach to reform thus opening up the possibility for even more radical behaviour later. While these groups began to demand further radical reform, the pragmatic reformers grouped around Zhao Ziyang began to outline a strategy to justify an elitist approach to pursuing Deng's top-down reforms. Ideas supporting neo-authoritarianism began to appear in 1986 but the theory became more important as a justification for holding power in late 1988 as the reforms began to falter.[33] Scholars such as Zhang Bingjiu, one of the major proponents of this view, see themselves as 'moderate democrats'. Zhang proposes that the gradual extension of market mechanisms will create the necessary basis for democracy. Neo-authoritarianism is justified as a means for producing democracy.[34] Zhang and his ilk argue that, at the present time, China does not possess the necessary cultural conditions for democracy. Thus, for the foreseeable future, a central authority is necessary to push through the policies that will create the basis for change.

Not surprisingly, this viewpoint has been sharply criticised by those who wanted more radical reform and who had already lost faith in the party's capacity to reform the system from the top down. Essentially, they questioned the basic premise that a neo-authoritarian ruler could lay the foundation for a democratic form of government that, in turn, would spell the demise of that person's rule. Critics argued that such an approach would strengthen the system of 'rule by man' thus perpetuating Chinese predilection for strong, authoritarian rule.[35] Such argumentation ran counter to the reformers intention of devising a system based on 'rule by law'.

To promote democratisation by strengthening the 'rule of law', critical intellectuals such as Cao Siyuan, Su Shaozhi and Yan Jiaqi began to propose a strategy based on institutional reform.[36] This process of increasing the parameters for democratic debate was to be supported by the emergence of independent groupings in society that would gain in strength as the economic reforms progressed. Especially the astronomer, Fang Lizhi, argued that the economic reforms were producing a new class of private entrepreneurs who would eventually compete with the state. Fang estimated that this process would take some twenty to thirty years before a sufficiently strong power base for an opposition party would be created that could enable it to challenge the CCP.[37]

Their main proposals included improving the representativeness and independence of the people's congress system, granting delegates immunity during debates[38] and reducing party interference in government organisations and society at large. The process of institutional reform was to be accompanied by expanding the freedom of speech, assembly and the press. Finally, there was the party itself. They stressed the need to make the party more accountable to outside organisations and to make it more democratic internally. Yan Jiaqi suggested that not only should different opinions be allowed to be expressed but also that factions should be permitted. He saw the formation of factions as providing the basis for the emergence of a multi-party system.[39] Su Shaozhi proposed that the party limit its role by returning to a genuine vanguard role. This would still give the party a leadership role. But Su suggested that it should 'not be such a large party but an elite'. Further he argued that intellectuals should have more influence in defining what the leadership's role meant in practice.[40]

RE-DEFINING PARTY-GOVERNMENT RELATIONS

Without doubt, the key issue in political reform is that of the party's role in society and its influence on other organisations. As noted above, while all could agree that some loosening of the party's deadening grip was necessary, there were strong disagreements about to what extent. Clearly, a major structural transformation would undermine deep-seated, vested interests and thus far-reaching reform was bitterly opposed. This section looks at the attempts that have been made to loosen the party's grip over the government sector.

Overlap and confusion about the division of responsibility between policy formulation and implementation have been a constant feature of political life in the PRC.[41] On occasions, the overlap of party and state has led to the party actually implementing policy. Normally, this is condemned but during the early phase of the Cultural Revolution with the creation of revolutionary committees, it was positively encouraged. Some of the resulting confusion was removed by the abolition of these committees in 1979 and initial moves to abolish concurrent holding of party and state posts by individuals. In July 1980, Hua Guofeng announced that he would hand over his post of Premier to Zhao Ziyang while retaining the position of Chairman of the Party.[42] At the Third Session of the Fifth NPC (August–September 1980), the practice was extended to the provincial level to prevent the 'over-concentration of power and the holding of too many posts concurrently by one person' and to separate party work effectively and clearly from government work.[43]

Such moves were more of a symbolic importance given that all key officials in the state apparatus were, and still are, leading party members. There was never any intention that such measures should lead to autonomy for the state sector and institutional dominance was retained through party groups in all state organs. Yan Jiaqi highlighted the problem, writing that in practice party organisations often undertook work that should have been handled by 'organs of state power, namely the executive branch and the legislative branch'.[44]

As the 1980s progressed, separation of powers became a key demand of reform-minded party intellectuals and calls were made for the termination of party identification with the government.[45] The need to loosen the party's overbearing involvement in government was broadly accepted by the leadership. Party interference was generally seen as a brake on promoting the rational decision-making needed for economic reform. To ease the brakes, the vested interests of party officials were to be broken up to prevent them from stifling the new emphasis on entrepreneurship. Reformers argued that the party's 'leading role' did not justify undue interference and sometimes made the more radical proposal that the party be moved out of government organisations, including state-owned enterprises, altogether.[46] Such a far-reaching idea did not persuade a majority among top leaders but a majority was found to support the downgrading of the role of party organisations within the government apparatus.

Party domination of the legislature, executive and judiciary is worsened by the fact that the party has no effective regulatory mechanism. The system of discipline inspection commissions revived in the late 1970s has not concerned itself with this kind of problem, concentrating instead on internal party discipline. As a result, when the interests of the state or of the individual are infringed, the legal system cannot automatically intervene as it is controlled by the party. Further, even where legal officials do possess powers to intervene, they are unlikely to do so where high-ranking officials are involved. Numerous cases are reported in the press of high-handed party secretaries acting in defiance, or perhaps in ignorance, of the law. To improve this situation critical intellectuals, such as Su Shaozhi, have even suggested that a Constitutional Court of Law be set up to adjudicate whether decisions taken by central and local party and government leaders are in line with the law of the land.[47] However, as long as 'rule by man', in this case 'party man', rather than 'rule by law' is the dominant ethos, the creation of new rules, regulations etc. will not fundamentally resolve the problem.

The problems with such a confusion of roles are evident and good practical reasons exist for trying to create a real division of responsibilities. As the American social scientist, Franz Schurmann, has pointed out, the more an organisation becomes a 'command-issuing body' the more it must 'grapple with the concrete technicalities of command'. This would lead to increasing bureaucratism and inflexibility thus thwarting the party's ability to innovate and adjust to changing circumstances.[48] This point was recognised by former General Secretary, Zhao Ziyang. Speaking in October 1987, just before the Thirteenth Party Congress, he warned that the party must not turn itself into an executor entrapped in the mundane technicalities of daily command.[49] Once it became a 'direct executive body', it would no longer be able to avoid bureaucratism.[50] Zhao further warned that if the party took on the work of other organisations, it would turn into an interested party, leaving it with little room to manoeuvre in resolving conflicting interests. One final worry to Zhao was that if the party became so involved in routine government matters it would be unable to look after its own party affairs. Zhao felt that party members would allow 'their own land to go barren while tilling the land of others'.[51] Given the reported lack of discipline, increasing corruption and ideological confusion among party members there is certainly enough work for party members keeping their own 'land' under control.

Relaxation of direct party control over economic activities has advantages other than simply facilitating the new development strategy. By distancing itself from the day-to-day running of the system, the party can seek to avoid the blame for economic failings. These can more readily be blamed on faulty implementation etc. Particularly at the level of the enterprise this can be important. Management can be held responsible for failings and thus be dismissed if necessary while, in theory, the party's reputation could remain intact. This would not be the case where party and management are synonymous.

While Zhao Ziyang resisted the demands for structural overhaul, he did present a number of new policies at the Thirteenth Party Congress. Zhao's report to the Congress while bearing the hallmarks of a compromise document and containing Deng Xiaoping's cautious approach, did put forward a number of ideas that would have significantly weakened party influence in the government sector. The most important measure Zhao proposed was the abolition of leading party member groups (*dangzu*) in units of state adminstration.[52] Previously it had been the normal practice for party members who were leading members in state administrative units, enterprises or research establishments to hold caucus meetings to discuss policy within their organisation. These groups became increasingly powerful taking over more and more work of the organisation concerned.[53] They were established by the party committee (*dangwei*) at the next highest level and were responsible to that committee. The abolition of these party groups was interpreted by scholars in the Chinese Academy of Social Sciences as a major weakening of party power in their research institutions.[54]

Further, most party committees that parallel a department in the government sector appoint one of the members of the standing committee to take charge of work in the government sector even if the person concerned holds no official position in that sector. Zhao Ziyang announced that this practice would be halted.[55] Thus, the Organisation Department of the Central Committee informed all provincial party committees in January 1988 that in the forthcoming elections to their committees the post of full-time deputy-secretary (*zhuanzhi shuji*) or standing committee member taking charge of government work without holding a government post should be abolished. The number of standing committee members of provincial-level party committees was to be reduced accordingly.[56]

In the same spirit, all CCP work departments that carry out overlapping functions with those of government departments were to be abolished. In April 1987, the Anyang city party committee closed all departments that overlapped with government departments, including the economic and rural work departments. Further, the city government took over the cultural, educational, sports, health, national affairs and overseas Chinese work that had been formerly controlled by the city party committee's propaganda and united front departments.[57] The list of these departments indicates just how far the arms of the party reached. Also, the party committee's organisational department's management of over eight hundred cadres above the section level was transferred to the city government.[58] The transfer of cadre management out of direct party control could have a significant impact. A common complaint of government officials is that often they cannot make decisions concerning their own personnel as this is an area where the party exerts ultimate authority.

Moderate reformers in the party also made an initial attempt to spell out the duties of party committees during the forth-coming period. Yet the duties reveal just how little real authority party officials are willing to hand over to other organisations. The Central Committee of the CCP is to retain leadership over the 'political principles and orientation' in major policy decisions concerning domestic and foreign affairs, the economy, national defence etc. Importantly, it will retain its power of *nomenklatura* by recommending the officials for major posts in the central state organisations.[59] Given that the Organisation Department is headed by Chen Yun supporter, Song Ping, traditionalist party members retained considerable say over official appointments. Similar powers are granted to local party committees. The list of candidates that the Anyang party com-mittee will 'recommend' shows how far the hand of the party will still reach into the local organs. It will recommend officials such as the chairman and vice-chairmen of the people's con-gress, mayor and deputy-mayors, chairman and vice-chairmen of the political consultative conference, chief judge, chief procu-rator and candidates for leaders above the county deputy head level.[60] The vagueness of the functions means that whoever is in control of the party apparatus at whatever level has consider-able leeway for interpreting just to what extent the party can interfere in other areas.

With the removal of Zhao Ziyang as General Secretary and the campaign by his opponents to reassert party dominance, the question arises whether these nascent reforms will be pur-sued or whether they will be allowed quietly to drop. Certainly, the important role of the party at the basic levels has been stressed since Zhao's dismissal. It was the intention of the pragmatic reformers to strengthen the position of enterprise managers vis-à-vis the party committees at the basic level. They had hoped that this would enable the enterprises to respond to market signals rather than to the political demands dictated by local party officials. This was in direct contrast to Chen Yun's strategy. In Chen's view, the relaxation of the central plan and the promotion of limited market stimuli had to be accompanied by the presence of strong party organisations. This was to ensure that enterprises did not get seduced by the anarchy of the market. A strong party presence would ensure conformity to the general outlines of the central plans as well as to other social and political goals decided by the party leadership.

THE CHALLENGE FROM BELOW: THE EMERGENCE OF CIVIL SOCIETY

Despite the impressive aggregate figures for rises in income and consumption levels, the party's attempt to create a new legitimacy based on economic success began to fall apart from the mid 1980s onwards. Not only was it becoming apparent that more than expected were excluded from the new found wealth but also many of those who had actually improved their situation felt themselves to be relatively deprived. The lack of sufficient reform of the political structure meant that the increasing economic and social grievances could not be adequately expressed. Political activity became increasingly anti-systemic. The tendency towards anti-systemic behaviour was facilitated by the relaxation of party control over society and fuelled by increasing disregard of the party and its self-ascribed leading role.

The party-sponsored reforms have produced major changes in society. Not only have the economic policies produced a variety of new organisations but also the more relaxed political atmosphere led to an increase in the expression of sectoral and even individual interests. A particular challenge to party authority was the expansion of private enterprise which led not only to an increase in economic activity outside of its control but also to a more direct political challenge. In this respect, it is important to note that two of the students' main support groups during the 1989 demonstrations came from the newly flourishing private sector. Firstly, there was the Flying Tiger Motor Brigade that provided the students with their information about troop movements after martial law was declared and which was able to spread information on demonstrations throughout the city. It is no surprise that the first arrests, on 30 May 1989 were of members of this group.[61] Secondly, there was the Stone Group Corporation, a computer company, which was instrumental in terms both of financing the students and providing them with advanced communications networks.[62] In fact, even before the demonstrations began, the Stone Corporation had challenged party dominance. On 26 March 1989, the corporation had financed a meeting at the National Library in Beijing at which those present decided to ask the CCP to remove all mention of Mao Zedong Thought and the 'Four Basic Principles' from the state constitution.[63]

Numerous professional organisations have sprung up and unlike the old-style mass organisations, they have consciously pursued the interests of their members. This meant a refusal to accept a political agenda set entirely by the party. This increase in political activity amounted to the emergence of civil society in the PRC. While mobilised participation and party-guided political study sessions declined, genuine politics began to emerge. This process was not de-politicisation as some have referred to it but a real politicisation of Chinese society. Demands were made to place issues of accountability, sub-group autonomy, and self-determination on the political agenda. Deng Xiaoping's 'revolution from above' was in danger of running into an even more powerful 'revolution from below'.

The enthusiasm for the reform programme that was observable throughout much of Chinese society in the early eighties had turned to disappointment tinged with cynicism and resentment as the second half of the 1980s progressed. This transformation came about through a variety of factors. Firstly, the rural reforms which had been the one area of spectacular success for the economic reformers had begun to go badly awry from 1985 onwards. The policy success of the early 1980s had turned into the headache of the early 1990s. Secondly, the urban economic reform programme that was launched with much fanfare in late 1984 not only failed to turn around the urban economy but was also extremely destabilising. Thirdly, frustration among large sections of the population increased. Even among those who had tangibly benefited from the reforms, there was the feeling that they were not doing well enough while others were doing still better.[64] Fourthly, many critical intellectuals and students became disillusioned with the lack of sufficient political reform. Finally, the increase in contacts with the outside world brought in a range of new ideas along with the technology. Urban China was becoming increasing cosmopolitan in its outlook and increasingly aware how far it lay behind much of the rest of East Asia in terms of development. This had the effect of increasing popular dissatisfaction with the pace of economic reform. Additionally, it provided critical intellectuals with alternatives to the policies offered by their own party leaders. Not only did China's intellectuals pick up ideas from the West but also, more importantly, some formed strong links with critical intellectuals in Eastern Europe, especially Hungary.[65] Reform ideas from other Socialist countries could not be so easily dismissed as those from capitalist countries as being 'bourgeois'.[66]

The peasantry is poorly represented at the national and provincial level in formal terms. In fact, most peasant representatives to national and provincial committees tend to be drawn from the new rural wealthy elite, a group that has little in common with the interests of the vast majority of China's peasantry. The selection of successful peasants was intended to signal the success of the reforms as well as trying to encourage others to emulate them in becoming rich. Thus, delegates from 10,000 *yuan* households replaced the poor and lower-middle-class peasants who had been given national prominence during the years of the Cultural Revolution. Yet, despite the generally poor representation the peasantry has been pursuing their interests at the local level through a variety of more informal mechanisms. The relaxation of controls in the countryside and the emphasis on the household as the key economic unit have provided the peasantry with a myriad of opportunities for pursuing their interests.

The lack of formal representation has not been an impediment to influencing policy-making: quite the reverse. By a mixture of resistance to policies with which they disagree and seizing on opportunities presented by other policies, indeed sometimes pushing far ahead of central policy, peasants have been able to modify significantly rural policy to their benefit. An example of the former is the strong resistance to the one-child family campaign and non-co-operation by not registering births or simply not complying by having more children. Also compliance in the extreme threw up the ugly and unacceptable incidences of infanticide. The development of the early phase of rural policy after the re-introduction of the responsibility system in 1979 provides a good example of the latter.[67] Watson has demonstrated convincingly how, at each stage, practice in the countryside was moving ahead of central policy.[68] Events in the countryside have led Zweig to comment that 'in essence we are witnessing the unbridled pursuit of peasant political and economic interest'.[69] Yet, the fact that these activities take place through informal channels means that the outcome can be unpredictable with the peasantry still prey to changing policy direction at the centre.

However, not all peasants have benefited from decentralisation and the new policies are leading to the emergence of new economically powerful strata in the countryside. Many peasants in the poorer areas and especially those not near to lucrative urban markets have actually seen their incomes fall as a result of recent policies. Those who have moved off the land are dependent on the success of collective industries in the small rural towns or on temporary labour in the urban areas. The austerity measures in place since September 1988 and tightened since June 1989 have caused large numbers of collective enterprises to close down and the lack of investment funds has caused the collapse of building projects throwing hundreds of thousands if not millions out of work. To prevent these newly dispossessed from becoming a political problem in the urban areas, the party will have to resurrect the strong barriers that previously kept the peasantry out of the urban environments.

Apart from the peasants in backward areas, and the new rural migrants, even the better off peasants have been affected by current policies. Many peasants have been forced back into grain production from which they had pulled out because of its lack of profitability. Not surprisingly, this has caused resentment among peasants who had been getting used to their new won freedoms. Stringent production quotas for grain have been reimposed and the reforms designed to dismantle the state monopoly over distribution have been effectively abandoned. Peasants in many areas are being forced to sell to the state at below market prices, something which has caused violent outbursts.

The peasants have no formal channels through which they can deal with political issues; the village committees and township governments do not seem to provide this function. The most radical political reform to date has been the abolition of the commune as a unit of government administration. The township, abolished in the Great Leap Forward, has been revived as a unit of government administration leaving the commune to arrange economic affairs. The production brigades were replaced by village administrative and economic committees. The hope was that these new, or revived, organisations would provide basic-level political institutions that would be more responsive to resolving the political and legal consequences that arose from the new economic situation in the countryside. While abolition of the commune seems to have been a generally popular measure, the new institutions have been unable to fulfil the roles assigned to them. In particular, they do not seem to have made rural officials any more accountable than in the past for their actions.[70]

As controls have been relaxed, peasants have shown themselves willing to undertake actions to defend or promote their interests outside of the formal channels. In 1987, for example, when officials responsible for chemical fertiliser production manufactured a shortage to drive up prices, some hundred thousand incidents of peasant response were reported ranging from looting fertiliser plants to capturing transport lorries.[71] Similarly, in 1988 when the state ran out of money to pay for the harvest and issued IOUs, there were many reports of violent resistance and many state tax collectors and other local officials were attacked.

The fact that most peasant political activity takes place through non-sanctioned channels indicates that the party has not been capable of creating formal institutions for the political participation of the peasantry. Although the peasants did not come out to join their urban brothers and sisters in 1989 in any great numbers,[72] it is dangerous for the regime if the overwhelming majority of society have to rely on political activities that are not sanctioned or exert their influence through withdrawal and non co-operation.

While the workers might not run the factories or the government, by comparison with other groups, they have enjoyed a favorable status since 1949 in terms of material gains and social status. Indeed, on the whole, the party-organised working class has shown little inclination for long-term political activity concentrating on more immediate concerns. However, the industrial working class perceived its privileged position to be threatened by the reform programme as it began to unfold. Whether true or not, there was a growing perception that those in the collective or private sector were doing much better. This perception derived partly from reporting of, or experience with, the exceptional cases rather than the norm.

Essentially, urban workers were being offered a deal that involved giving up their secure subsidy-supported low-wage lifestyle for a risky contract-based system that might entail higher wages at the possible price of rising costs and unemployment. Many urban workers decided to reserve their judgement. Their reservations were exacerbated by the leadership's indecisiveness about urban reform that resulted in a stop-go pattern throughout the 1980s. Their insecurity mounted after 1986 when the reforms resulted in spiralling inflation without consequent improvements in material standards. Not surprisingly, talk of further price reform and reductions in subsidies created a sense of panic. Zhao Ziyang's attempts, with Deng Xiaoping's support, to produce rapid economic results created the inflation of 1988 and 1989 that threatened all those on fixed incomes. As a result, much of urban China was frustrated with the progress of urban reforms. In fact, one third of all urban households suffered from a drop in real incomes during 1988 and this number must have gone up in 1989. Many of the remaining households were also feeling the economic pinch and incomes were being subsidised by taking on a second and sometimes even a third job.[73]

This situation did not lead to greatly increased political action by China's urban industrial working class. There were occasional go-slows and strikes but no mass action. It is important to note that urban workers only took to the streets some time after the students had led the way. This reticence by workers in state-owned enterprises to engage in open political activity came not only through the tighter political and social controls at the urban work-place but also because of their rela-

43

tively privileged position with respect to other members of the working class.

The existence of the officially sponsored trade unions directly under party control makes it difficult for workers to organise spontaneously. The space for autonomous political activity is thus contracted. Yet, there have been fairly consistent complaints from workers, and even on occasion, from their representatives that the unions have neglected the workers' interests in their efforts to reduce industrial conflict and promote production.[74] During the reform period, the leadership's response has been to try to restore their credibility by granting workers greater freedom within carefully defined limits. Most of the time, the majority of workers seem to have been happy to operate within these party defined constraints.[75]

It was only once the student demonstrations created the possibility that some workers established their own organisation. In mid-May, the Capital (or Beijing) Workers' Autonomous Federation was set up as well as active organisations in Shanghai, Nanchang (where a solidarity organisation was also founded), Guiyang, Wuhan, Nantong, Jinan, Hangzhou, Changchun and Changsha.[76] Orthodox party leaders interpreted the formation of a city-wide workers' federation as a major threat. The existence of such an organisation was a direct affront to the party's claim to represent the highest form of working-class consciousness. Such a challenge could never be accepted by orthodox party leaders and it merely served to convince them that they were confronted by a 'counter-revolutionary' organisation. Throughout the 1980s, the party has been afraid that it would be confronted by a Solidarity type opposition and this fear seemed to be realised in May 1989 when the workers joined the students. As a result, a majority was constructed to use the coercive power of the state to crush the rapidly expanding student-led protests.

In terms of getting issues on the political agenda, if not in material terms, intellectuals and students have been main beneficiaries of the new policy programme pursued since 1978. Yet, ironically they became its most vociferous critics and the staunchest promoters of their own interests. As noted above, the emphasis on practice and a more empirical approach to decision-making has led to a greater value being placed on consultation and discussion and this has resulted in key groups of experts being drawn into the decision-making process on a more systematic basis.

Initially, measures were introduced to improve both the material situation and the prestige of intellectuals. Gone are the references to the 'stinking ninth category', as they were called during the Cultural Revolution, and instead intellectuals are defined as an integral part of the working class. This 'ideological upgrading' was accompanied by attempts to improve their work, housing and salary conditions.[77] To facilitate their contribution to the modernisation process, intellectuals have been granted greater freedom within their fields of professional competence. There has been an explosion of professional journals and convening of congresses to enable the exchange of views. Professional societies have been mushrooming as a further forum for the exchange of ideas and as organisations on which the party and state leading bodies can draw for expertise. In addition, senior intellectuals and tens of thousands of students have been allowed much greater access to the world intellectual community. As a result, intellectual debate became increasinglv linked to issues that absorbed the world academic community.

Intellectuals were also given an unparalleled chance to influence the decision-making process throughout the 1980s both in terms of policy-making on specific areas and in terms of being able to advance publicly their own particular interests. They have played a prominent role in drafting reform legislation for the overhaul of the agricultural, industrial and science and technology sectors.

The importance of intellectuals to the party leadership was reflected in the attempts to promote more of their number to leading positions and to co-opt more of them into the party. Calls were consistently made to appoint more experts to run research institutes and factories.[78] Yet within research institutes and other work units, some officials, who owe their position to their political and administrative skills at working the old system, have moved to block the advance of those who derive their power from their detailed technical knowledge. While those with technical skills push for greater autonomy, many administrative cadres have fought to exert control over the enterprise's work in order to maintain their own position. Quite rightly, increase in autonomy for a professional manager is seen as undermining the role of the party committee in an enterprise.

Since June 1989, the emphasis on the leadership role of the party in all spheres at the work-place has been renewed. This stands in marked contrast to the reformers' attempt to limit the influence of party committees.

Party secretaries have resorted to a variety of measures to prevent being by-passed by the new generation of better educated party members. This friction has resulted in attempts to block the applications of intellectuals to join the party, or putting them onto unlimited probation while their 'complicated' backgrounds are investigated.[79] Despite these problems, increasing numbers of intellectuals have been joining the party and have been appointed to leadership positions but often both groups have been frustrated. Many older cadres have felt resentment at being by-passed by 'party yuppies', while intellectuals who have had their advance blocked have become disillusioned with the party's promises of a bright new future.

Membership of organisations such as the NPC and the Chinese People's Political Consultative Conference have also provided intellectuals with inputs into the decision-making process. Further, intellectuals played important roles in a number of the think-tanks that were set up by Zhao Ziyang to give concrete form to his reform programmes. Such expanded consultation was also apparent at the provincial level. For example, leaders of Heilongjiang Province gave their seal of approval to regular contacts and consultations between leading personnel and experts in order to make use of their 'brain-trust role as advisers' in formulating macroeconomic strategy and important economic policy decisions.[80]

The revival of the 'united front' approach and the increased reliance on experts has led to a revitalisation of the eight other political parties in the PRC. Contrary to the view that these parties would pass away with the generation that spawned them, they have flourished again and have even begun to recruit new members.[81] The CCP sees these other parties as providing a useful link to the intellectuals who it cannot draw directly under its own influence and as playing a pivotal role in mediating with influential Chinese abroad.[82] For example, the Jiusan Society is composed mainly of intellectuals from scientific and technical circles and the CCP has sought to take advantage of those connections.

These parties have used the new opportunities to press the

interests of their own members. Indeed, the Democratic National Construction Association composed mainly of people from financial and business circles even contemplated the possibility of setting up a genuine opposition political party rather than one which operated under the tutelage of the CCP.

Since the repression of the demonstrations in June 1989 and the emergence of multi-party systems in Eastern Europe, the CCP has been at pains to stress the unique nature of its own multi-party system. Of course, this is intended to forestall any moves to genuine independence by the already existing parties. Articles have stressed the acceptance by the other eight parties of the CCP's leadership.[83] In an interview, the Chairman of the Democratic National Construction Association, Sun Qimeng, stated that Communist party leadership was the prerequisite and guarantee for multi-party co-operation. Contrary to views expressed by his association a year or so before, Sun noted that his party was not a 'party out of office or an opposition party'.[84]

The late-1980s exposed problems with this system of regime patronage for intellectuals. As the CCP leadership divided over fundamental issues the parameters of debate were continually redrawn in such a way that many of the 'loyal intellectuals' fell outside of the realms of the acceptable. Hu Yaobang's effective dismissal in January 1987 as a result of student demonstrations was a major turning-point for many pro-party intellectuals.[85] Hu was seen by many as supporting further experimentation with political reform and as the most important patron of intellectuals within the top leadership. His dismissal caused critical intellectuals to question the validity of their tacit agreement. It seemed that the party could not be relied upon to keep its part of the bargain. Many of the harsh judgements that had been reserved for private discussion were thrown into the public domain. The disillusionment with incomplete reform in the political sphere caused critical intellectuals to question the validity of working within the constraints laid down by Deng Xiaoping and the feasibility of 'revolution from above'.[86]

Independent intellectual activity increased at the beginning of 1989.[87] Of particular importance was the petition movement begun on 6 January by Fang Lizhi's open letter to Deng Xiaoping calling for the release of political prisoners.[88] On 28 January the 'new-enlightenment salon' was founded by Su Shaozhi, Fang Lizhi, Wang Ruoshui and others. This salon and the journal it published provided an important forum for the discussion of unorthodox ideas. Once the students provided the lead, the intellectual community radicalised even further and began to mobilise on the students' behalf against the traditionalists in the party. On 14 May, twelve prominent intellectuals issued an appeal saying that they would join the students' hunger strike if the movement was not termed patriotic. On 16 May, they set up the Beijing Intellectuals' Autonomous Federation. Finally, on 17 May, Yan Jiaqi and Bao Zunxin, among others, signed a manifesto reaffirming that the student-led movement was patriotic and demanding the abolition of the dictatorship. They claimed the movement would lead to the destruction of the dictatorial and autocratic regime. Alluding to Deng Xiaoping, they wrote that although 'the Qing dynasty has been gone for 76 years, China is still ruled by an old and aging emperor, although he does not wear the crown'.[89]

Hu Yaobang's enforced 'resignation' also came as a shock for the students.[90] After all, their demonstrations had been used as the excuse to dismiss him. As the incipient elite, China's students had been offered a place of prestige in China's future in return for acquiescence to the party's overriding goals. What the party did not realise was that the students themselves wanted to play a major part in defining what that future would be. It is noticeable that the two major rounds of demonstrations (December 1986 and April–June 1989) erupted after a perceived set-back for the reformers.[91] In particular, they have to be seen in light of the unfulfilled promises for political reform that had been presented by Deng Xiaoping himself as an important part of the reform programme.

Indeed from 1980 onwards, campus-based radicalism had been increasing and many students began to express iconoclastic ideas. They were less willing than the critical intellectuals to accept the idea of a revolution from above and to operate within the guidelines laid down by the party. A number of factors created for them the time and space to think more critically about China's future. They were not yet integrated into the system of regime patronage that entrapped most intellectuals; they were relatively free from the political and social controls that inhibited spontaneous activity among other groups of urban society; and although by no means well off, the students were not concerned so directly with financial and social problems.

The students constructed the view of themselves as the moral guardians of the Chinese nation. They saw themselves as standing in a direct line of descent from the students who had demonstrated in the May Fourth Movement of 1919 and the Anti-Japanese movement of 1935. This identification with such previous movements gave the students the feeling of righteousness in their cause. The fact that their continued complaints were rejected by the authorities led them towards a fundamental critique of the state itself, something that became clearly apparent in the demonstrations of 1989. The general view prevailed that if the state could not see the necessity to redress the 'just grievances', then there must be something fundamentally wrong with the state itself. The idea of moral righteousness found its most extreme expression in the hunger strike that was begun on 13 May 1989.

In 1980, students at Beijing University had shown themselves willing to challenge the authorities on questions of genuine political reform. Hu Ping, a student at the University, won an election for the local people's congress against the official candidate, only to discover that he was not allowed to take his seat and not assigned to a job upon graduation. For many students this showed that there were very clear limits to what the party would tolerate.[92]

The student demonstrations of 1986 gave further impetus to campus radicalism, and demonstrations sporadically continued thereafter though they tended to be linked to specific student grievances. Thus, the demonstrations of 1988 found little support among the population at large because of their preoccupation with such issues as the hours at which lights were turned off on campus, the poor canteen facilities and the crowded dormitories. This provided no threat to the authorities, and the situation was defused quickly when university authorities made limited concessions.

These demonstrations were accompanied by on-campus lectures and the establishment of 'democratic salons' that provided students a chance both to hear and discuss unorthodox viewpoints. Key leaders of the 1989 protest movement Wang Dan, Shen Tong and Wu'er Kaixi, all ran radical discussion groups. These three young men already had been planning some political activities for 1989 before events overtook such planning following the death of Hu Yaobang.[93]

Thus, when the death of Hu Yaobang provided a spark, the students were well prepared to fan the flames. The students formed the first major autonomous organisations since the foundation of the PRC and the strength of the support that they were able to muster as the movement progressed presented the party with its greatest challenge to date.

By spring 1989 disillusionment and cynicism had replaced optimism about the reform programme. Urban anger was increased by the higher visibility of official corruption. Abuse of public positions and the privatisation of public function had reached extreme proportions by the late 1980s. Chinese society had become one 'on the take' where, without a good set of connections and an entrance through the 'back door', it was very difficult to partake of the benefits of economic reform. The sight of children of high-level officials joy-riding in imported cars was a moral affront to many ordinary citizens. It was not surprising that the student slogan of 'down with official speculation' found a large, enthusiastic audience.

By 1989, it was clear that in the eyes of many urban dwellers, the party's incompetence and moral laxness had eroded any vestigial notions that the party was a moral force in Chinese society. Once the dams were breached by the students, a flood of supporters was waiting to defend the students and attack the authorities.

THE PARTY'S RESPONSE TO A CHANGING SOCIETY[94]

The events of June 1989, clearly showed that the party as a whole was incapable of responding to the new challenges facing it. As the system came under pressure from without, the political stability and unity that had been carefully constructed during the reform period crumbled.

Within the top leadership, opinions on political reform polarised around two main viewpoints: the pragmatic reforming and the traditional orthodox. They were not the only views expressed and some individuals such as Deng Xiaoping moved between the two. On occasion, Deng has seemed to give the green light to far-reaching change yet, at crucial moments, has supported the traditional viewpoint on political issues in order to preserve his economic reforms from attack. The two view-points are linked to the question of the extent of economic reform. Clearly the nature of the party depends on the kind of economic system over which it is to preside.

The pragmatic view was presented by Zhao Ziyang at the Thirteenth Party Congress. The term pragmatic is used as the reforms proposed are designed primarily to improve economic efficiency. Picking up the theme first put forward by Deng Xiaoping in August 1980, Zhao contended that political reform was indispensable if economic reform was to continue, without it economic reform would grind to a halt. In linking the two processes, he stated '[t]he process of developing the socialist commodity economy should be a process of building socialist democratic politics'. As a result, the Central Committee had decided that 'it was high time to put political reform on the agenda for the whole party'.[95]

The fact that Zhao neglected the 'Four Modernisations' in his speech was significant.[96] This reinforced the link between economic and political reform. The appeals to modernise agriculture, industry, national defence and science and technology demonstrated concern with economic reform and ignored the need for an accompanying 'modernisation' of other aspects of society. Those concerned to push ahead further with political reform referred to 'socialist modernisation', a term that included 'modernisation' of culture and ways of thinking.[97]

Reformers argued that the tendency of a Leninist party to concentrate power in the hands of a few is exaggerated in the PRC by the lingering influences of a feudal political culture. Such a party structure does not suit the demands of a more decentralised, market-influenced economy where flexibility, efficiency and the encouragement of initiative are key values. This idea was also taken over by Zhao. He noted that:

China's existing political structure was born out of the war years, basically established in the period of socialist transformation and developed in the course of large-scale mass movements and incessantly intensifying mandatory planning. . . . It fails to suit, economic, political and cultural modernisation under peacetime conditions or the development of a socialist commodity economy.[98]

The statement suggested that future reforms would have to deal with some of the core issues of the party's role and structure as inherited in the Leninist model, developed during the pre-1949 struggle for power and intensified under the centrally planned economy. The intention was to move beyond the superficial reforms initiated after Mao's death.

Zhao's proposals reaffirmed the need for a redistribution of power both horizontally to state organs at the same level and vertically to party and state organs lower down the administrative ladder. Moreover, breaking with the monistic view common to CCP thinking and the idea of uniform policy implementation, Zhao acknowledged both that 'specific views and the interests of the masses may differ from each other' and that 'as conditions vary in different localities, we should not require unanimity in everything'.[99] Zhao seemed to be feeling his way towards the acceptance of a 'loyal opposition', something that was alien not just to the Maoist political system but also to the Chinese tradition. However, Zhao's acknowledgement of a limited pluralism was not intended to accommodate factions within the party. Nor was it intended to sanction the setting of the political agenda by civil society.

It is clear that the over-centralised political system is no longer congruent with an increasingly decentralised economic system, or at least a system where much economic activity takes place outside of the centrally planned system. The economic reforms are giving rise to new forces within Chinese society. If the party continues to pursue economic reform, it will have to adopt strategies to accommodate the demands of these new forces. In addition, the party will become dependent on new strata such as professional managers, traders and entrepreneurs as well as the technicians and scientists who were already important for the functioning of the centrally planned economy,[100] to implement the more market-oriented policies. The development of institutions to accommodate the interests of these new forces will be a difficult task for the party given their more diffuse nature than the forces on which the old centrally planned system depends.

Yet even the pragmatists have made it clear that any increase in political activity should not be allowed to disrupt stability or the overriding goal of achieving economic modernisation would be undermined. This, in turn, produces the need to 'institutionalise' such activity in order to prevent the increased heterogeneity in society leading to instability. Further, tacit recognition by the party of the existence of other groups should not be interpreted as the emergence of a 'pluralist' political system. Indeed, the attempts to integrate these groups can be interpreted as an attempt to prevent that plurality by revising the structure of the regime and the party's relationship to state and society.

To this end the party can pursue two policies. Firstly, it can recruit as party members those new groups on which it has become reliant for its continued rule. This allows the party to expand its presence in significant sectors of society while maintaining its privileged ruling position. Of course, this has the effect of importing the interests of these groups into the party with the possibility that they prove a threat to the former dominant ethos. Secondly, it can seek to influence key groups in society more indirectly by binding them into organisations that become dependent on regime patronage. To head off mass opposition, the party will seek to extend its organisation, coordination and supervision of as much of the population as possible.

Traditionally, for this purpose, the party has relied on what it terms mass organisations such as the trade unions and the Women's Federation. This is, of course, a two-edged sword as it provides a mechanism of participation to officially sanctioned groups. However, as noted above, it makes the formation of autonomous union organisations or women's organisations extremely difficult. Further, it ensures that sectoral interests are subjugated to general party policy. The party allows such organisations the autonomy to organise their own activities, within a broadly defined framework, and to support the pursuance of legitimate rights of their members in so far as they do not override the common good, as defined by the party. In return, the party expects unconditional support for its broader political, economic and social programmes. However, even at times when control, economic and political, has been much tighter these organisations have proved themselves to be unwieldy for serving this purpose.

While neither Hu Yaobang in late-1986 nor Zhao Ziyang in mid-1989 saw the student protests as a major threat, the traditionalists in the party saw them as a challenge to the very fundamental principles of party rule. Crucially, Deng Xiaoping decided to side with them. Whereas Zhao appeared willing to make concessions to the students' demands, his opponents felt that no retreat was possible as it would lead to a collapse of Socialism.[101] Since June 1989, the traditional party members have set out their policy programme. This has two main elements. First, a programme of economic austerity that is also intended to restore to pride of place the centrally planned economy. Second, tight political supervision over society combined with a major political campaign to eradicate the influences of 'bourgeois liberalisation'.

While Deng Xiaoping has supported the second, the programme of economic austerity has entailed attacks on his own reform programme. Deng has always maintained a traditional view of political activity that occurs outside of party control and resisted Mao's attempts to open up the party to criticism from outside forces. In August 1989, the *People's Daily* carried a thirty-two-year-old speech from Deng in which he argued that too much democracy was undesirable for China. To ignore the masses was dangerous as this might lead to greater unrest, a view reinforced by the events of the Cultural Revolution. However, the party itself would decide whether to take any notice of the views expressed and whether it was qualified to continue in its leadership role was a matter for the party alone. This was an explicit rejection of 'Big Democracy' as proposed by Mao Zedong through which non-party masses would be allowed to have a say in party affairs. Its republication in 1989 was a clear indication of Deng's belief in the primacy of the party in China's political life.[102]

The group with which Deng sided seek to run the party and its relationship to society along orthodox Leninist lines. Efforts to relax the party's grip over state and society are resisted and they seek continually to institutionalise party dominance. Thus, the stress on the need for party strengthening at the basic level and the concern that political and ideological work continues to be taken seriously.

The student-led demonstrations of 1989, have convinced this group that it was the rejection of their view that ideological campaigns were necessary to combat the adverse effects of the economic reforms that enabled the political challenge to grow. They have blamed former party secretaries Hu Yaobang and Zhao Ziyang for not taking the problem seriously enough at an early stage and thus allowing it to get out of hand.[103] One of the specific accusations against Zhao is that he refused to include the need to 'oppose bourgeois liberalisation' in his speech to commemorate the seventieth anniversary of the May Fourth Movement as had been requested by Premier Li Peng and various other 'comrades'.[104]

The re-launching of a campaign to combat 'bourgeois liberalisation' in the summer of 1989 has been backed by calls to strengthen the party's role throughout the Chinese political system. Again prominence was given in the Chinese press to the need to uphold the 'Four Basic Principles'.[105] These vague principles are used by the traditionalists to extend their control over society by party organisations and give them the chance to criticise anything with which they disagree as negating socialism and the party. This reassertion of control was clearest in the tightening of controls over intellectuals and the media. Propaganda chief Wang Renzhi has reminded intellectuals that it is wrong for them to think of themselves as the 'most advanced and outstanding of the working class'.[106] However, treatment of intellectuals has become a tricky issue and other party leaders are clearly worried that intellectuals will withdraw their services from the economic modernisation programme.

General Secretary, Jiang Zemin, gave intellectuals an ambiguous message in a speech to commemorate the 1990 anniversary of the May Fourth Movement. He acknowledged that the vast majority of intellectuals were patriotic and that the growth of heterodox ideas among young people was the fault of the party.[106] The fact that the source of the problem is traced to faults in the party indicates that younger people can expect tougher party control over their lives as long as traditonal party members retain influence. This essentially patronising attitude of traditional party members is seen most clearly in the revival of the calls for young people to study various model heroes such as Lei Feng.[107] However, Jiang displayed no ambivalence when presenting a highly orthodox view of the relationship between the party and journalists. Essentially, he stressed that all media must follow the line set by the Central Committee and that those promoting unorthodox ideas would be punished.[109]

This drive to maintain institutionalised party dominance provides stability and assurances as well as status for party cadres. However, at the same time, it does much to explain the stifling of initiative that has been increasingly apparent during the reform period. In combination with the dual-pricing system, it provides the structural basis for corruption that has been heavily criticised not only by student demonstrators but also in the official Chinese press. The concentrated nature of power and the lack of a genuine system of accountability mean that party officials at all levels are in a unique position to turn professional relationships into personal connections for financial gain.

A major problem for Deng Xiaoping has been that while he shares these political views, he wishes to protect and push ahead with the economic reforms. Yet, the orthodox leaders clearly see various aspects of the economic reforms as giving rise to the political and ideological problems. They have been able to use Zhao Ziyang's dismissal to launch a critique of the economic reforms. They also attempted this in 1987 after Hu Yaobang's fall but their attempts were blunted very quickly. While Deng Xiaoping sanctioned the campaign against 'bourgeois liberalisation' in 1987, he quickly terminated it once it became clear that the air of uncertainty created was undermining the economy. In this, Deng was helped by the appointment of Zhao Ziyang as General Secretary as the latter used his position to blunt the political campaign and to continue to exert influence over economic policy.[110] In 1989 and 1990, it has been harder for Deng to rein in the attacks in part because the manner and circumstances under which Jiang Zemin was appointed as Zhao's successor give him no room for manoeuvre on these issues even should he wish to influence them. However, by May 1990 there were clear signs that the attack by the traditonal leaders on economic policy was being blunted.

Traditional leaders recognise that the economic reforms not only create the basis for 'disruptive ideas' but also call into question traditional notions of socialism. They challenge what the Hungarian economic theorist, Kornai, calls the 'ethical goals' of socialism such as equality, solidarity and security.[111] Thus, it is not surprising that despite calls for continuing the economic reforms, in August 1989 attacks began in the official press on the private economy and the inegalitarian consequences of Zhao's (not Deng's!) policies.

In using the military to crush the demonstrations of 1989, the traditonal leaders believe that they acted in the best interests of their revolution and have shown no remorse for the actions undertaken. Yet this does not mean that they have been oblivious to the consequences of their actions but the measures offered have been symbolic rather than real. Celebrating forty years of party rule on 1 October 1989, General Secretary Jiang Zemin rather than offering an olive branch to his own society and the international community as many had expected, presented a policy prescription that can be summed up as 'back to the future'. Such leaders wish to take China back to an imagined 'golden age' when there was social stability, solid economic growth under an essentially Soviet-style economic system and when it was clear who were enemies and who were friends. Thus Jiang called for vigilance against efforts by the West to subvert the Chinese government and institute capitalism, for vigorous repression of dissent, economic retrenchment and a return to central planning.[112]

This traditional approach to managing the party's role in the political system is clearly out-dated in a modern society where economic reform and technological development are creating a more diversified and sophisticated society. Zhao's acknowledgement that a limited plurality is inevitable has been rejected and the traditionalists prefer to think in terms of a single undifferentiated mass of people who work harmoniously for the creation of Socialism. The party's role, of course, is to tell the masses what their interests are as they strive to build Socialism. Should the current leadership decide to push ahead with the economic reforms, inevitably they will be confronted by precisely the kinds of problems that they so manifestly refused to deal with in April–June 1989. Eventually, if it wishes to have a chance of staying in power, at some point the party will have to move back to the kind of relationship between party and state and society that was envisaged by Zhao Ziyang and his supporters.

POSSIBILITIES FOR THE FUTURE

In part, the tough approach in China can be explained by the continued grip on power by the revolutionary generation. Having fought some fifty years to establish and maintain the power of an orthodox Communist party, they were ill-equipped to come to terms with the nature of the challenge that confronted them. It was much easier for them to simply interpret the movement as a counter-revolutionary uprising thus making it quite clear how it had to be dealt with.

Clearly, the power wielded by ostensibly retired veteran leaders has undermined the official stress on the institutionalisation of Chinese politics and the idea that an orderly succession can be achieved. One of the main stresses of the reform programme noted above is that China would be governed by a legal, predictable system with rules and regulations applicable to all. However, when the system came under stress, individual power relationships built up over decades proved to be more important than the rule of law and the formal functions people held. In this respect, it is important to note that the decision to implement martial law in May 1989 was not taken by a formal party or state body but by an ad hoc meeting held at Deng Xiaoping's home following discussions between Deng and other supposedly retired veterans. It was only after this decision had been made that it was pushed through party and state bodies so that it could be announced formally by Li Peng in his capacity as Premier.[113]

The veterans eased into retirement by Deng between 1985 and 1987 clearly retained considerable power behind the scenes through their personal connections and institutionally through membership of the Central Advisory Commission. This Commisssion, headed by Chen Yun, has functioned as a rival to the Central Committee where Zhao Ziyang and Deng Xiaoping had built up a pro-reform majority.

Despite assurances to the contrary, Deng has been unable to deal with the issue of succession. He has repeated Mao's methods of anointment by the paramount leader. Deng Xiaoping's attempts to boost the position of the current General Secretary Jiang Zemin as his successor is merely the latest in a series of attempts to ensure that a successor is in place before the paramount leader dies. However, to date all attempts to manage succession by transferring legitimacy from the paramount leader to a chosen disciple have failed. Deng has proved no more successful than Mao in this respect. His first two protégés Hu Yaobang and Zhao Ziyang were both dismissed from their posts ostensibly for being too liberal in their reactions to student demonstrations.

Neither has the system been able to rid itself of the need for a 'supreme leader' to balance the competing factions in the top party leadership. This was made clear by Deng Xiaoping's role during the protests and by Zhao Ziyang's revelation to Gorbachev that a secret decision had been taken in 1987 that all important issues should still be referred to Deng. This over reliance on Deng is another factor seriously undermining the long term stability of the current leadership and accounts for the panic that hits shares in Hong kong each time his death is rumoured.

However, it is important to note that both at Central Committee and provincial levels and below, major personnel changes have been pushed through that suggest time is on the reformers' side. The events of June 1989 revealed a party that was deeply divided and where considerable support for the demonstrators existed. While three pro-reform members of the Politburo have gone (Hu Yaobang, Zhao Ziyang and Hu Qili), five of the remaining eight members have a pro-reform orientation.[114] The Central Committee elected at the Thirteenth Party Congress was thought of as being Zhao's committee. A number of leaders who had been associated with previous campaigns against 'bourgeois liberalism' failed to gain election or suffered an embarrassingly low vote. The traditionalists' ability to control decision making will depend on their capacity to orchestrate the election of a new Central Committee before they run out of momentum. As one moves further down the administrative ladder, the process of regeneration of the leadership has moved further with the majority of the appointees having had the benefit of higher education and having been appointed when issues of reform were high on the political agenda. However, Premier Li Peng stands as a good warning to the simple equation that a higher education training in a technical subject means that one has a more progressive political attitude.

To deal with the crisis that it faces, the senior party leaders are attempting a process of internal regeneration. This capacity for self-regeneration should not be underestimated given the number of times that the party has been almost destroyed only to rise phoenix-like from the ashes. With the erosion of the importance of ideology during the reform period, most of the party realise that legitimacy, or simply acquiescence in its continued rule, can only be regained through economic success, a prospect that is hampered by the traditionalists' stress on the need for debilitating ideological campaigns.

The current leaders have pointed to their success in curbing excessive economic growth and bringing down inflation as evidence for trust in their economic competence. The growth in GNP for 1989 was only 4 per cent, the lowest increase since the death of Mao Zedong. The slow-down is seen more clearly by the fact that growth in industrial output on an annual basis in the last quarter was only 0.7 per cent. While retail price inflation for 1989 as a whole was calculated at 17.8 per cent, figures suggest that by the end of the year it had been brought down to 3 or 4 per cent, possibly even lower.

In addition to perseverance with the programme of economic austerity, the leadership has responded, or is trying to give the impression, of responding to the movement's political demands. A widely publicised campaign against official speculation and corruption has been launched. On 28 June 1989, the Politburo adopted a seven-point programme to deal with corruption. This addressed issues such as closing down firms that had engaged in potentially corrupt activities, preventing the children of senior officials from engaging in commercial activities, limiting perks derived from official positions – such as entertaining, travel abroad, special supply of scarce goods and driving around in imported cars.[115] Further, one of the students' main demands was met when, on 9 November 1989, Deng Xiaoping stepped down from his last official position as Chair of the Party's Military Affairs Commission.[116]

Such a process of internal regeneration will not prove successful over the long term and a number of the measures are cosmetic. The high profile campaign against corruption has floundered and run aground quite quickly. Indeed the base for official corruption can only be eradicated through a radical restructuring of the economy, something which the current leadership is unlikely to contemplate. Finally, the resignation of Deng Xiaoping will fool no one. Whether Deng wants to or not, he will have to remain active in politics to try to keep his third choice as successor Jiang Zemin in power and to try to salvage something of his original reform programme.

More important will be whether the leadership can turn the economy around. This seems extremely unlikely over the long term and indeed the current leaders lack the imagination to construct new policies. Clearly, balance needed to be restored to an economy that was running out of control in late 1988. The question is whether the current austerity measures can provide anything more than a temporary respite. The present policies do not deal with the fundamental structural problems of the economy and are exacerbating many of them by denying their existence. While the economic squeeze has succeeded in dampening demand, it has not improved productivity and remodelled the irrational structure as promised. By early 1990, there were clear signs that the austerity measures were pushing the economy towards a major recession. In October 1989, for the first time in a decade, industrial output fell on a month-to-month basis by 2.1 per cent. In the period January–March 1990, industrial output recorded recorded no growth while that of light industry fell 0.2 per cent. The collective sector has been hard hit and the growth in the monthly industrial output dropped from 16.6 to 0.6 per cent in September 1989. A number of large factories were idle at the end of 1989 because of the slowdown in output. In the first two months of 1990 alone, this resulted in 1.5 million urban residents losing their jobs. This deteriorating economic situation is clearly adding to the leadership's worries.

Shaken by the economic downturn, and fearing social dislocation, measures have been quietly introduced to ease the austerity programme despite resistance by fiscal conservatives at the centre. Two main arguments have been used against the austerity measures as enterprises began to suffer shortages and economic growth slowed. First, there are those who have argued for a loosening of controls on bank loans and secondly, those who go further and have called for a halt to austerity and the increase of society's spending power by expanding investment in fixed assets and by expanding consumption funds. In fact, in 1989 national investment in fixed assets was only reduced by 50 billion *yuan* rather than the proposed 90 billion.[117] Monetary policy has been eased with the government planning to issue 40 billion *yuan* in new currency in 1990 as opposed to 21 billion in 1989.[118] However, resistance is shown by the fact that reports were still being carried in the Chinese media on the need to persist with the austerity programme.[119]

The divisions and lack of ideas about the way forward have also been reflected in debates about the collective sector and the coastal policy for export-led growth. The clampdown on collectives that was apparent in autumn 1989 was obviously

eased and articles appeared praising their contribution to economic growth. Finally, there has been a reaffirmation of the
strategy of coastal development that was closely associated with
Zhao Ziyang. Following a visit in early February 1990 to the
Special Economic Zone of Shenzhen, Li Peng proclaimed that
the establishment of Special Economic Zones and the further
opening of coastal areas were still a major component of the
reform plan.[120]

While the traditionalists' attack might have been blunted, the
current formal leaders clearly lack the necessary imagination to
chart a new way forward. Even should they wish to launch
further policy initiatives, they are hampered by their dependence on the patronage of the veteran revolutionaries. This
makes it difficult for them to establish their own power base
that could be used to support them in any forthcoming struggle.
This confirms the view of them as a transitional leadership and
the real struggle of succession will start when the veterans die.
Their dependence on the patronage of the old men means that
the system has become frozen and they will be unwilling to take
risks or launch new initiatives to deal with China's problems. As
a result, the current leaders will not be able to guide China out
of the stop-go policies pursued in the 1980s. As long as they
remain in power, periods of loosening of control will be followed by the quick re-application of central control mechanisms
once prices begin to rise and potential unrest appears imminent.

The likelihood of a crisis arising with future succession struggles might suggest a greater role for the PLA and some
observers have speculated on the possibility of a *coup d'état*.
While the events of June 1989 showed that control of the PLA
is the vital factor in Chinese politics, the scenario of a coup is
unlikely unless China really begins to disintegrate. The military
as an institution has shown a reluctance to become too involved
again in government. Many of the military commanders remem-
ber being dragged into the political arena during the Cultural
Revolution and the subsequent criticism of their role. In
addition, the military itself is divided along precisely the same
lines as the party. While discipline held up pretty well during
the crushing of the 'rebellion' in June 1989, evidence before and
since indicates that deep divisions exist. In mid-February 1990,
official reports confirmed the rumours of dissent in the PLA
and that a political campaign had been under way to persuade

soldiers to remain loyal to Socialism and the party. An article later in the month noted that the PLA had become a target for infiltration by 'hostile forces within and without the country'. The primary task of future political work was 'to guarantee that guns are in the hands of those politically reliable'.[121]

The fear that the army might defect to the opposition should worry the current leaders as their power came through the 'barrel of the gun' and their continued rule will rely on the threat of force for some time to come. The worries of being confronted by another major movement in urban China has been combined with the worries about increasing political activity among China's 'national minorities'.

The army will clearly play an important role in any succession struggle and its support will be crucial for any aspiring General Secretary. Should it act, there is no guarantee that it would be to support the traditional party leaders. The new style army had begun to do rather well from the reforms after the problems of adjustment and it may be concerned by too great an economic reversal. In fact, it has been the first victim of the West's economic sanctions against China. The last few years had seen a booming arms trade and the idea of China as a bulwark against Soviet aggression in the Far East meant that it acquired the kind of high-level military technology denied to other Socialist countries. Indeed the most likely initial breakthrough in the current impasse is for sections of the military to support the seizure of power by a pro-reform faction within the party.

The current party leadership must rule without the support of key sections of its urban population which makes its attempts at economic renewal all the more difficult to attain. It has clearly lost the support of the younger generation and no amount of study of Lei Feng is going to win them back. The fast changing events in Eastern Europe and the Soviet Union have left China's leaders looking increasingly out of touch with reality and as ossified as the Brezhnev leadership in its later years.

Recent events in Eastern Europe and the Soviet Union make even the most far-reaching scenario of the collapse of Communist party rule look feasible. A return to reform policies at some point in the future is inevitable and it remains to be seen how skilfully party leaders will deal with the issues that arise. Not only will economic reform be pursued but many of the political issues will be put on the agenda including a re-evaluation of the events of June 1989. As Gorbachev has discovered in the Soviet Union once the snowball of reform starts moving quickly downhill, it is very difficult to stop and party leaders will be pushed into adopting increasingly radical postures to avoid the avalanche. Should the people come out onto the streets a second time to demonstrate against the Communist party, it is debatable whether the PLA would let itself be used again to put down popular unrest.[122]

It is difficult to see beyond Communist party rule to state what might replace it and thus no attempt will be made. At the present time in China there is no person who can rally support as an independent moral authority such as Vaclev Havel in Czechoslovakia or Lech Walesa in Poland. Neither are there any alternative structures around which opposition can rally such as the Church in some Eastern European countries. One possibility might be for the reformers within the party to break away and form a coalition with one, or some, of the eight political parties in the PRC. Yet these parties are also tainted with 'guilt by association', and if a genuine multi-party sytem were to be established most, if not all, of the parties would be left behind with the CCP.

It is likely that the various groups in exile will play a role in the regeneration of China. While no one in China would, at the present time, suggest that an alliance be formed with them, it may be propitious once major changes have already begun. An alliance with such groupings outside of China could provide increased legitimacy among the urban population.

If the centre continues to flounder, the regions will use this to pursue their own agendas and programmes. Apart from the fears of secession in Tibet, the growing problems in Xinjiang and possibly Inner Mongolia, there is now the growing *de facto* economic independence of Guangdong and the coastal areas. Already they are pursuing as far as is possible their own policies and it is to be expected that regionalism will become an even stronger feature than is currently the case. Over the longer term, perhaps the only viable option to develop a more democratic China is to allow a genuine decentralisation to take place within a federalist structure that allows both economic and political pluralism. However, two thousand years of striving towards centralised rule warns against thinking that such an option will be easy to achieve.

Thus, whoever China's future rulers are, one thing is certain – they will inherit an extremely difficult economic situation and an unstable political and social system. Unless the CCP can come to terms with the implications of its own desire for economic growth swiftly and in a manner that creates a real forum for dialogue between the different interests in Chinese society, it will not be the CCP.

NOTES

* The author would like to thank Yves Chevrier, Jon Unger and Gordon White for comments on parts of this paper. In particular, I would like to thank Kathy Hartford for her many comments on an earlier draft.

1 In April 1973, Deng was introduced by Premier Zhou Enlai at a reception for Cambodian military officials as a Vice-Premier of the State Council.

2 Part of the decline in these average wage figures is explained by the addition of many young workers in the lowest wage scales. The statistics used here are taken from various official PRC publications.

3 *Zhonggong jimi wenjian huibian* (Collection of Secret Documents of the CCP) (Taibei: Institute of International Relations, 1978), pp. 443–5.

4 Zhou Enlai had originally put forward this programme at the First Session of the NPC in December 1964.

5 Li Yizhe was a combination of the names of the three main authors of the poster. The poster contained a major attack on the political system as it had emerged from the Cultural Revolution. It denounced the authoritarianism of the system and called for the 'revolutionary supervision by the masses of people over the leadership at various levels in the party and state'. The Democracy Movement of late 1978 and early 1979 was initially tolerated by Deng Xiaoping while it focused its criticisms on the 'abuses' of the Cultural Revolution and his political opponents. However, once it became clear that the criticisms were broadening out to a more general critque of the Chinese party–state system, he moved to bring it to an end.

6 Gordon White, 'Chinese Development Strategy After Mao', in Gordon White, Robin Murray and Christine White (eds), *Revolutionary Socialist Development in the Third World* (Brighton: Wheatsheaf Books, 1983), p. 163.

7 Gordon White, 'The New Course in Chinese Development Strategy: Context, Problems and Prospects', in Jack Gray and Gordon White (eds), *China's New Development Strategy* (London: Academic Press, 1982), p. 6.

8 Tony Saich, 'Party Building Since Mao – A Question of Style?', *World Development*, Vol. 11, No. 8, 1983, p. 750.

9 This growth rate of some 12 per cent per annum was far above the 4 to 5 per cent rates achieved between 1970 and 1977.

10 In January 1977, Hua had put forward the slogan, 'We must resolutely uphold whatever policy decisions Chairman Mao made and unswervingly carry out whatever Chairman Mao instructed.' This became known as the 'Two Whatevers' policy.

11 Chen is said to have criticised Deng at a meeting of senior members of the Central Advisory Commission in April 1990 for causing the trends that culminated in the student-led demonstrations of 1989. See also, Chen Yun, 'Shoulder Heavy Responsibilities and Study Philosophy', *Renmin*

ribao (People's Daily), 15 April 1990. This was a talk of Chen Yun's delivered on 17 July 1987. Chen's speech stressed the need for leaders to listen to different opinions.

12 This process was completed with the promulgation in June 1981 of the 'Resolution on Certain Questions in the History of Our Party Since the Founding of the People's Republic of China'. A translation can be found in *Beijing Review*, No. 27, 6 July 1981. It should be noted that the attempts to liberalise economic practice were closely associated with Chen Yun.

13 On this point in particular and the strategy in general see Thierry Pairault, 'Industrial Strategy (January 1975–June 1979): in Search of New Policies for Industrial Growth', in Gordon White and Jack Gray (eds), *China's New Development Strategy*.

14 For an excellent account of the earliest phase of the agricultural reforms see Andrew Watson, 'Agriculture Looks for "Shoes that Fit": The Production Responsibility System and its Implications', in Neville Maxwell and Bruce McFarlane (eds), *China's Changed Road to Development* (Oxford: Pergamon Press, 1984).

15 It was essentially based on Chen Yun's 'Three Freedoms and One Guarantee' policy of the early 1960s that had been introduced to revive Chinese agriculture after the disaster of the Great Leap Forward. Under this policy, private plots were restored, rural markets revived, small rural enterprises were encouraged to take responsibility for their own profits and losses, and output quotas were fixed at the household level.

16 Deng Xiaoping, 'Reform of the Leadership System of Our Party and State' 18 August 1980, in *Deng Xiaoping wenxuan 1975–1982 (Selected Works of Deng Xiaoping 1975–1982)* (Beijing: Renmin chubanshe), p. 282.

17 This was a speech to an enlarged session of the Politburo and was approved by the Politburo on 31 August. The speech was re-released by Xinhua's Chinese service on 29 June 1987. Importantly, this version included a new point four in the speech that discussed the need for major reforms in the system of enterprise management to put more power in the hands of enterprise managers and to remove the party committee from involvement in 'routine affairs'. This re-release was in preparation for the Thirteenth Party Congress that was held in October 1987 and signalled a willingness to push ahead again with political reform.

18 Liao Gailong, 'Historical Experience and Our Path of Development', *Zhonggong yanjiu* (Research on the CCP), Vol. 15, No. 9, September 1981, p. 159.

19 The principles are adherence to the socialist road, the dictatorship of the proletariat, the leadership of the Communist Party, and Marxism–Leninism and Mao Zedong Thought. See Deng Xiaoping, 'Uphold the Four Basic Principles', 30 March 1979, *Deng Xiaoping wenxuan 1975–1982*.

20 Personal communication from participants at the conference.

21 Deng Xiaoping, 'Not Reforming the Political Structure Will Hamper the Development of Productive Forces', 3 September 1986 quoted in *Beijing Review*, No. 20, 18 May 1987, p. 15.

22 See, for example, Wang Huming, 'Heading for an Efficient and Democratic Political Structure', *Shijie jingji daobao (World Economic Herald)*, 21 July 1986.

23 On this notion see Cyril Zhiren Lin, 'Open-Ended Economic Reform in China', in Victor Nee and David Stark (eds), *Remaking the Economic Institutions of Socialism* (Stanford: Stanford University Press, 1989).

24 The re-definition of party–government relations is dealt with below. For a review of the reform of the bureaucracy see John Burns, 'Civil Service Reform in Post-Mao China', *The Australian Journal of Chinese Affairs*, No.

18, July 1987; the initial phase of reform of cadre policy is traced in Tony Saich, 'Cadres: From Bureaucrats to Managerial Modernisers?', in Birthe Arendrup et al. (eds), *China in the 1980s – and Beyond* (London: Curzon Press, 1986); and the question of citizen participation is dealt with in Tony Saich, 'Modernization and Participation in the People's Republic of China', in Joseph Y.S. Cheng (ed.), *China: Modernization in the 1980s* (Hong Kong: The Chinese University Press, 1989).

25 Hua Guofeng, 'Report on the Work of the Government', in *Main Documents of the Second Session of the Fifth National People's Congress of the People's Republic of China* (Beijing: Foreign Languages Press, 1979), p. 72.

26 This measure had been first suggested by Zhou Enlai in his 1957 'Report on the Work of the Government'.

27 Lü Cheng and Zhu Gu, 'Conscientiously Safeguard the People's Democratic Rights', *Hongqi (Red Flag)*, No. 17, 1980.

28 See, for example, Chen Yun, 'Speech at the National Conference of the CCP', *Renmin ribao*, 24 September 1985, p. 2; and Chen Yun, 'Combating Corrosive Ideology', *Beijing Review*, No. 41, 14 October 1985, pp. 15–16; and *Renmin ribao*, 4 October 1985.

29 'The Decision of the Central Committee of the Communist Party of China on Party Consolidation', in *Beijing Review*, No. 42, 17 October 1983, p. 1. The decision was adopted at the Second Plenum of the Twelfth Central Committee.

30 The restructuring reduced the previous eleven regional commands to seven; with a 50 per cent reduction in the total of senior officers and the appointment of 'younger, better educated, and professionally more competent' officers. Such major reshuffles have occurred very rarely and usually mark a leader trying to assert or consolidate his control over the military. Thus, in 1973 in the wake of the purge of Lin Biao, Mao Zedong reshuffled his regional military commanders; the 1985 reshuffle can be seen as an attempt by Deng Xiaoping to consolidate his authority; and a reshuffle in May 1990 may have represented an attempt by President Yang Shangkun to increase his control over the military regions.

31 Cheng Hsiang, 'News From Beidaihe', *Wen Wei Po*, 8 August 1986, translated in *SWB:FE*, 8335.

32 Some of the concrete reform measures proposed by Zhao are discussed below.

33 For an excellent overview of this theory and other strategies for democratisation in recent years see William Howe, 'Which Way to Go: Strategies for Democraticisation in Chinese Intellectual Circles', to be published in *China Information*. Information included here is drawn from this article.

34 Zhang Bingjiu, 'Radical or Moderate Democracy', in Liu Jun and Li Lin (eds), *Xinquanwei zhuyi: dui gaige lilun gangling de lunzheng (Neo-authoritarianism: a Debate on the Theoretical Programme of Reform)* (Beijing: Beijing Economic Institute Press, 1989). See also, Wu Jiaxiang, 'Democratisation through Marketisation', *Shijie jingji daobao*, 10 April 1989.

35 See for example, Hao Wang, 'On Transitional Democracy', *Zhengzhixue yanjiu (Research on Political Science)*, No. 3, 1989.

36 Cao Siyuan was an adviser to Zhao Ziyang and a top executive with the Stone Computer Corporation. He was arrested in June 1989 but released in May 1990. Su Shaozhi was a researcher at the Chinese Academy of Social Sciences. He had been dismissed as Director of the Institute of Marxism–Leninism and Mao Zedong Thought after Hu Yaobang's fall. At present, he is researching in the USA. Yan Jiaqi was Director of the Institute of Political Studies until 1987. After his flight from China, he

became Chair of the Front for a Democratic China based in Paris. For the evolution of Su's views through the first half of the 1980s see *Democratization and Reform* (Nottingham: Spokesman, 1988). For his current thinking see his contribution in this volume (Chapter 6) and *Understanding Democratic Reform in China* (Milwaukee: Bradley Institute for Democracy and Public Values, Papers on Democracy, 1990). For a selection of Yan's writings see *Zouxiang minzhu zhengzhi. Yan Jiaqi zhongguo zhengzhi lunwenji (Towards a Democratic Politics. Essays on Chinese Politics by Yan Jiaqi)* (Teaneck, New Jersey: Global Publishing Co., 1990).

37 See, *Zhengming*, July 1987, p. 21 and October 1988, p. 25.
38 The suggestion was also made that deputies who were party members be given the right to disagree with the party organisation to which they belonged.
39 Interview with Yan Jiaqi, summer 1986.
40 A.J. Saich, 'Political and Ideological Reform in the People's Republic of China: An Interview with Professor Su Shaozhi', *China Information*, Vol. 1, No. 2, p. 25.
41 This section is drawn from Tony Saich, 'Much Ado About Nothing: Party Reform in the Eighties' in G. White (ed.), *From Crisis to Crisis: China Under Economic Reform* (Basingstoke: Macmillan Press, forthcoming).
42 Even when Hua was replaced as Chairman, the posts were kept in separate hands with Hu Yaobang taking over the leading party function. At the Twelfth Party Congress (August 1982), the post of Chairman was abolished altogether and replaced by General Secretary.
43 Hua Guofeng, 'Speech at the Third Session of the Fifth National People's Congress', in *Main Documents of the Third Session of the Fifth National People's Congress of the People's Republic of China* (Beijing: Foreign Languages Press, 1980), p. 196. Exceptions to this rule could still be found even in 1988. In Heilongjiang Province, the Secretary of the Provincial Party Committee also served as the Chairman of the People's Congress. See, 'Separation of Party and Government in Heilongjiang', *SWB:FE/0065* B2/2, 3 February 1988.
44 Yan Jiaqi, 'Our Current Political System and Political Democracy', *Jiefang ribao (Liberation Daily)*, 13 August 1986.
45 See, for example, Tan Jian, 'Reform and Strengthen China's Political System' in B. Stavis (ed.), *Reform of China's Political System, Chinese Law and Government*, Vol. 20, No. 1, 1987, p. 49.
46 See Tony Saich, 'The Chinese Communist Party at the Thirteenth National Congress: Policies and Prospects for Reform', *Issues and Studies*, Vol. 25, No. 1, January 1989.
47 A.J. Saich, 'Political and Ideological Reform in the People's Republic of China: An Interview with Professor Su Shaozhi', p. 24.
48 F. Schurmann, *Ideology and Organisation in Communist China* (Berkeley: University of California Press, 1968), p. 111.
49 Zhao Ziyang, 'On Separating Party and Government – Part of a Speech at the Preparatory Meeting for the Seventh Plenary Session of the Twelfth Central Committee', *Renmin ribao*, 26 Novemeber 1987, p. 1. The meeting was held on 14 October.
50 Zhao Ziyang, 'Advance Along the Road of Socialism with Chinese Characteristics', *Renmin ribao*, 4 November 1987, p. 3. An official tanslation can be found in *Beijing Review*, Vol. 30, No. 45, 9–15 November 1987.
51 Zhao Ziyang, 'On Separating Party and Government – Part of a Speech at the Preparatory Meeting for the Seventh Plenary Session of the Twelfth Central Committee', p. 1. Ironically, one of the major accusations made

against Zhao since his dismissal is that he ignored party work and thus allowed internal discipline to disintegrate.

52 Zhao Ziyang, 'Advance Along the Road of Socialism with Chinese Characteristics', p. 3.
53 Interview with members of the Institute of Politics and Law, Jiangsu Provincial Academy of Social Sciences, June 1988.
54 Ibid., and interview with members of the Institute of Marxism-Leninism and Mao Zedong Thought, the Chinese Academy of Social Sciences, June 1988.
55 Zhao Ziyang, 'Advance Along the Road of Socialism with Chinese Characteristics', p. 3.
56 CCP Guidelines on Forthcoming Elections', *Xinhua* in Chinese translated in *SWB/FE*: 0059, B2/1, 27 January 1988. These guidelines also proposed that no new post of government adviser be created and that government advisers over the age of seventy should retire. This was presumably to prevent the party member simply carrying out the same function under a different name.
57 It is important to note that Anyang is Zhao Ziyang's home town. Local examples of successful policy implementation are often used to promote a shift in national policy. In most instances, one or other senior leader has links to the locality concerned.
58 Lu Yun and Feng Jing, 'Anyang Begins Political Reform', *Beijing Review*, Vol. 31, No. 12, 21–7 March 1988, p. 18.
59 Zhao Ziyang, 'On Separating Party and Government', p. 1.
60 Lu Yun and Feng Jing, 'Anyang Begins Political Reform', p. 19.
61 Arrested at the same time were three leaders of the Capital Worker's Autonomous Federation suggesting that the party was particularly worried by political activity among the working class.
62 According to Stone's former General President Wan Runnan, the student movement cost some 40,000 *yuan* per day and that most of the financing came from the Stone Corporation and other private enterprises. See, *Jiefang yuebao*, August 1989, p. 22.
63 This meeting was timed to coincide with the annual session of the NPC meeting in Beijing. See, Jasper Becker, *The Guardian*, 28 March 1989.
64 See Anita Chan, 'The Challenge to the Social Fabric', in David S.G. Goodman and Gerald Segal (eds), *China at Forty. Mid-Life Crisis?* (Oxford: Clarendon Press, 1989).
65 The experiences of reform in Hungary had a major influence on the drafting of the document for urban economic reform adopted by the Central Committee of the CCP in October 1984.
66 This idea is developed in Andrew G. Walder, 'The Political Sociology of the Beijing Upheaval of 1989', *Problems of Communism*, Sept–Oct 1989, pp. 31–33.
67 An earlier example would be during land reform when the party had to strive hard to hold in check 'peasant excesses'.
68 A. Watson, 'Agriculture Looks for "Shoes that Fit"'.
69 D. Zweig, 'Opposition to Change in Rural China', *Asian Survey*, Vol. 23, No. 7, 1983, p. 885.
70 On this and related issues see Thomas P. Bernstein, 'The Limits of Rural Political Reform' in Victor C. Falkenheim (ed.), *Chinese Politics From Mao to Deng* (New York: Paragon House, 1989).
71 Quoted in Anita Chan, 'The Challenge to the Social Fabric', p. 84.
72 While peasant participation was very limited in Beijing, demonstrations in Nanjing and relatively small cities, such as occurred in Anhui province,

involved some peasant participation. See Lawrence R. Sullivan, 'The Emergence of Civil Society in China, Spring 1989' in Tony Saich (ed.), *The Chinese People's Movement: Perspectives on Spring 1989* (White Plains, New York: M.E Sharpe, 1990).

73 See Han Guojian, 'Moonlighting Craze Hits China', *Beijing Review*, Vol. 32, No. 45, 6–12 November 1989, pp. 21–23.

74 See, for example, *Gongren ribao (Workers' Daily)*, 10 October 1979.

75 There were accounts in the early 1980s that with the formation of Solidarity in Poland attempts had been made in Central China to set up similar independent organisations.

76 Talk by Ding Xueliang at the Conference *Perspectives on Tiananmen* held at Brandeis University, 16–17 September 1989 and Lawrence R. Sullivan, 'The Emergence of Civil Society in China, Spring 1989'.

77 Anita Chan notes that despite what the academics themselves might have felt about the situation, they were doing financially better than the average worker. Among the eight occupational groups in civil service pay scales, academics rank second highest, behind only state-organ officials. Anita Chan, 'The Challenge to the Social Fabric', p. 71.

78 Zhao Says Experts Should Run Factories', *China Daily*, 17 November 1984, p. 3.

79 Sun Jian and Zhu Weiqun, 'What is the Current Situation in Implementing Policies on Intellectuals?', *Renmin ribao*, 8 July 1984, p. 3.

80 *SWB:FE* 8176.

81 They have also begun to rejuvenate their own leadership in order to ensure their continued existence. *Xinhua* in English, 22 November 1985, in *JPRS–CPS–85–* 121, p. 45.

82 See, for example, 'Chinese Democrats Tour Abroad', *Beijing Review*, No. 29, 16 July 1984, pp. 8–9.

83 See, for example, Liu Lantao, 'Stability, Multi-Party Cooperation', *Renmin ribao*, 23 April 1990.

84 Lu Yun, 'Democratic Party Leader on Multi-Party Cooperation', in *Beijing Review*, Vol. 33, No. 2, 8–14 January 1990, pp. 23–4.

85 Formally speaking, Hu resigned his position but it is quite clear that there was nothing voluntary about this.

86 In interviews conducted in both the summer of 1987 and 1988, a number of intellectuals specifically referred to Hu's dismissal as marking a key turning-point in their belief that the regime was capable of reforming itself. Zhao Ziyang was not seen as a leader who had a high regard for issues of intellectual freedom.

87 For a discussion of the increased political activities of China's intellectuals during the first part of 1989 see Woei Lien Chong, 'Present Worries of Chinese Democrats: Notes on Fang Lizhi, Liu Binyan and the Film "River Elegy"', in *China Information*, Vol. 3, No. 4, spring 1989, pp. 1–20.

88 Fang and the later signatories of the petition argued that the anniversary of the May Fourth Movement of 1919 would provide a good opportunity for the release of such prisoners. In particular, they called for the release of Wei Jingsheng who had been imprisoned as a result of the Democracy Movement of 1978–9.

89 See *Zhengming*, June 1989, p. 42 and 'Mayor Chen Xitong's Report on Putting Down Anti-Government Riot', *Information Bulletin of the Embassy of the PRC*, n.d., pp. 23–4. This report was delivered on 30 June 1989 to the 8th Meeting of the Standing Committee of the Seventh NPC. Bao Zunxin was an associate research fellow at the Institute of Chinese History, Chinese Academy of Social Sciences. For the text of the 14 May appeal

and the 17 May manifesto see Wu Mouren et al. (eds), *Bajiu zhongguo minyun jishi* (*Chronology of the 1989 Chinese Democratic Movement*) (n.p.:n.p., 1989), pp. 196–7 and pp. 248–9 respectively.

90 This section draws from information in Tony Saich, 'The Beijing People's Movement, Spring 1989', *The Australian Journal of Chinese Affairs*, July 1990.

91 In fact, on the economic front it was clear that the reformers were on the retreat from September 1988 when the austerity measures were introduced by Premier Li Peng and Vice-Premier Yao Yilin. However, the NPC meeting of March 1989 made it clear that inroads were to be made into the political reforms.

92 In numerous interviews with Beijing University students they referred to the Hu Ping case as the origins of the student activism that culminated in the demonstrations of 1989.

93 The year 1989 was an important one for anniversaries. Apart from being the 40th anniversary of the founding of the People's Republic, it was the 70th anniversary of the May Fourth Movement, the 200th anniversary of the French Revolution and the 10th anniversary of the imprisonment of Wei Jingsheng.

94 This draws on information contained in Tony Saich, 'Much Ado About Nothing: Party Reform in the Eighties'.

95 Zhao Ziyang, 'Advance Along the Road of Socialism with Chinese Characteristics', p. 3.

96 The 'Four Modernisations' were put forward by the then Premier, Zhou Enlai, in January 1975 but fell into disuse during the subsequent succession struggles. The early revival of the slogan after Mao Zedong's death (September 1976) and the arrest of the 'Gang of Four' (October 1976) had indicated the new leadership's intention to deal with the pressing economic problems.

97 See for example, Jin Xiong, 'Socialism and Social Modernisation', *Guangming ribao*, 21 September 1987. The fact that it is not just China's economy that needs modernising has been a common theme of the country's reform minded intellectuals. See for example, A.J. Saich, 'Political and Ideological Reform in the People's Republic of China: an Interview with Professor Su Shaozhi'. Here Professor Su refers to the need for 'Comprehensive Modernisation' and criticises the view that sees modernisation solely in economic terms.

98 Zhao Ziyang, 'Advance Along the Road of Socialism with Chinese Characteristics', p. 3.

99 Ibid., pp. 3–4.

100 Before the reform period began even the integration of these groups was more difficult to achieve than in the Soviet Union because of the general hostility displayed towards intellectuals in general.

101 See for example Yang Shangkun's speech of 24 May 1989. 'Key Points of Comrade Yang Shangkun's Speech to an Emergency Enlarged Meeting of the Military Affairs' Commission', 24 May 1989, printed speech, p. 3. Yang specifically mentions Deng Xiaoping, Chen Yun, Peng Zhen, and Wang Zhen as supporting this viewpoint.

102 Deng Xiaoping, 'The Communist Party Must Accept Supervision', 8 April 1957 translated in *SWB:FE* 0543 B2/1, 24 August 1989.

103 Wang Zhen is even said to have accused Zhao of 'surrendering to the bourgeoisie', when he warned new party leader Jiang Zemin not to stray down the same road. See the report in *Wen Wei Po*, 24 July 1989 translated in *SWB:FE* 0518 B2/4, 26 July 1989.

104 See Li Peng's speech of 22 May 1989 in 'Key Points of Speeches by Li

Peng, Yang Shangkun, Qiao Shi and Yao Yilin at the Meeting of 22 May', printed pamphlet distributed to party members on 25 May 1989, pp. 2–3.

105 See the extracts of comments by Deng Xiaoping on the 'Four Basic Principles' carried prominently in *Renmin ribao*, 24 June 1989.

106 Wang Renzhi, 'On Opposing Bourgeois Liberalisation', *Qiushi (Seek Truth)*, No. 3, 15 February 1990. The speech was originally delivered on 15 December 1989. This is the most complete expression of the critique.

107 Jiang Zemin, 'Patriotism and the Mission of China's Intellectuals', *Renmin ribao*, 4 May 1990.

108 In March 1990, Jiang Zemin, Yang Shangkun and Li Peng all wrote inscriptions calling on the nation to learn from Lei Feng. *Xinhua* in English, 4 March 1990, *SWB:FE* 0704 5 March 1990, B2/6. Lawrence Sullivan has argued that PRC leaders have strengthened their authority by 'infantilising' the population, that is, treating the entire Chinese nation (including the elderly) as though they were children. Lawrence R. Sullivan, 'The Emergence of Civil Society in China, spring 1989'.

109 The speech was delivered on 28 November 1989 but was only released on 1 March 1990. Jiang Zemin, 'Several Questions Concerning Journalistic Work – An Outline of a Speech at a Study Class on Journalistic Work', *Qiushi*, No. 5, 1990.

110 It is rumoured that a decision was taken at the summer 1988 party meetings in Beihaide to prevent Zhao from speaking out on economic issues.

111 J. Kornai, 'The Dilemmas of a Socialist Economy: the Hungarian Experience', *Cambridge Journal of Economics*, No. 4, 1980. I am grateful to Gordon White for drawing my attention to this work.

112 Jiang Zemin, 'Speech at the Meeting in Celebration of the 40th Anniversary of the Founding of the People's Republic of China', 29 September 1989, *Beijing Review*, Vol. 32, No. 41.

113 See Yang Shangkun's speech of 22 May 1989 in 'Key Points of Speeches by Li Peng, Yang Shangkun, Qiao Shi and Yao Yilin'.

114 Those with a more pro-reform orientation are Chairman of the National People's Congress, Wan Li; the Minister of National Defence, Qin Qiwei; the former Foreign Minister and current Vice-Premier, Wu Xueqian; Vice-Premier, Tian Jiyun; and the party secretary of Sichuan Province, Yang Rudai.They are opposed by the head of the Education Commission, Li Tieying; the party secretary of the Beijing Municipality, Li Ximing; and State President, Yang Shangkun.

115 'CPC Vows to End Corruption', *Beijing Review*, Vol. 32, No. 32, 7–13 August 1989, p. 5.

116 He gave up his position as Chair of the State Military Affairs Commission at the subsequent NPC meeting in 1990.

117 *Xinhua* in English, 23 February 1990 'National Deputies Call for Continuation of Economic Retrenchment', *SWB:FE* 0700 B2/4, 28 February 1990.

118 Nicholas D. Kristof, 'China, Fearing Unrest, Eases Policies', *International Herald Tribune*, 20 February 1990.

119 See, for example, 'Continuing Austerity is Best Plan, Expert Says' in *China Daily*, 14 February 1990, p. 4. This is based on an article by Zhao Haikuan published in *Jingji ribao (Economic Daily)*, 19 January 1990.

120 'Li describes SEZs as part of nation's major reform plan', *China Daily*, 10 February 1990, p. 1.

121 *Jiefangjun bao (Liberation Army Daily)* editorial 28 February 1990, 'A Programmatic Document that Strengthens the Political Construction of Our Army' translated in *SWB:FE* 0703, 3 March 1990, B2/1–2. See also, *Xinhua*

in Chinese, 'Central Committee Document: Ensure Guns in the Hands of "Politically Reliable"', translated in *SWB:FE* 0701, 1 March 1990, B2/1–4.

122 In May and June 1990, senior party fgures Deng Xiaoping and Jiang Zemin stressed that should there be future demonstrations, they would be dealt with by the armed people's police and not the military.

3

NO WAY OUT?
RURAL REFORMS AND FOOD
POLICY IN CHINA

Kathleen Hartford

Scratch reform in Socialist systems and the word dilemma emerges with remarkable regularity. From Kornai's *Contradictions and Dilemmas* to Colton's *Dilemma of Reform in the Soviet Union* to Connor's *Socialism's Dilemmas*, reforming Socialism would seem to be beset not by mere problems but by gargantuan, and insoluble, contradictions.

China, for several years after beginning its reform process, appeared to offer more grounds for hope. There, a massive transformation from the ground up in rural areas signalled success in introducing market mechanisms and private initiative, while the fruits of that transformation promised a reservoir of both goodwill and resources that might fund the early phases of urban industrial reform. Some six years after the Third Plenum of the Eleventh Central Committee announced the reform emphasis and launched the initial rural reform policies, all looked rosy. And urban reform began in earnest.

Two Central Committees later, another Third Plenum met in early autumn 1988 to take stock of what by then was looking like imminent economic disaster. The outcome of this meeting was a combination of emergency measures that essentially froze some reforms while reversing others, but achieved little more than the embitterment of many Chinese and a slight deceleration of the rate at which the economic crisis mounted. In the aftermath of the brutal crackdown on the mass movement of spring 1989, even more severe austerity measures have been announced, and there are persistent signals emanating from some quarters among the still divided CCP leadership indicating that the past pattern of economic reform will be drastically

74

altered if not repudiated altogether. Meanwhile, the much-vaunted political reforms are, for now, clearly a dead letter.

The Beijing spring movement underlined the contradictions of reform and the erosion of the party's legitimacy in the urban arena. Yet one might well contend that the roots of these problems, and the obstacles to their solution, are to be found precisely in that arena where the reforms had such resounding early success: in the rural sector, in rural incomes and employment, and in food production. Failure to construct a credible (and popular) solution to the difficulties in this sector helped to create the deep divisions within the leadership that led to the tragic events of June; failure to resolve the social and economic ills of the countryside now threatens to stymie efforts at economic recovery and to put an end to all reform for some time to come.

In this chapter, I address the question of how the rural reforms developed, how they have arrived at this apparent impasse, and then why they will prove difficult if not impossible to 'solve'. Ultimately, as I hope to demonstrate, the Chinese situation illustrates not one but two sets of dilemmas: one related to the problems of reforming a Socialist system, the other related to eliciting economic development in a poor, heavily populated, and largely agrarian nation. These dilemmas, I contend, converge in a crisis of the Chinese *political economy*, in the fullest sense of that term. Rural reforms, by virtue of their very success, have dismantled the previous Maoist–Stalinist political economy in the rural areas, and fatally eroded its underpinnings in the urban areas. The result has been the collapse of the previous implicit social contract that bound together the Chinese body politic, a social contract that represented certain concrete guarantees to certain social groups and created a political elite whose authority rested ultimately on their capacity to sustain those guarantees. Performance of this social contract was grounded in the economic institutions of the Maoist system. With the demise of those institutions, a new social contract, grounded solidly in new economic and political institutions, is essential. It requires painful choices in the economic realm, and creative solutions in the sociopolitical realm. With an ageing, unimaginative, and illegitimised group of leaders at the helm, however, China is unlikely to enjoy such a new social contract in the foreseeable future.

75

THE MAOIST SYSTEM AND MAOIST SOCIAL CONTRACT

Among the large, populous developing nations only China seems to have brought its agricultural development into an approximate balance with demand.[1]

China has within a short period of twenty-four years already abolished absolute poverty; there is no unemployment in China and no inflation. These are the three problems which most developing countries of Asia, Africa and Latin America have failed to solve so far and see no hope of solving in the foreseeable future.[2]

'Reform' by its very nature implies a pre-existing system; reform is the reshaping of some thing, for some end. And thus we must, before plunging into the rural reforms, examine the baseline: what came before? And why was reform pursued with such seemingly desperate urgency? The rhetoric of the post-Mao reformers has been consistently negative in its treatment of the Maoist rural system, depicting it as a dreadful failure. Western scholars differ in their interpretations on this point, but most tend to go along with the reformers' generally negative assessment of the Maoist years.

And yet, by many standards, the Maoist rural system by the mid-1970s had registered considerable achievements – achievements all the more impressive when set against the performance of other Asian giants with similar developmental problems, rather than against the dynamic Asian 'little dragons' with which the reformers have tended to draw invidious developmental comparisons. Daily per capita calorie supply in China in 1977 was 2,467; in India, 2,021; and in Indonesia, 2,272.[3] From 1970 to 1976, per capita cereals production in China grew at a rate considerably outstripping both India and Indonesia.[4] Other indicators commonly taken as evidence of performance in guaranteeing basic food supply and its relatively equitable distribution – infant mortality rates and life expectancy – made China look good by comparison with its two large, poor neighbours. Indeed, the comparison was drawn to China's advantage by no less authority than the World Bank:

Chinese agriculture has sustained (under conditions of virtual self-sufficiency) a population that accounts for about 22 per cent of the world's total with less than 8 per cent of the world's arable land. With some notable exceptions, such as in 1960 and in 1961, supply of basic necessities has been maintained while the population increased by some 430 million in the 30–year period since 1949 – an average rate of increase of 2.0 per cent p.a. Provision of the basic necessities, together with the maintenance of a good security system to ensure their availability in times of local or national misfortune, has been a continuing policy preoccupation. *No large developing country has done as well as China in this regard.*[5]

While the comprehensive explanation of such a huge accomplishment is necessarily complex, for our purposes here it is sufficient to take into account certain basic factors, some institutional and some not, but all related certainly to the Maoist approach to rural development and the national food system. Efforts at agricultural development certainly went beyond purely organisational measures, to investments in rural infrastructure (using vast amounts of peasant labour) and agricultural research. By 1978, China had extended irrigation to 48 per cent of its arable land, compared to 22 per cent for India and 37 per cent for Indonesia.[6] Yet even such ostensibly non-institutional factors were related to the system of collectivised agriculture, the commune. The communes provided an alternative to the epidemic problems of rural landlessness, rural–urban migration, and urban unemployment and sectoral imbalances faced by most other developing nations. For over twenty years the communes served as the local linchpin for an integrated system of agricultural planning, organisation of production, provision of basic consumption needs and employment opportunities, marketing of surplus, manufacture of essential production inputs and financing of rural infrastructure investments. Building upon this foundation, China was thought by many not uncritical observers to have achieved a notable record in ensuring urban food supply, reducing differences between urban and rural incomes and living standards (by developing country standards) and integrating agricultural development into a coherent general development strategy.[7]

In the countryside, during the latter part of the Maoist era, that strategy was epitomised by the Dazhai production brigade, elevated to the status of national model. Dazhai represented in microcosm what Mao and his supporters saw as the preferred strategy for agricultural (and national) development based on the commune system. This included self-sufficiency and self-reliance, collectivised forms of production, group-material and normative incentives, popular participation in management and decision-making, and political education and struggle.[8]

Within the commune, there were three tiers of organisation, from the 'people's commune' at the top (usually corresponding to the old natural economic unit of the standard market area), the production brigade (generally equivalent to a natural village), and the production team (approximately twenty to forty households within the brigade). The most important level of agricultural management was the team, which organised agricultural and other production, and served as the basic 'unit of account' and thus of income distribution.

Most compensation methods were based on a 'workpoint' system. Team members received a certain number of workpoints for their labour input. The team accountant kept records of these and at year's end the value of each workpoint was determined by dividing the team's distributable net income by the grand total of workpoints earned within the team. An individual's income thus depended upon both his/her own labour contribution and the income of the team as a whole. Within this common framework, numerous local methods developed to distinguish among the labour contributions of team members. The principal types were based on time rates and task rates. In the mid-1960s, the Dazhai method of workpoint calculation came into national prominence, with vigorous promotion from the highest levels in the CCP. The method, 'self-report with public evaluation', was intended to reward peasants both for physical effort and for political consciousness, but in practice in most units using it, degenerated into a relatively pro forma, and quite egalitarian, public assignment of workpoint values to individuals' work days.[9]

Distributions according to workpoint totals were made only at the end of the year. In the meantime, households drew out necessary cash and grain or other food from the team, which were recorded against the year-end distributions. Minimum rations for all households were effectively guaranteed by this method. Households or individuals qualifying for public assistance were partially supported out of the team's welfare fund. Others who did not so qualify and who had drawn more from team stores than their year's workpoints earned, went into debt to the team for the overdrawn amount. Sometimes such families accumulated debts to their team for years.

Significant differences in living standards might be found within the team, depending upon the worker:dependant ratio, industriousness and skills of household members, and so forth. Average incomes also varied widely between local units and even provincial averages could differ radically.[10]

The 'private sector' within the villages continued to play an important part in both production and incomes even after collectivisation. Altogether, 'private' land in the team was generally to run from 5 to 10 per cent of the total, with the legal maximum set at 15 per cent.[11] Local cadres responded to intermittent pressures from above to restrict private plots, but often encountered strong resistance from peasants, and adjusted to that resistance at times by pro forma or token restrictions.[12] Families might also engage in household handicrafts production. Income from all of these sources belonged entirely to the family.

Rising production at the level of teams and individual households accounted for much of the rise in production and rural incomes through the 1960s and 1970s. Another element spurring rural development was added at the brigade, and commune, and county level. This was the expansion of rural small-scale industries, a critical part of a comprehensive strategy of self-reliant, integrated local development.

The emphasis lay particularly on the 'five small industries' – iron and steel, cement, chemical fertilisers, energy, and agricultural machinery. By 1971, half of China's counties had complete sets of these industries.[13] Many communes, brigades, and teams also established food processing and textile plants and a wide range of special manufacturing enterprises. These small-scale industries figured prominently in the Maoist programme for 'self-reliant' regional development.

From 1965 to 1977, the gross output value of the commune and brigade enterprises grew over three times as fast as that of agriculture.[14] From 1974 to 1977, their share of gross agricultural income rose from 14.7 to 30.5 per cent.[15] By the late 1970s, commune- and brigade-run enterprises employed roughly one-tenth of the rural labour force.[16] These industries also helped to finance a rapid expansion of infrastructure investment and social services.

For the basic agricultural and industrial products, China's commercial system relies on purchases and sales through the supply and marketing co-operatives, owned and operated by the state. Through this system, the state in the 1970s bought, in addition to roughly 20 per cent of the grain output, nearly 100 per cent of cotton output, and huge quantities of oil-bearing crops, pigs, eggs, aquatic products, and sugar crops. State laws stipulated that grain, edible oils and cotton could only be sold to state procurement agencies; supply of these items to consumers was rationed. Many other food items whose supply to consumers was more loosely controlled could also be sold by producers only to the state.[17] Generally, the producer prices of such items were fixed by the state. Two different levels of prices for these were in effect: 'quota prices', the lowest, for the basic procurement quota amount; 'over-quota' prices, slightly higher (20 per cent higher, in the case of grain) prices for, in effect, an additional procurement quota above the basic quota. Technically, there were three levels, with an additional category of 'negotiated prices', for surplus over the procurement quotas, arrived at through negotiation between state procurement agencies and rural producers. In practice, however, the over-quota and negotiated prices seem to have been collapsed into one, and may not have been subject to negotiation. Former rural residents interviewed, including some former team and brigade cadres, mentioned only a two-price system and no negotiations.[18] By the mid-1960s, as production increased more rapidly than quotas, the more productive units' income often increased rapidly as growing proportions of their sales brought the higher over-quota or negotiated prices.

Aside from those agricultural products delivered as raw materials for light industry, the lion's share of the produce procured by the state went into the state-run urban retail food system. Consumption of basic foodstuffs for registered urban residents was guaranteed by a ration system providing low-priced basic grains, meat, oils, and some vegetables. This was the urban end of the Maoist era's food system, and dated from the 1950s. It was intended to ensure basic nutrition, but because the procurement prices of foods were held relatively low, it served as well to transfer surplus from the countryside to the cities. The emphasis on regional economic self-sufficiency, and particularly the increasing emphasis on grain cultivation throughout the 1970s, had the effect of reducing competition for food supply between urban and rural areas by, in effect, ruling out rural areas' claims on any grain output other than their own, except in extraordinary circumstances. By thus reducing their 'claims on the state', they could glory in the thought that they were helping accelerate national economic development.

And yet, there were considerable costs of the Maoist system. These prompted opposition to some of the Maoist policies or to the Maoist project altogether, from the highest to the lowest levels of the Chinese system. The struggle between Maoists and their opponents buffeted the villages with campaigns and frequent reversal of policy over the twenty years of collectivised agriculture. Two years of policy experimentation and political manoeuvres after Mao's death culminated in the CCP Central Committee's verdict on the agricultural system adopted at the Third Plenum in December 1978:

[V]iewed on the whole, the speed of our country's agricultural development over the past twenty years has not been fast, and extremely sharp contradictions exist between [the level of agricultural development] and the needs of the people and of the four modernizations. From 1957 to 1977 the national population increased by 300 million, of which 40 million were nonfarming population; the area of cultivated land, due to land used for basic construction and other reasons, decreased by over 100 million *mu*.[19] Therefore, although there had been increases in per-unit yield and grain production, in 1977 the average per capita grain nationally was still a little less than in 1957, and in the rural areas 100 million-odd people had insufficient grain rations. In 1977 the national average of the agricultural population's annual per capita income was only 60-odd *yuan*. [This figure refers only to income from collective distribution, not from private pursuits.] In nearly a quarter of the production teams, team members' income was under 40 *yuan*. . . . If agricultural development is not accelerated, industrial and other construction projects cannot be achieved.[20]

The record in grain production was certainly not negligible in light of China's population:land ratio or its level of development. Grain output *had* kept pace with the growth of population, for all the Central Committee's gloomy statements.[21] But other food products and industrial crops had not increased commensurate with grain. Maintaining consumption levels for non-grain foodstuffs was an increasingly serious problem, and this was reflected in the pattern of China's foreign trade, with agricultural products imports taking up increasingly large chunks of foreign currency during the first half of the 1970s. And, due in large part to its disappointing production performance, the collective economy provided little more than basic security of food and shelter.[22]

Three principal aspects of Cultural Revolution decade practices were identified as the major culprits: excessive demands upon production teams and their members, enforced engagements in economically irrational production, and excessively egalitarian distribution practices. At every level from the state down to the production team, cadres were accused of demanding far too much of the peasants, in return for, at most, next to nothing. At all levels of the agricultural policy establishment in the Cultural Revolution decade, many cadres became so preoccupied with behests from above to achieve grain self-sufficiency that grain not only crowded other developmental requirements out of their heads, but also began to crowd other crops out of the fields. The 'Gang of Four' cadres who curtailed the initiative of production teams came in for a heavy share of criticism. Theirs was a double crime: first, forcing the teams to grow *grain*, and second, *forcing* them to do anything. Moreover, the leftist disapproval of private sidelines seems to have had a generally deleterious impact on production, and certainly had a pronounced effect on rural consumption standards.[23]

The post-Mao Chinese critiques thus point to the shortcomings of the Maoist policies, and eventually to the institutional framework within which those were implemented. There is of course no dearth of Western critiques that pursue similar themes, particularly exploring the disincentives and economic irrationality of the Maoist approach.[24] Yet a number of Western studies have carried the critique further, into examinations of the ways the Maoist policies and institutions were articulated with rural society and culture.[25] These works all begin with the premise that the Maoist project did not work upon rural society as a sculptor upon inanimate clay; rather, the *interaction* between the Maoist state and rural society tended to remould both, and not necessarily in either case for the better. The interpretations of individual scholars as to the nature and the extent of the remoulding vary considerably. Claude Aubert, for example, suggests in an eloquent passage that the party–state may have been the one more transformed:

> Pourtant sous cette facade de soumission unanime, le pouvoir du parti ne fut jamais total et son ambition hegemonique s'est en réalité brisée sur une société villageoise restée intacte dans la coherence de ses comportements malgré les divisions apportées en son sein par les interventions extérieures. Et de façon paradoxale, c'est l'ampleur même de l'ambition hegemonique du parti qui a été cause de sa faiblesse inherente. En effet, son pouvoir n'étant plus, comme celui des dirigéants villageois d'autrefois, d'arbitrage ou de médiation, mais au contraire de gestion, il lui a fallu obtenir l'adhesion de l'ensemble de la population active et les actions menées, pour être realisées, devaient benéficier d'un consensus minimal de la part des interessés. Des lors, les communautés villageoises, avaient les môyens de manifester leurs propres interets, de faire transparâitre leur propre identité et de limiter ainsi le champ d'action des nouvelles autorités.[26]

Richard Madsen, on the other hand, argues that the repeated struggles between Maoist and non- (or anti-) Maoist initiatives within the village articulated with two different visions of community, both grounded in the traditional ethos, but corresponding to conflicting interests 'shaped by' different groups' 'objective position within the village's economic and social structure'. As local leaders manipulated the discourses characteristic of each of these visions, however, the language of morality became entangled with personal self-interest, factional squabbling, and dissolution of community bonds. Nor was an antidote to such 'demoralization of culture' offered by the pure but deracinated (Maoist) 'moral revolutionary' or the (Liuist) 'pragmatic technocrat'. In brief, Madsen sees the 'traditional' moral culture of the village as shattered and the Maoist ethos discredited by the struggles of the Maoist years, while the utilitarianism of the techno-pragmatists serves merely to justify the narrow pursuit of individual self-interest; there is no longer any glue binding rural society.[27]

Whether the peasantry is seen as fundamentally altered or not by the Maoist project, most Western analysts taking rural society as their point of focus have concluded that the era of collectivised agriculture intensified and institutionalised traditional 'closed' patterns of localism – and tended to suppress perhaps equally strong traditional patterns of 'openness' to the larger world, to markets, to the state system.[28] However, as Madsen's analysis suggests, this was not simply the elevation of a peasant 'moral economy' (as conceived by James Scott), above the concerns of the 'rational peasant' 'political economy' (as conceived by Samuel Popkin). [29] Rather, the discourse concerning legitimacy of policies and leaders ran along two different dimensions: one, concerning the appropriate *unit* of reference (national entity, village community, class/interest group, or individual/household), and the other concerning the appropriate *values* (subsistence guarantees or material prosperity).

The common perception of the Maoist project, with the hindsight of the 1980s is that it focused on a peasant 'class' that came to stand for nearly the entire village community, and emphasised for that community – and for that matter, for the nation as a whole – the value of subsistence guarantees. The result, many would argue, was merely an egalitarian sharing of poverty. This may indeed have been the concrete result. But that should not blind us to the fact that the Maoist *promise* was that material prosperity and subsistence guarantees could be achieved together, if people worked together for the good of the whole. For most communities at most times, the subsistence guarantee did obtain. Rural collectives guaranteed some form of employment and basic food rations to all members; urban residents could count upon basic employment and secure access to food. To the extent that this was true, the Maoist system lived up to the social contract that secured the compliance of Chinese citizens with the party–state. However, by late in the Maoist era, the system's failure to live up to the remainder of the social contract was becoming increasingly apparent, and caused increasing disaffection throughout the polity. It was in this context that the reforms were introduced by a new set of leaders, offering a new social contract in an urgent bid to reconstruct the legitimacy of the party–state as well as to build an economically powerful modern nation.

THE EVOLUTION OF RURAL REFORM

But Maoism had politicised the rural economy and subordinated economic growth to political goals. It is not surprising, then, that the rural reforms aimed first and foremost at maximising economic growth through the depoliticisation of rural economic institutions and economic policy implementation. In effect, the new party leadership sought political legitimacy on the basis of economic performance.

The rural reforms developed in two somewhat overlapping stages, the first running roughly from 1978 to 1984; the second, roughly from 1984 to 1989. In the first stage, reform policies focused primarily on reforming producer incentives to evoke both increases in output and a restructuring of the composition of output. The measures used included market liberalisation (including expanded freedoms for household production for the free market), producer price increases and tax and quota reductions, and – the most highly touted of the reform measures – introduction of contractual 'responsibility systems' that eventually restored household farming and paved the way for the formal end to the commune system.

Greater tolerance for peasants' trade in rural free markets came earliest in the reform era. By 1980, attempts to combat 'leftist' thinking included removing strictures against peasants' long-distance trading. Local authorities were urged to provide better physical facilities for market trade. The state later relaxed restrictions on private grain sales and most cities quickly witnessed the proliferation of private grain markets.[30] The number of rural markets rose from 33,000 in 1978 to 50,000 by 1984, while the number of urban markets (in many of which agricultural products brought into the city by peasants were the main commodities) nearly tripled between 1979 and 1984.[31]

The early changes in the system of agricultural prices and procurement included increased producer prices, decreased or stablised levels of mandatory state purchases, and promises of reduced input prices. The Central Committee announced its decision to raise state procurement prices for major agricultural commodities in early 1979, the increases to become effective with the summer 1979 harvest. State procurement prices for quota purchases of grain rose an average of 20 per cent; over-quota purchases were awarded a 50 per cent bonus over the new quota prices (the old bonus was only 20 per cent). Prices for cash crops also increased. Over the next several years, further price increases and the growing proportion of sales at over-quota prices had brought the average procurement prices much higher. The average prices of grain, cotton, and oilseeds rose by 50 per cent from 1978 to 1984; the average procurement price of sugarcane rose by 67 per cent.[32]

The Central Committee also proposed 'reducing the burden' on China's peasantry, by reducing state agricultural taxes and quota grain requisitions.[33] The new policies also called for 10 to 15 per cent reductions in the prices of fertilisers, insecticides, machinery, and so forth. However, the promised price cuts did not materialise; in fact, input prices have risen steadily since 1979.[34]

Despite the large increases in producer prices, official policy during the first phase of reforms aimed to keep staple food prices for urban consumers largely constant. This policy necessitated increasing the subsidies to make up the difference between procurement costs and selling prices. The size of subsidies for retail food prices rose by nearly 500 per cent from 1978 to 1984. By that latter year, these subsidies claimed 22 per cent of the central state budget.[35] When food prices did rise, state employees (mostly urban office and factory workers) received wage increases or supplements to help cover the difference.[36]

The price increases and tax and quota reductions had several different objectives. First, they were to redress a 'price scissors' that was affecting rural incomes relative to urban ones.[37] Second, they were to put into peasants' hands money that would be used on productive investments.[38] Third, and by no means last in importance, they would provide a strong incentive for increased output, and for adjustments in cropping patterns. However, it seems clear that neither the types of changes nor their magnitude (as for example in the case of producer price increases) were carefully thought out beforehand. Rather, in a climate generally favorable to reform – and not only reform, but rapid and highly visible reform – the price and procurement changes emerged from a whirlwind round of bargaining in which some of the appropriate players (e.g., the Finance Ministry) were left out of the process.

The Third Plenum (1978) proclaimed production team autonomy an essential corrective to the excessive demands previously made upon teams. Most of the new leadership believed that fundamental changes in the incentive system had to accompany producer autonomy. Each team, the plenum declared, must be permitted to structure incentives in keeping with its own special circumstances. The wave of this new future was the 'production responsibility system'. The term originally covered a wide variety of practices, virtually all of which involved two common features: first, some form of contract (oral or written) for production, concluded between the team and smaller units within the team; and second, some method for differential compensation that distinguished the work contribution of each producer, thus satisfying the principle of 'to each according to his work'. The Central Committee explicitly ruled out household contracting in its initial call for responsibility systems.[40] Two principal types of responsibility system received early official approval. The first was termed 'small-lot contracting, fixed compensation' and the second, contracts 'linking compensation to output'. The small-lot contracting system assigned individuals or work groups to specific tasks, setting in advance the number of workpoints to be paid for task completion.[41] Clearly this method bears a strong resemblance to the task rate system in use earlier.

The second general type of system, 'linking compensation to output', consisted of longer-term contracts with variable remuneration.[42] The two most prevalent variants through 1979 were contracts with individual labourers and with groups. During 1980 and 1981, responsibility systems developed in both more highly collectivised and very loosely collectivised directions. In the less collective direction, the new household contracting arrangements were revived through 1979 and 1980, especially in Sichuan and Anhui provinces, and finally received formal Central Committee approval in September 1980.[43]

Household contracting includes two basic methods. In the first, 'contracting production to the household', the team

assigns plots of land to household by contract; the size of allot-
ment may be based on population, labour power, or a combined
household population and labour power index. The contracts
generally stipulate the inputs other than land to be provided
by the team, the output targets, and the workpoints to be
awarded upon fulfilment of the contract. In addition, the contracts generally specify bonuses for overfulfilment and penalties
for substandard performance.[44]

In the second type of household contracting system, 'comprehensive contracting', individual households receive contracts
for plots of land in return for a fixed payment to the team,
which is supposed to satisfy state and collective requirements
(taxes, welfare fund, collective investments, etc.). The household keeps all other produce, for its own use or for sale. Unlike
all other responsibility systems, this method features no 'unified
distribution' of the team's product. Peasants are basically self-
employed and they 'compensate' themselves directly with their
own output. They must also provide their own grain rations.[45]

The type of responsibility system used in any team was supposed to be entirely up to the 'democratic decision' of its members. The household contracting methods were used particularly widely in the more backward or poorer provinces. More
highly collectivised methods were most popular where commercialisation and mechanisation of agriculture had already reached
farily high levels.

In early 1982, the Central Committee seemed willing to solid-
ify the status quo by proclaiming a new stage of 'summary,
perfection, and stabilisation'.[46] Rather than stabilising, however,
the countryside made an astounding leap towards general adoption of household contracting. In October 1981 the household
contracting system took in not quite half of all production teams;
by June 1982 the proportion was up to 74 per cent, and by July
1983 it was reported at 93 per cent. By 1984, 99 per cent of all
teams were reported as using the 'comprehensive contracting'
system.[47]

In some cases, the authorities may have bowed to the need
to approve household contracting to prevent complete demo-
lition of the collective. But despite the centre's rhetorical emphasis on voluntarism, the trend would appear not to have been
wholly spontaneous, particularly in more developed areas.
Initiatives from above were crucial in pushing the countryside

to household contracting, and may have been even more important in the accelerated changes after late 1981.[48] In the party rectification drive launched after the centre opted for household contracting, rural party members were scrutinised for their responsiveness to the new policies. In Hebei's Tong county, for example, it was reported that the party rectification drive included the replacement of nine out of the sixteen township secretaries, who apparently had been obstructing (or bore the brunt of the blame for obstructing) reforms. The result: the proportion of household contracting rose from 18.3 per cent in 1983, to 83.7 per cent in 1984.[49]

The theoretical arguments for China's 'new-style family economy' in agriculture have hinged on two basic premises. The first is the relatively low level of development of the 'productive forces', even in the most economically advanced areas.[50] Chinese economic analysts who saw this relative backwardness as the determining factor leave open the possibility that with the long-run modernisation of Chinese agriculture, development of productive forces may require 'large-scale production' and more collective organisation.[51] Other writers contended that the special characteristics of agricultural production at *any* level of modernisation require household management for maximum efficiency and flexibility.[52]

Either emphasis was consistent with the conclusion that household-based management of agricultural production was most advisable for the foreseeable future. By the beginning of 1984, the Central Committee's Document No. 1 on rural work urged that peasants' contracts to given plots of land should be set for fifteen years or longer,[53] thus spelling a formal commitment to a substantial period of family farming.

Structural and managerial changes at the team and household levels created pressure for fundamental transformation in the nature of the commune. Those initiatives have altered the standing and remuneration of cadres at all levels, introduced new 'collective' ventures that compete with established collective or state-owned industries and commercial organs, and yielded forays into the organisational separation of economic activities and political/administrative functions.

Changes attendant upon introduction of household contracting bade fair to remove cadres' incentives entirely, as many cadres lost their rights to significant remuneration for adminis trative work, and sometimes lost their administrative posts. At the brigade level cadres did have some alternatives to manual labour, or to swallowing the loss of salaries. They could resort to work in collectively owned enterprises or rely on those enterprises' earnings to maintain the level of their salaries.[54] At the team level, however, most cadres did indeed turn their attention to their own responsibility fields.

Shortly after introduction of the production responsibility systems, some Chinese agricultural specialists began to argue that the contract systems obviated the need for most of the commune's or brigade's functions. Initially it was considered necessary merely to improve the management and accounting systems in 'collective' agriculture; but after the early 1980s, the very term 'collective' was increasingly dispensed with, in favour of a 'co-operative' rural economy based on the new family farming.[55] The change in nomenclature represented a shift in the official conception of the nature of these institutions.

The revised national constitution stipulated the gradual divorce of governmental functions from the commune structure.[56] By late 1983, the Central Committee and the State Council had called for completing the establishment of township (*xiang*) governments to assume all governmental functions of the communes by the end of 1984.[57]

On paper, at least, the transition to separate governmental and economic bodies occurred on schedule. By the end of 1984, the State Statistical Bureau reported that only 249 communes, 7,046 production brigades, and 128,000 (out of over 5 million) production teams had not yet created separate structures. By contrast, over 91,000 township governments and over 28,000 'economically organised people's communes' were in place, and more than 926,000 'village people's committees' had been formed.[58]

The second major change in the nature of the commune concerns its strictly economic functions. Reform policy began to call for the formation of specialised bodies ('associations', 'companies', or 'co-operatives') which performed on contract the technical or special functions heretofore handled by communes and brigades.[59] Moreover, rather than building up productive and service capacities in collective structures, central party policy increasingly encouraged the development of privately owned capacity. 'Central Document No. 1' of 1983 extended permission to individuals to purchase trucks and large tractors, or to build warehouses and other such facilities, charging other peasants for their use.[60] Households or groups of households began to invest in agricultural machinery or small-scale commercial ventures. These 'new economic associations' might compete with collectively owned ventures, co-operate with them, or provide goods and services the collective could not provide.[61]

As is implied by the foregoing descriptions, the rural reform policies in the first phase encouraged a considerable degree of diversification and restructuring of rural economic activity. Agricultural producers were exhorted to develop the 'five great industries' in the rural sector: crops (now to include much more than grain), livestock, aquatic products, forestry, and household sidelines.[62] Up to 1981, several major changes occurred. First, areas considered unsuitable for grain production reverted to their traditional emphases on pastoralism, forests, fisheries or cash crops. Within grain-producing areas, many areas that had grown three grain crops a year dropped to two, while some double-cropped areas dropped to one grain crop yearly.

For certain areas, 'diversification' meant regional specialisation in particular cash crops. In Shandong province, the area planted to cotton increased by nearly 150 per cent from 1979 to 1982, by which time it equalled over 17 per cent of the area sown to grain; grain acreage fell by 12 per cent. Fujian and Guangdong provinces expanded sugarcane areas by 18 and 53 per cent respectively.[63]

But for most areas, diversification meant development of new products within the framework of the existing grain economy. This local diversification was encouraged both under responsibility contracts (i.e., on land contracted from the collective) and in household sidelines and private plots.

The emphasis on diversification stemmed at first from a concern with soaking up rural surplus labour (estimated at 30 to 50 per cent of the rural labour force) as the contracting systems made agricultural labour use more efficient. That employment concern led to an expanded meaning of diversification, from production (the initial emphasis), to a far wider range of activity including commerce, transport and service trades. This expanded sense, and achievement of, diversification has been articulated with new organisational forms linked with the second phase of rural reform and development strategy that began taking clear shape in 1984.

The second stage of rural reforms, while intended to continue promoting the output of agricultural products, had also to adjust some of the imbalances arising out of the first phase of reform, and to push reform of the rural economy along the road of development, not just growth. Thus in the years after 1984, reform policy in the rural sector placed primary stress upon 'commercialisation' (with both domestic and international orientation) of the rural economy and upon the development of industry and other non-agricultural enterprises in rural areas. These emphases emerged in a number of concrete policies.

The first such policy, which actually had its roots in developments as early as 1981 or 1982, was the encouragement of 'specialised households', which came to play such an important part in the programmatic model for rural development that their formation constituted one of the criteria for evaluating progress in the nationwide party rectification campaign.

The major distinguishing feature of the specialised household is that all or nearly all of the household labour force is used in the specialised line of production. The authorities were quick to note their high productivity, cost effectiveness, and orientation towards commodity production (with some 70 to 90 per cent of the household's output being for sale). Because the specialised households are considered to contribute to the overall rise in rural prosperity and the national supply of agricultural commodities, they are often entitled to state-supplied 'award grain', to team allocations of fodder land or feedgrains, and to preferential credit from agricultural banks and credit co-operatives.[64] Perhaps the most irresistible element of the specialised households' appeal as a model, to be sure, is that they often get very wealthy pursuing their specialities. Hard work and *risk*-taking, two of their fortes, are thus demonstrated as worthwhile for other peasants.[65] However, not all of China is thought to be able yet to develop specialised households extensively. They appear most successful in the most modernised regions, and often fare poorly in poor, mountainous regions.[66]

Some areas, however, have found that a variety of factors dictate the rapid concentration of grain lands in the hands of specialised grain households. This is particularly the case where numerous off-farm employment opportunities beckon and peasants are especially reluctant to grow grain, or cannot do so efficiently.[67] After Document No. 1 of 1984 proposed the concentration of land for specialisation, local authorities could adjust land contracts on the principle of 'voluntary transactions and mutual benefit'. In one county in Guangdong province, after such adjustments some areas devoted only one-third of their labour power to agricultural production.[68] However, too-rapid expansion of specialised households even in otherwise appropriate contexts can still be harmful, as some Chinese analysts have noted. They stress that specialised lines must be in balance with the resources of the given region, which requires some limitation on how many can specialise and in what.[69]

The second set of policies under the phase of reform also has its roots in earlier developments. These policies have fostered the development of rural industry and other enterprises to soak up surplus rural labour and provide new avenues for sustaining income growth in the countryside. The new departures have included an explosion of credit for rural entrprises,[70] the contracting of some collectively-owned enterprises to individuals, and encouragement of individual entrepreneurs (including permission for the hiring of wage labour).

The general trend towards greater private investment and private employment of labour was confirmed and intensified in Central Committee Document No. 1 of 1984, and again in 1985. By 1985, the Central Committee approved peasants' moving into small cities and market towns to set up shops and service trades, and peasants' private mining enterprises.[71] Given such encouragement, 'private and individual enterprise' has grown apace. By 1987, 10.3 million non-agricultural individual household businesses were registered in the countryside, employing 16.7 million people.[72] 'Rural economic associations' of households outside the old territorial collective framework but quasi-co-operative in nature, numbered 484,000 by 1987 and employed 4.2 million people.[73]

Meanwhile, the township and village enterprises (formerly commune and brigade enterprises) enjoyed their own spurt of mushroom growth. Between 1980 and 1987, the numbers of such enterprises grew modestly (expanding from 1.4 to 1.6 million), but their employment rose dramatically (from 30 to 47 million).[74]

The proliferation of non-agricultural employment opportunities was reflected in a shift in structure of the rural labour force. While in 1978, 90 per cent of the rural labour force was engaged in 'agricultural' (including forestry, fisheries, husbandry, and water conservancy) work, by 1987 that proportion had fallen to 80 per cent.[75]

Equally significant for the constellation of power and interests in the countryside, as the household contracting systems dried up the accustomed source of funds for rural local government (for roads, waterworks, social expenditure, salaries, etc.), rural enterprises and private entrepreneurs became increasingly important sources of legitimate and illegitimate public revenues. The potential profitability and, therefore, taxability, of collective and private rural enterprises prompted local officials to channel more bank credit and scarce fixed-price inputs their way, and thus away from agriculture. While the draining of resources away from agriculture was not necessarily the intention of the central government's policies, any emphasis on 'encouraging' nonagricultural enterprises, given the institutional realities in rural areas, was likely to have that effect.

The third set of phase two reform policies pertained to the revamping of the state commercial system.[76] As agricultural output grew and the variety of products proliferated during the early 1980s, it grew increasingly clear that meshing plan and market required something more sophisticated than patching market trade onto the margins of the old planning system. With the Agricultural Work Conference held at the end of 1984, the new line of approach was hammered out in some detail, working in some of the changes already in progress and introducing bold new steps. This approach aimed at a transformation of the state system for agricultural procurement, replacing the mandatory planning system for agriculture, with its imposed sales quotas at fixed prices ('unified purchase and marketing' or UPM), with a new system of voluntary contractual sales at prices shaped by market forces.

For decades, the state had bought just about anything peasants would sell, at prices set with an eye as much – or more – to the income-distribution function of prices, as to adjusting supply and demand. But by 1984 the state could no longer afford the luxury of continuing with this practice. (Recall the steeply mounting retail food subsidies.) At the beginning of 1985, then Premier Zhao Ziyang announced that the 'unified purchase and marketing' system for agricultural products would be gradually phased out beginning with that year's procurements.[77] Thenceforth all sales to the state were to be made on a voluntary contractual basis, and the price of farm products other than grain was to be released to reach market levels in the cities (but with wage subsidies to cushion urban residents against the increase). Grain prices, however, were still held low for both producers and consumers.

Underlying these changes was a basic shift in the conception of the role of planning in the agricultural system, from command to 'indicative' planning.[78] To induce sales in, or reduce them to, the desired quantities, the state would have to rely increasingly on price incentives.[79] Agricultural producers' decisions on what and how much to produce therefore would eventually respond to price indicators as an index of demand for commodities whether sold to the state or on the market.

In its dealing with individual peasant producers, the glue expected to hold the Socialist system together is the new Little Red Book: the contract.[80] The contract dictates, firstly, which households will be permitted to engage in what kinds of production, unless they are willing to take their chances on the market not only for selling their produce but also for obtaining inputs; and secondly, what quantities of produce thay can count on selling, for what price, and at what cost of production.

The state's planned purchase and sales policies included provisions for enabling some areas more easily to specialise in products destined for market trade – Guangdong's Pearl River Delta area and South Jiangsu, for example. These areas were permitted to 'adjust' their production away from grain (thanks to reduced grain sales obligation) in order to capture comparative advantages in specialised products for export or for nearby urban markets; their procurement targets were reassigned to interior areas.[81] Central Document No. 1 of 1986 called for contracts between processing factories and peasants, in which the factories would take some responsibility for assisting peasants in developing production; and for the construction of coastal export bases.[82] Other *market*-promotion functions of state agencies included fostering the development of facilities to spark market town growth, and 'mobilising' means of transportation to make the most of scarce transportation facilities for individual traders.[83]

In other words, the commercial reforms announced in 1985 were not intended to do away with the state commercial system entirely, but rather to reform its way of doing business. The assumption was that if both state commercial agencies and peasant producers reoriented themselves towards responding to market signals, state commerce and free markets could coexist to the advantage of all.

At the same time, however, the reforms at this stage held back from moving entirely towards market signals: state producer prices of grain and certain other basic foodstuffs were exempted from subjection to market mechanisms. This reservation, we will see, has virtually ensured the development of one of the major bottlenecks in economic growth and continued reform; and yet, as I will argue, the party leadership could not have done otherwise without precipitating a major crisis of political legitimacy.

RESULTS OF THE REFORMS

Let us look at the good news first, for the good news poses a knotty analytical problem if we are to explain the speed and intensity of the collapse of party–state authority since 1988. Put quite simply, the ten years of rural reform produced phenomenal increases in rural output and peasant incomes, and unprecedented improvements in consumption for both rural and urban residents.

Agricultural output grew in both physical and value terms. From 1978 to 1988, grain production rose a total of 29 per cent, cotton by 94 per cent, oilseeds by 154 per cent, meat by 155 per cent, and sugar crops by 162 per cent.[84] From 1978 to 1988, the gross agricultural output value rose by 83 per cent, after correction for inflation. From 1980 to 1987, in nominal terms agriculture increased by 143 per cent, while the gross output value of all other rural economic activity (industry, construction, transportation, and commerce) rose by 446 per cent.[85] Peasant incomes rose at an almost dizzying rate, with per capita income averaging 134 *yuan* in 1978, 355 *yuan* in 1984, and 545 *yuan* in 1988.[86] The value and income figures are mostly in nominal terms, because the Chinese statistical sources provide very few figures in real terms. The unreliability of official price indexes and, for incomes, of sampling procedures means that we cannot determine just how far those nominal numbers should be revised downwards, although revised they should be.[87] Nevertheless, the fact remains that the real increases were tremendous.

This was clearly reflected in enhanced food and nutrient availability. The average per capita consumption of certain basic agricultural products indicates the general trend of improvement (see Table 3.1).[88] The consumption increases were enjoyed by both urban and rural residents. The quality and variety of food products in cities improved rapidly; by early 1989, free markets even in the depths of winter offered a virtual cornucopia of foods.[89] For rural areas, moreover, the quality of life improved in a manner difficult to capture in quantitative terms, with the proliferation of rural services and processing facilities.

Table 3.1 Average per capita consumption of basic agricultural products, 1978–87

	1978	*1987*	*% increase*
grain (kg)	195.5	251.4	29
pork (kg)	7.7	14.5	88
confections (kg)	3.4	6.7	97
tobacco (boxes)	30.8	66.3	115
alcohol (kg)	2.6	10.5	304

Space does not permit going in detail into the reasons for these improvements; I have developed that argument at length elsewhere.[90] Suffice it to say that one must account for the improvements on the production side not only by referring to the shift to household farming, but perhaps more importantly, to the increases in state producer prices (especially up to 1984); technological change in crops, animal breeds and production techniques; increased availability of chemical fertilisers; the proliferation of private market opportunities; and the liberalisation of planting quotas and reduction of procurement quota amounts. On the incomes side, the *number one reason for improvement* has been structural change in the rural economy, which has meant a decline in the proportion of agriculture in total rural output value, a decline of crops' share in agricultural output value, and finally, a decline of grain among crops' output value.

In addition, the rise in *urban* consumption levels has been sustained only by mounting state subsidies, both in the form of retail price subsidies, and in increments added directly to urban wages. The subsidy costs are hard to gauge accurately. Ostensibly, these rose from 9.4 billion *yuan* in 1978 to 37 billion *yuan* in 1984, but have been brought down since then; the 1986 subsidies were reported at 25.7 billion *yuan*.[91] That decline is partly a function of the decline in state procurements, but may be more largely a function of regional and local governments' having shouldered the burden of subsidising procurement prices in order to meet their delivery quotas of grain and other crops.[92] The subsidy bill probably made an enormous leap in 1989, as the procurement price increases announced for grain and other products were expected to cost the state an additional 9 billion *yuan*.[93]

The subsidy issue brings us to the more negative side on the results of reform, where problems in eliciting certain types of progress in the rural sector have become entangled with problems of macroeconomic and urban reform. The nexus of the tangle is what has come to be discussed increasingly in China as the Grain Problem.

Grain supply is a burning issue in the Chinese context, in part because of the very real concern with feeding 1.1 billion people, in part because of the symbolism (national integrity, solution of historical problems). In this context, it is important to note the trends in grain production over the reform years. Grain output has essentially stagnated since 1984. The record harvest in that year raised hopes that China could meet its ambitious target of 450 million metric tonnes of grain by 1990. In subsequent years, however, output has consistently failed to reach the 1984 level. The target set for 1988 was 410 MMT; actual output fell well short of that. For 1989, the target was once more set at 410 MMT, but despite prognostications during the summer of a bumper harvest, fell short of the target.[94]

The potential danger posed for the entire nation by such trends is apparent when one compares the trends in grain output with population growth. From 1976 to 1984, grain output roughly kept pace with population growth. Since 1984, population growth has continued at a slightly elevated rate, leaving grain output behind.

The crux of the problem is the grain procurement system,

which has proven impossible to reform without causing major problems for urban residents' access to food, but which in the absence of reform will exacerbate the grain production problem by undermining peasant producers' incentives to grow grain.

This is not to say that China faces an immediate shortfall in consumption needs. The country still produced, in 1988, sufficient grain to feed its population. Local shortages of certain items have cropped up; in January 1989, for example, a Chinese economist living in Beijing maintained that there was no rice available either in state grain shops or in free markets in the city – and took me on a short guided tour of the markets to prove his point. But substitute commodities have generally been available. Thus Minister of Agriculture He Kang could with perfect sincerity claim at the NPC meeting in March 1989 that 'although there is some pressure on our grain supply, it seems that this is not a crisis'. For, even with the disappointing grain harvest of 1988, state procurement agencies had collected 98 per cent of the planned grain quota purchases, and 90 per cent of the negotiated purchases.[95]

However, crisis has thus far been averted at the price of increased dependence on the international market, and intense alienation of rural producers. After a short spell as a net exporter of grain, China began importing significant quantities of grain again in 1986. By 1987, net grain imports were nearly 10 million tonnes.[96] Imports declined slightly in 1988, but were expected to rise in 1989. What is of potentially enormous significance, both for future import needs and for China's general food security, national grain reserves at year's end in 1987 were the lowest since 1974.[97]

The need for imports has been kept down only by increasing the harshness of the methods for forcing farmers to grow grain, and to sell it to the state. Although some peasants did increase their output and their investment in grain cultivation in response to the more favourable price situation during the first phase of reform, escalating input prices and a widening gap between state and market prices have all but eradicated any producer interest in selling grain to the state.[98] A recent survey showed that peasants now grow mostly for their own consumption and to fulfil the procurement quotas that were reimposed after being briefly lifted in 1985. By 1988, even the quota deliveries were in many instances made only under virtual coercion by local cadres, who might, for example, refuse to allocate jobs in the booming rural enterprises, or to permit children to attend school, for families that refused to fulfil their sales quotas.[99]

Coercion may only have become more necessary in 1989 in light of peasants' experiences with 1988's 'voluntary' procurement. As local governments ran short of cash for the quota and negotiated purchases in autumn 1988, they began issuing IOUs to peasant producers in return for grain deliveries. Beijing instructed local governments to redeem these IOUs by the Chinese New Year, and announced that all such outstanding payments had been made. However, revelations by delegates to the NPC in March 1989 made it clear that many peasants still awaited payment – and in the meantime, could not purchase seeds and fertilisers for the spring planting.[100] With the contraction of credit and the general decline in rural economic growth resulting from the tightened austerity programme, local governments this year are already facing a cash shortage of mammoth proportions. For example, Xiangfan Municipality, the second highest grain-producing area in Hubei, needs 650 million *yuan* in cash in 1989 to make its rice, cotton, and oil purchases. Local officials were thrown into a panic by the shortage of cash in autumn 1989; according to a report in *Farmer's Daily*:

> Regarding the funds needed for procurement . . . for autumn, excluding the funds raised by the grain departments from selling grains to other localities, withdrawing currency from circulation, borrowing capital, collecting debts, and collecting repayment of leans ahead of schedule; the funds handed down from the city and province; and the funds handed down by superior departments to compensate for the price increase, the shortfall is 310 million *yuan* (i.e., nearly half the amount needed).[101]

Here we see the state caught in the contradictions between trying to reduce inflation (at runaway levels by early 1989, thanks to the mounting government deficits) while encouraging grain production and sales. The first is necessary to make progress in industrial development; the second, to maintain essential urban food supplies.

Austerity measures taken with the aim of reducing inflation have had and will continue to have a deleterious impact on the welfare or rural residents, in terms of employment, incomes and consumption. The rural labour force in 1978 was 306 million; by 1987 it was 390 million. The rural sector, despite rapid growth rates up to 1987, was unable to provide employment for these numbers. With the loosening of urban migration restrictions, in the mid-1980s, millions of peasants voted with their feet. Thousands of young women from rural Anhui province flocked to Beijing to find work as maids; tens of thousands of young men from Gansu moved to Guangzhou (Canton) and the Pearl River Delta area for temporary and contract labour in construction and other unskilled jobs. Beggars appeared on the streets of the capital city (notably, near the major hotels catering to foreigners) and prostitutes appeared in hotel lobbies.

Before the austerity programme was announced in fall 1988, an estimated 50 million rural transients had moved into China's cities and more prosperous rural areas, while an estimated 180 million underemployed remained in the rural areas. The contractionary policies since then spell nothing but trouble for these people. After the Chinese New Year holiday in winter 1988-9, hundreds of thousands of peasants from the impoverished north west poured into Guangdong province looking for work, only to be quite vigorously discouraged by the authorities. In April 1989, Premier Li Peng was urging these peasants to 'return to their villages to engage in agricultural production'.[102] After the June crackdown, the public security forces were exhorted to hasten the departure of migrants from the major cities. But back in the villages, jobs have dried up as the austerity programme began to reduce both the availability of credit and demand for the output of the rural enterprises.[103] Recent unconfirmed reports suggest unemployment and underemployment have swollen enormously, despite the rather modest official figures

RURAL REFORM, FOOD POLICY, AND SOCIAL CONTRACT

It is impossible to create a closed and consistent socio-economic normative theory which would assert, without contradiction, a politico-ethical value system and would at the same time provide for the efficiency of the economy. It is impossible if that theory seeks to be realistic and wishes to take into account the true behavioral characteristics of people, communities, organizations and social groups.[104]

From a strictly (neo-classical) economic perspective, the solution of China's current developmental impasse requires the austerity measures described above; and the solution of the food policy impasse, also from this perspective, requires thoroughgoing price reform and the elimination of most state subsidies. Economically speaking, China has no other choice if it is to meet its growth and development goals. Adjustments in the economic system and structures, the elimination of entitlements, the marginalisation of some producers, the bankrupting of inefficient enterprises, may be painful but are certainly essential adjustments for the long-run health of the economy, and thus, for the success of reforms.

The problem with this perspective is that it is a limited one, and excludes some of the factors which must be central in constructing any resolution of the problems that Chinese reform now faces. It is tempting to cast the problem simply (if this complex could be called simple!) in terms of the dilemma of *Socialist reform*: that of making the transition from a centrally planned command economy to a mixed ownership responding to market signals.

For China, state-Socialist development during the entire era from 1949 to the late seventies created and fostered the institutional entrenchment of social groups and social interests connected with centralised planning and state enterprises (not just bureaucrats and managers, but also state sector workers). Efforts at economic reform *outside* this sector may receive considerable support from these influential groups insofar as those reforms increase the resources available to the state sector (as raw material, revenues, or consumption goods). Economic reforms that are immediately costly either directly or indirectly to these groups will be opposed with all the political resources at their command – which are considerable[105] – even though the eventual outcome of such reforms might be to increase the net resources in the state sector. Where a reform coalition is able to push through such reform policies despite resistance, the affected groups will lobby for, and get, a variety of specific exceptions or special treatment, roughly in proportion to their relative power in the state system. The result is a snowballing scramble for patched-together 'deals' that turn the reform edifice into a jerry-built structure, one that may distort market signals and inflate inefficiencies beyond those of the previous centrally controlled system.

Here is the first shoal upon which the rural reforms have run aground. Producer prices have risen, but will not be permitted to rise so high as to undermine urban claims on a cheap basic food supply. State funds go into retail food subsidies rather than into agricultural investment,[106] thereby sacrificing future productive capacity to current consumption. When credit must be cut back and scarce producer goods at controlled prices must be conserved under austerity programmes, preference goes to the large state industries, and rural enterprises are allowed to die on the vine, ostensibly because they are less 'efficient'.

This is not to say that if reforms were actually carried to full fruition, all problems would be solved. As Kornai has observed:

> In the course of history, whenever an advanced stage of some main economic disease came to prevail in an economic system, and a radical therapy was started, at least one other main disease developed to a conspicuous extent.[107]

The particularly virulent problem in the Chinese case is that it has got stuck at a stage where the rural sector can languish from both diseases simultaneously.

But let us not stop with the Socialist reform dilemma, for there is a type of solution proposed for rural development that, it is hoped, will get around the problems. The strategy more or less consciously pursued since the early 1980s has essentially been to bet on the strong, concentrating the economic opportunities and resources that *are* available to the rural sector among the individuals, lines of production, and regions that are expected to be most profitable. (The supposition being, of course, that the benefits will trickle down, some day, somehow.)

The significance of the selective impact of this strategy cannot be underlined too strongly, especially in view of the common tendency both within and outside China to attribute successes in the rural reforms to the loosening of political or politically dictated shackles on economic forces. True, such unshackling has occurred, but it has been neither uniform nor unidirectional.

103

As the bonds of state quota sales have grown looser for some, they have been accordingly tightened for others. As access to credit or cheap inputs has been opened to some, it has accordingly closed off for others. The particular strategy of selective unshackling and the resultant pattern of growth have endangered politically tinged clashes of interest between town and countryside, between coastal and interior provinces, between more richly and more poorly endowed areas, and between the new economic elite (some of them former cadres, or clients of cadres) and the general run of farmers in the villages.

This has brought China to a second type of dilemma, that of *Third World development*, and especially of Third World rural development as it has been pursued under state auspices in non-Socialist countries. The basic developmental approach of many governments has been to adopt 'industrialisation first' policies reflecting urban bias (these include protection of industry, priority investments in heavy industry, and cheap urban food supply). Johnston and Clark have argued that:

> the measures that governments sometimes adopt to counteract the adverse effects of their economic policies on agriculture usually benefit only the larger farmers and therefore reinforce other polarising factors which lead to a bimodal pattern of agricultural development. This ... applies in large measure to subsidies on inputs and low-interest-rate policies. Because of the excess demand situation that results from holding prices artificially low, some form of administrative rationing of inputs and credit becomes necessary. And the larger and more influential farmers generally receive the lion's share of those scarce resources.[108]

Exploring just such a pattern of agricultural modernisation in Latin America, Merilee Grindle has summarised its results:

> A decline in the production of staple crops, rising food import bills, higher rates of rural unemployment and underemployment accompanied by massive rural-to-urban migration, the increased concentration of landholdings, and higher levels of international dependency – these were the costs of agricultural modernisation in Latin America.[109]

The irony, in the Chinese context, is that the socialist state, under reforms, deliberately fostered the development of such a class of large farmers where none had existed for nearly thirty years following land reform! The dilemma posed by bimodalism is that growth in the highly capitalised and commercialised, rapidly modernising, large-farmer segment of the rural sector occurs at the expense of, rather than in advance of, the small subsistence farmer sector. Chinese rural policy has been some-what ambivalent on the implications of this issue. On the one hand, there are occasional murmurs against letting the big far-mers get *too* big and powerful; on the other, there are whispers and even shouts that local cadres should foster and even become such large farmers.

The ambivalence on this may relate to policy differences at the top in Beijing, of which there were many; or to doubts as to the economic efficiency of many of the new specialised farms. But a significant part of the ambivalence most likely stems from the party–state's uncertainty over just who is the reliable social base under the new order in the countryside. For Latin America, Grindle argues that the developmental state after World War II played an interventionist role in rural areas which altered its social foundations:

> Legitimacy was accorded to the state apparatus to initiate these policies and to expand its presence in the agricultural economy and in rural areas. At the same time, these poli-cies supported the emergence of a small class of capitalist entrepreneurs . . . who subsequently developed both the economic and the political power to demand continued favourable treatment from the state.[110]

This new class of entrepreneurial farmers, Grindle contends, managed to constrain the options available to the state when resentment exploded over the 'vulnerability and exploitation of the rural poor'. In this setting, redistribution was impossible, and the state resorted instead merely to 'disaggregation, dif-fusion, and co-optation through the timely distribution of state resources and services and increased repressive capabilities'.[111]

Is this the future for rural China? Probably 'reformers' and 'conservatives' alike would shy away from such a prospect, when it is posed so baldly. And yet, the regime faces a potential crisis of legitimacy in rural China before which the urban legit-imacy crisis of spring 1989 may pale in comparison. The Maoist social contract held together as long as it did because it was linked with certain values that resonated with the moral perspectives and at least some of the material interests of a relatively undifferentiated peasantry; and where party–state initiatives were at odds with peasant interests, the regime could evoke compliance from rural leaders by offering a share in power and some prospects of mobility. Ultimately, of course, the inability to deliver on the promise of prosperity and the clash of state and peasant interests eroded the foundations of the Maoist party–state. The reforms since then have changed the face of the rural social landscape tremendously, satisfied some interests, created new ones, raised tremendous hopes and then dashed many of them. But with its main claim to rule for the past decade or so having been its immediate contributions to rising standards of living, the state is on shaky political ground during a period of contraction and austerity.

This is not to say that a solution is impossible. Ideological creativity might yield some appeals that can evoke a strong positive response from rural and urban constituencies, for long enough to allow the painful adjustments to be made. More careful policy planning might meet the subsistence concerns as well as the desire for greater prosperity of the rural and urban populace. Intelligent political institution-building could knit together new constituencies in a renewed organisational framework for the party–state. But to name these challenges in the current situation is to make a declaration of pessimism. For who can imagine their being met by any one who played a part in the butchery in Beijing?

NOTES

1 W. David Hopper, *Scientific American*, 1976.
2 Sartaj Aziz (Deputy Executive Director of the World Food Council), *Science and Public Policy*, 1976.
3 World Bank, *World Development Report, 1980* (New York: Oxford University Press for the World Bank, 1980), pp. 100–11. With these, and with any other quantitative indicators of performance, it must be noted that the choices of different indicators or different years may yield conflicting impressions. The point here is not to demonstrate that China had, beyond a shadow of a doubt, performed consistently better than India or Indonesia in all respects, but merely that there were some good grounds for evaluating its performance favourably in a comparative context.
4 *FAO Production Yearbook*, Vol. 33 (1979) (Rome: Food and Agriculture Organization of the United Nations, 1980, pp. 50–1, 57.

5 World Bank, *China: Socialist Economic Development* (Washington, DC: World Bank, 1983), Vol. 2, p. 54; emphasis added.

6 *FAO Production Yearbook*, Vol. 33 (1979), pp. 50–1, 57.

7 See for example Dwight Perkins, 'Development of Agriculture', and Jon Sigurdson, 'Rural Economic Planning', in Michel Oksenberg (ed.), *China's Developmental Experience* (New York: Praeger for the Academy of Political Science, 1973).

8 See Tachai, *Standard-Bearer for China's Agriculture* (Beijing: Foreign Language Press). For discussions of the Maoist strategy as applied to agriculture, see John G. Gurley, *China's Economy and the Maoist Strategy* (New York: Monthly Review Press, 1976), esp. Ch. 5; E.L. Wheelwright and Bruce McFarlane, *The Chinese Road to Socialism: Economics of the Cultural Revolution* (New York: Monthly Review Press, 1970), esp. Ch. 10.

9 William L. Parish and Martin King Whyte, *Village and Family in Contemporary China* (Chicago: University of Chicago Press, 1978), pp. 62–3. Some rough sense of the complexity of record-keeping in the task rate system can be garnered from Hubeisheng Yingshanxian Songcixian, *Zhiding laodong ding'e lanben jingyan* (Beijing: Nongye chubanshe, 1981), passim, esp. pp. 10–23. Many more methods were in use – sometimes seriatim – in China's rural communities. On the Dazhai workpoint system, see Byung-joon Ahn, 'Political Economy of the People's Commune in China', *Journal of Asian Studies*, Vol. 34, No. 3, May 1975, p. 647.

10 Jan Myrdal, *Report from a Chinese Village* (New York: Random House, 1972; originally published by William Heinemann Ltd, 1965), pp. 121–2, 154–5, 198–9. I am indebted to Carl Riskin for pointing out the substantial difference between household and per capita averages for Myrdal's data. For a comparative perspective, see Martin King Whyte, 'Inequality and Stratification in China', *China Quarterly*, December 1975, pp. 688–9. On differences in provincial averages, see World Bank, *China: Socialist Economic Development* (Washington, DC: The World Bank, 1983), Vol. 1, p. 84.

11 'Regulations of the Work of the Rural People's Commune', September 1962, reprinted in Jurgen Domes, *Socialism in the Chinese Countryside* (London: C. Hurst, 1980), pp. 148–9.

12 David Zweig, *Agrarian Radicalism in China, 1968–1981* (Cambridge, MA: Harvard University Press, 1989).

13 John G. Gurley, *China's Economy and the Maoist Strategy*, p. 254.

14 World Bank, *China*, Vol. 2, p. 57.

15 Ministry of Agriculture, Policy Research Office (ed.), *Zhongguo nongye jiben qingkuang (Basic Conditions of Chinese Agriculture)* (Beijing: Nongye chubanshe, 1980), pp. 104–5.

16 *SWB:FE* W1162/ A/ 1–2.

17 The procurement figures are from *Jiben qingkuang*, pp. 39–40. Details on categories of commodities may be found in Audrey Donnithorne, *China's Economic System* (New York: Frederick A. Praeger, 1967), pp. 284–5. Hartford interviews, Hong Kong, June 1983.

18 Hartford interviews, Hong Kong, June 1983.

19 One *mu* is equal to one-sixth of an acre.

20 'Decision of the CCP Central Committee on some problems concerning accelerating agricultural development (draft)', *Zhonggong yanjiu (Research on the CCP)*, Vol. 13, No. 5, 1979, p. 151. This document was passed down to lower-level party organs for discussion; it was formally adopted, with revisions, at the Fourth Plenum in September 1979. *Zhonggong yanjiu*, Vol. 13, No. 1, 1979, p. 128; *Zhonggong yanjiu*, Vol. 14, No. 10, 1979, p. 132.

The revised document is published in *Renmin shouce 1979* (*People's Handbook*, 1979) (Beijing: Renmin ribao chubanshe, 1980), pp. 37–45.

21   The 1977 harvest year was a bad one, and grain production per capita indeed only equalled 98.68 per cent of the 1957 figure. However, per capita grain output in 1976 was 101.27 per cent, and in 1978 104.95 per cent, of 1957's. Calculated from unmilled grain output figures in *Nongye nianjian 1980* (*Agricultural Yearbook 1980*], p. 34, and population figures in USDA, Economic Research Service, *Agricultural Statistics of the People's Republic of China, 1949–82*, Statistical Bulletin No. 714 (1984), p. 9. If the USDA's figures on grain output (which include some items, such as soybeans, not counted in the Chinese system as 'grain') are used (p. 12), the 1976 per capita output is 103.59 per cent compared to that of 1957; 1977's, 100.95 per cent; and 1978's, 107.36 per cent.

22   This is not to say that China had no malnutrition. At the beginning of the 1980s, a number of Chinese sources reported 'hunger' or low grain rations among somewhere between 100 million and 200 million peasants. Generally the definition of 'hunger' is not given in such sources, but one article did cite national statistics for 1978 showing 150 million peasants receiving grain rations below 150 kg for the year (200 kg in southern rice-growing areas), and claimed that 'a large part' of them had received such low rations for most years since the communes had formed. Lu Xueyi, 'The Trend of Contracting Output to the Household and a Question that Must be Made Clear', *Nongye jingji congkan* (*Materials on Agricultural Economics*), No. 5, 1981, reprinted in *Nongye jingji* (*Agricultural Economics*), No. 21, 1981, p. 79. Another source, claiming 100 to 200 million hungry peasants, mentioned 'semistarvation' conditions in some areas in 1972. See Yang Jiangbai and Li Xuezheng, 'The Relations between Agriculture, Light Industry and Heavy Industry in China', *Social Sciences in China*, No. 2, (1980). Personal communications from a number of Western scholars who resided in China in the late 1970s also made it clear that many peasants were going hungry. The causes of the hunger are not entirely clear; Jean Oi's work suggests that at least part of the problem may well have stemmed from local cadres' or the state's excessive insistence on stockpiling grain reserves or forcing grain sales by grain-deficient teams. Jean Oi, 'State and Peasant in Contemporary China: The Politics of Grain Procurement', unpublished Ph.D. dissertation, University of Michigan, 1983, esp. pp. 96–168. However, because of the general practice of distributing some minimum basic ration to all team members before making workpoint distributions, it is unlikely that China had anywhere near the incidence of long-term, severe malnutrition that is so common in many other parts of Asia.

23   David Zweig, *Agrarian Radicalism*; Sun Deshan and Wu Yan, *Sheyuan jiating fuye he jishi maoyi* (*Commune Members' Household Sidelines and Collective Commerce*) (Beijing: Nongye chubanshe, 1982), pp. 5–6.

24   E.g., David Zweig, *Agrarian Radicalism*; and Claude Aubert, 'Le triple échec de la collectivisation, ou le piege de la tradition', in Claude Aubert et al., *La société chinoise après Mao* (*Chinese Society After Mao*) (Paris: Fayard, 1986). But Nicholas Lardy argues that the 'fundamental shortcomings of agricultural development policy . . . stem from the introduction of compulsory procurement of farm products in . . . 1953 and the collectivisation of agriculture in 1955–56', not from the 'Cultural Revolution' decade. Moreover, Lardy argues that 'distorted prices and restricted markets for inputs and outputs' pose the greatest stumbling block to China's agricultural development. Nicholas Lardy, *Agriculture in China's Modern Economic*

Development (Cambridge, England: Cambridge University Press, 1983), pp. 220–1.

25 Claude Aubert, 'Le triple échec de la collectivisation'; Richard Madsen, *Morality and Power in a Chinese Village* (Berkeley: University of California Press, 1984); Helen F. Siu, *Agents and Victims in South China: Accomplices in Rural Revolution* (New Haven: Yale University Press, 1989); Vivienne Shue, *The Reach of the State: Sketches of the Chinese Body Politic* (Stanford: Stanford University Press, 1988).

26 Claude Aubert, 'Le triple échec de la collectivisation', pp. 35–6.

27 Richard Madsen, *Morality and Power*. Siu, while seconding the proposition that the Maoist years have wrought some fundamental transformation of rural society, which no longer fits the simple rubric of 'traditional', nonetheless underlines the message that one cannot hear too often in analysing rural China: localities differ tremendously. Helen F. Siu, *Agents and Victims in South China*.

28 See G. William Skinner, 'Chinese Peasants and the Closed Community: An Open and Shut Case', *Comparative Studies in Society and History*, Vol. 13, No. 3, 1971, pp. 270–81, for a discussion of the cyclical changes in the openness of the traditional village community. The argument that the Maoist party-state forced the encapsulation of localism may be found in Claude Aubert, 'Le triple échec de la collectivisation', and in Vivienne Shue, *The Reach of the State*.

29 James Scott, *The Moral Economy of the Peasant* (New Haven: Yale University Press, 1976); Samuel Popkin, *The Rational Peasant* (Berkeley: University of California Press, 1979).

30 *Nongye nianjian 1981 (Agricultural Yearbook 1981)*, pp. 141–2; Terry Sicular, 'Rural Marketing and Exchange in the Wake of Recent Reforms', in Elizabeth J. Perry and Christine Wong (eds), *Political Economy of Reform in Post-Mao China* (Cambridge, MA: Harvard Council of East Asian Studies, 1985), p. 104.

31 *Zhongguo tongji nianjian 1983 (Statistical Yearbook of China 1983)* (Beijing: Zhongguo tongji chubanshe, 1983), p. 386; State Statistical Bureau, *Statistical Yearbook of China 1985* (Oxford: Oxford University Press, 1985), p. 477.

32 State Statistical Bureau, *Statistical Yearbook of China 1985*, pp. 546–8.

33 'Decision of the CCP Central Committee on Some Questions Concerning Accelerating Agricultural Development (Draft)', *Zhonggong yanjiu*, p. 155.

34 'Decision of the Central Committee of the Communist Party of China on Some Questions Concerning the Acceleration of Agricultural Development (Draft)', translated in *Issues and Studies*, Vol. 15, No. 7, July 1979, p. 112; and *Beijing Review*, 28 September 1981, p.3, notes a 10 to 15 per cent reduction of major farm input prices in 1979 and 1980. Costs of production, however, seem to have increased in Chinese industry, thereby preventing the projected input price decreases. State Statistical Bureau, 'Report on Fulfillment of the 1981 Economic Plan', translated in *FBIS*, 30 April 1982, p. K19. See also *Zhongguo tongji nianjian 1983*, p. 460; Nicholas Lardy, *Agriculture in China's Modern Economic Development*, p. 192.

35 USDA, China *Agriculture and Trade Report*, June 1988, p. 12, reports the subsidy figures; comparison with state budgetary revenues from *Zhongguo tongji nianjian 1987 (Statistical Yearbook of China 1987)*, p. 634.

36 A five *yuan* monthly subsidy for nonstaple food prices amounted to 180 *yuan* per worker in three years. Yang Shengming, 'Incomes, Prices, Living Standards', *Renmin ribao*, 16 April 1982.

37 Lardy notes that the official price indexes 'suggest that peasants have benefited from a significant long-run improvement in prices of agricultural

products they sell relative to industrial products they purchase'. However, he finds these indexes misleading because they do not seem to have been adjusted to reflect the changing composition of commodities bought by rural producers. Looking at several other factors to evaluate the terms of trade between city and countryside, he tentatively concludes that 'the state transferred significant resources out of the agricultural sector over a sustained period'. Nicholas Lardy, *Agriculture in China's Modern Economic Development*, pp. 108–27. Numerous articles by Chinese economists in the early reform period referred to the need to redress the price scissors differential in favour of agriculture.

38 Michel Oksenberg, 'Economic Policy-Making in China: Summer 1981', *China Quarterly*, No. 90, June 1982, pp. 188, 190; Ji Long and Lu Nan, 'A Discussion of the "Scissors" Differential in Prices between Industrial and Agricultural Products', Hongqi, No. 6, March 1980, pp. 45–8.

39 Michel Oksenberg, 'Economic Policy-Making in China', pp. 165–94, esp. pp. 187–94.

40 'Decision of the Central Committee of the Communist Party of China', pp. 110–11.

41 'On Fixed Production Quotas and Calculations of Workpoints on the Basis of Work Done', *Renmin ribao*, 19 July 1978.

42 For a detailed description of several types of responsibility system which later came to be described under the umbrella of 'compensation linked to output', see Office of the Central Committee and Investigation Department of the Central Party School, 'Investigation and Views on the Several Responsibility Systems Linking Compensation to Output Current in the Countryside', *Renmin ribao*, September 1982, p. 2.

43 See David Zweig, 'Context and Content in Policy Implementation: Household Contracts and Decollectivisation, 1977–1983', in David M. Lampton (ed.), *Policy Implementation in Post-Mao China* (Berkeley: University of California Press, 1987); and Thomas P. Bernstein, 'Reforming China's Agriculture', paper presented at the Conference 'To Reform the Chinese Political Order', 18–23 June 1984, Harwichport, MA. Both provide rich detail on the political manoeuvres over the introduction of household contracting and the roles of the main protagonists.

44 Examples of these systems abound in the Chinese economic literature. For one sample, see Management Bureau of Rural Work Bulletins, *Nongcun renmin gongshe shengchan zerenzhi leibi* (*Types of Production Responsibility Systems in the Rural People's Communes*) (Beijing: Nongye chubanshe, 1981), pp. 110–13. See also Liu Xumao, 'A Brief Introduction to Several Principal Systems of Production Responsibility Now Practised in Our Country's Villages', *Jingji guanli* (*Economic Management*), No. 9, September 1981, p. 13.

45 A variety of different translations have been used for this type of household contracting. Some have termed it 'comprehensive contracting' or 'full responsibility for task completion'. 'Comprehensive contracting', while less faithful to the Chinese terminology, is perhaps more accurate.

46 *Renmin ribao*, 3 April 1982, p. 1.

47 Su Xing, 'Responsibility Systems and the Development of the Rural Collective Economy', *Jingji yanjiu* (Economic Research), No. 11, 1982, p. 6; JPRS-CAG 276, 24 October 1983, p. 5; State Statistical Bureau (ed.), *Zhongguo tongji zhaiyao* (*China Statistical Abstract*) (Beijing: Zhongguo tongji chubanshe, 1985), p. 28.

48 Hartford interviews with GGR, QIU, GQW, Hong Kong, June 1983.

49 Xiong Yongnian and Dai Xiaohua, 'Clean Out "Leftist" Thought, Advance With Great Strides', *Renmin ribao*, 19 December 1984, p. 4.

50 Louis Putterman, 'The Restoration of the Peasant Household as Farm Production Unit in China: Some Incentive Theoretic Analysis', in Elizabeth J. Perry and Christine Wong, *Political Economy*, p. 70.

51 Dan Kangming, 'More on the Family Economy', *Nongye jingji wenti* (Problems in Agricultural Economics), No. 6, 1984, pp. 23–6.

52 Zhao Ruizhang, 'On the New-style Family Economy in Our Socialist Agriculture', *Nongye jingji wenti*, No. 6, 1984, pp. 17–23, 40.

53 'Notice of the Central Committee of the CCP Concerning Rural Work in 1984', *Renmin ribao*, 12 June 1984, p. 1.

54 Hartford interviews with GGO, QIU, GQW.

55 Officially, the term 'collective' has not been applied to the rural producer units for quite some time. In Wuxi county in January 1989, however, local officials still referred to the collective as a matter of course.

56 'Draft of the Revised Constitution of the People's Republic of China', *Beijing Review*, 10 May 1982, p. 43; Hu Sheng, 'On the Revision of the Constitution', *Beijing Review*, 3 May 1982, pp. 17–18.

57 'Complete the Work of Establishing Township Governments by Next Year', *Renmin ribao*, 23 November 1983, p. 1.

58 *Zhongguo tongji zhaiyao*, p. 28.

59 Mu Qing, Guo Chaoren, and Chen Fuwei, 'A Corner of China's Countryside', *Hongqi*, No. 4, 1982, pp. 22–8; Liu Zheng and Chen Wuyuan, 'Nongcun quanli tizhi gaige di chubu chanqshi' ('Initial Attempts at the Reform of Rural Management Systems', *Jingji guanli*, No. 4, April 1981, pp. 37–41.

60 'Some Problems Concerning Current Rural Economic Policy', *Xinhua yuebao* (*Xinhua Monthly*), No. 4, 1983, pp. 73, 75.

61 Ma Renping, 'New Problems Arising Since the Implementation of the Rural Production Responsibility Systems', *Jingji guanli*, No. 8, 1981, pp. 4–6; and Zhou Qiren and Wang Xiaoqiang, 'On the Changes . . . ', p. 30.

62 'Decision of the Central Committee of the Communist Party of China on Some Questions Concerning the Acceleration of Agricultural Development (Draft)', pp. 107–9, 111–12.

63 *FBIS*, 9 February 1982, pp. 02–4; *SWB:FE* 6891 BII/ 2–3.

64 Yu Guoyan, 'Discussion of Problems in Specialised Rural Households', *JPRS-CAG*-245, January 1983, p. 28. A related type known as the 'keypoint household' is frequently mentioned in conjunction with the specialised households. Keypoint households are, like the specialised ones, engaged in some specialised occupation and market much of their output. But generally it is the 'supplementary' (i.e., female, retiree, or child) labour power in the household which is engaged in the specialised production. Many local authorities tend to conflate the two. In fact, because their economic activities and functions are so similar, they are most easily treated as one type. In this essay, the term 'specialised households' may be taken to refer to both types.

65 Wan Li, 'Developing Rural Commodity Production', *Beijing Review*, No. 9, 27 February 1984, p. 19; *JPRS-CAG*-254, 18 April 1983, p. 104.

66 Huang Huanzhong, 'A Discussion of Some Problems in the Rural Specialised Households', *Nongye jingji wenti*, No. 12, 1983.

67 Wuxi Municipal Committee Agricultural and Industrial Bureau, 'The Relative Concentration of Grain Fields is the Starting Point for Realising the Specialisation of Grain Production', *Nongye jingji wenti*, No. 9, 1984, pp. 30–31.

68 Li Hu, 'Farming Experts in Guangdong's Zhongshan City Have More Land to Till', *Renmin ribao*, 3 November 1984, p. 1.

69 *JRPS-CAG*-281, 12 December 1983, p. 53.

70 See for example Christine Wong, 'Interpreting Rural Industrial Growth in the Post-Mao Period', *Modern China*, Vol. 14, No. 1, January 1988, p. 11.

71 'Ten Policies of the Central Committee of the CCP and the State Council for Enlivening the Rural Economy', *Xinhua yuebao*, No. 3, 1985, pp. 52–5.

72 State Statistical Bureau, *China Rural Statistics 1988* (New York: Praeger, 1989), p. 10.

73 Ibid., pp. 6–7.

74 Ibid., p. 8. Note that these figures do not include county-owned enterprises, which would raise the rural non-agricultural employment figures considerably. For an enlightening, though sobering, discussion of the problems of interpretation of rural enterprise statistics, see Christine Wong, 'Interpreting Rural Industrial Growth in the Post-Mao Period'.

75 *Zhongguo tongji nianjian 1988*, p. 172.

76 It should be noted here that the Chinese themselves refer to 1985 as the year when the 'second phase' of rural reforms began, largely referring to this revamping of the commercial system, and corresponding to the beginning of the 7th Five-Year Plan. However, my periodisation puts the beginning of phase two a bit earlier, because I see the reform of rural commercial structures as part of a larger process of commercialisation of the countryside, in which the problems of truly eliminating command planning in agricultural procurement and meshing with the market have continued to bedevil the reform process.

77 'Economic System Reform Must Be Firm and Steadfast', *Renmin ribao*, 2 January 1985, p. 1. See also the discussion in Ding Shengjun, 'Reform of the System of Grain Commodity Buying and Selling', *Jingji yanjiu*, No. 8, 1984.

78 See for example, 'Guangxi on Planning System Interim Provisions', *FBIS*, 17 January 1985, pp. P1–2.

79 For the time being, however, 'award sales' of fertilisers or other inputs and grain (for cash crop sales) might still be relied upon. See for example, *FBIS*, 4 April 1986, pp. 02–3; and Document No. 1 of 1986, *FBIS*, 24 February 1986, p. K4. An interview with a Chinese agricultural economist in Beijing in January 1989 revealed that award sales of fertilisers continued to figure prominently in the incentive mix the state planned to offer farmers for 1989 grain output.

80 In fact, some of the contracts now being distributed are bound as red plastic booklets, just like the old sayings of Chairman Mao.

81 Zhao Ziyang, 'Release the Prices of Agricultural Products, Promote Adjustment of the Rural Production Structure', *Hongqi*, No. 3, 1985, p. 12.

82 'Plan of the CPC Central Committee and the State Council for Rural Work in 1986', translated in *FBIS*, 24 February 1986, pp. K3, K5.

83 Li Yingcan and Zhang Xiyun, 'Construction of Small Market Towns is an Effective Means of Accelerating Rural Commodity Production', *Jingji wenti* (*Economic Problems*), No. 10, 1984; 'Important Rules for the Development of the Commodity Economy in the Countryside', *Jingji ribao* (*Economic Daily*), 9 May 1984.

84 *Zhongguo tongji nianjian 1988*; 'Communiqué on the Statistics of 1988 Economic and Social Development Issued by the State Statistical Bureau of the PRC', *Renmin ribao*, 1 March 1989, p. 2 t2. FBIS-CHI-89–042 (6 March 1989), p. 38.

85 *Zhongguo tongji nianjian 1989*, p, 21; *China Rural Statistics 1988*, p. 13. It is

extremely difficult to find strictly comparable figures; not only do we have the difficulties with national figures, but also certain lines of production were shifted out of 'agriculture' and into other categories in 1985.

86 *Zhongguo tongji nianjian 1988*; 'Communique on the Statistics of 1988 Economic and Social Development', p. 43.

87 See the informative discussion of this issue in Lee Travers, 'Bias in Chinese Economic Statistics: the Case of the Typical Example Investigation', *China Quarterly*, No. 91, September 1982.

88 *Zhongguo tongji nianjian 1988*, cit., p. 42.

89 The meaning of cornucopia has regional variations, however. My observations in Wuxi and Nanjing in January 1989 were that the variety and quantity of produce could rival most American supermarkets; while in Beijing, produce was more limited in variety and quantity but still quite ample.

90 Kathleen Hartford, *Dilemmas of Socialist Reform: Rural Development and Food Policy in China, 1978–1989*, manuscript under revision for Harvard Council on East Asian Studies.

91 USDA, *China Agriculture and Trade Report*, June 1988, p. 12; *Zhongguo tongji nianjian 1988*, p. 763.

92 Those subsidies by local governments may take a direct form, in subsidies raising the producer price to a level at which local producers are willing to sell. But untold amounts of subsidy may also be rendered indirectly. In a field visit to one township in Wuxi county in January 1989, for example, my colleagues and I learned that local 'peasant' factory workers received wages for the days when they were required to work on their grain fields.

93 According to the 1988 budget report by Wang Bingqian, in *FBIS-CHI-89–054*, 22 March 1989, p. 14.

94 State Statistical Bureau, 'The Communique on the Statistics for 1989', in *FBIS-CHI-90–045*, 7 March 1990, p. 37. This report claimed a harvest (407 MMT) nearly meeting the target, but givern the clampdown on press reporting, and the pressure on the Li Peng government to display some economic successes, one may remain suspicious of the reliability of these claims until time has sifted them somewhat. I have queried a number of agricultural experts concering the credibility of the claim: some find it plausible, others (especially some who had paid local rural visits in 1989) do not.

95 'He Kang Holds Press Conference', *FBIS-CHI-89–054*, 22 March 1989, p. 16.

96 USDA, China: *Agriculture and Trade Report*, June 1988, p. 23. The USDA's own calculations, which use different starting months for trade years for different grains, yield different figures from those based on Chinese customs statistics. So long as comparisons are only made between figures from the same data set, however, they are not problematic.

97 Ibid.

98 In 1985, the gap between state prices and market prices for grain was small. The gap widened considerably even by 1986. By the end of 1988, it was pronounced. For example, the free market price of wheat was about one-third higher that the state price; for maize, 50 per cent higher; for millet, 100 per cent higher. The impact on grain production has been all the greater in that state prices for other agricultural commodities have been adjusted over these years, so that the relative profits of grain cultivation have fallen steadily. Hartford interview with Chinese agricultural economist, January 1989.

113

99 Hartford interview with Chinese economist, Beijing, January 1989.
100 Nicholas D. Kristof, 'Local Governments across China are Said to Face a Cash Shortage', *New York Times*, 15 April 1989, p. 3.
101 *Nongmin ribao* 1. My thanks to Tyrene White for calling this report to my attention.
102 *Far Eastern Economic Review*, 13 April 1989, p. 14.
103 See for example *Far Eastern Economic Review*, 28 September 1989, p. 8.
104 Janos Kornai, *Contradictions and Dilemmas: Studies on the Socialist Economy and Society* (Cambridge, MA: MIT Press, 1986), p. 137.
105 Just one example of how such political clout might arise in the Chinese context, apart from personal contacts and bureaucratic consonance of interests: the monopoly of the Chinese tobacco industry is held by the state-owned China Tobacco Corporation. In 1987, this single state corporation delivered 17 billion *yuan* in taxes and profit to the state treasury. That amounted to over 7 per cent of total state revenues in that year. *1988/89 People's Republic of China Yearbook*, (Hong Kong: New China News Agency, n.d.), pp. 269, 307.
106 Nearly every year the state has promised to increase agricultural investment. Nearly every year the real value of such investment has fallen.
107 Kornai, *Contradictions and Dilemmas*, p. 151.
108 Bruce F. Johnston and William C. Clark, *Redesigning Rural Development: A Strategic Perspective* (Baltimore: Johns Hopkins University Press, 1982), p. 73. A bimodal agricultural development strategy, in Johnston and Clark's usage, refers to settings where 'the increases in productivity and output, especially commercialised production, were concentrated to a large extent in a subsector of large farms which adopted labour-saving, capital-using technologies'. Ibid., p. 71.
109 Merilee Grindle, *State and Countryside: Development Policy and Agrarian Politics in Latin America* (Baltimore: Johns Hopkins University Press, 1986), p. 7.
110 Ibid.
111 Ibid.

4

FROM MODERNISATION TO INVOLUTION: FAILED PRAGMATISM AND LOST OPPORTUNITIES IN DENG XIAOPING'S CHINA

Yves Chevrier

We have witnessed the emergence in Eastern Europe and in the Soviet Union of a 'new regime' of reforms centered on political change, that is in an area which Deng Xiaoping's 'ancien rgime' carefully avoided. As a result, in no time but in a dramatic way, China has been pushed from the front to the rear of the reform movement in socialist countries. The Chinese leaders were not overtaken on their own ground: quite to the contrary, they made repeated choices over the last two years, indicating that they decided to maintain their style of economic-without-political reforms, although they are faced with economic and social problems as acute and as troublesome as those which elsewhere, from Poland and Hungary to East Germany, have led to a political breakthrough and then to the collapse of Communist regimes.

The spring 1989 crisis in the People's Republic of China was primarily a political phenomen, resulting from the contradiction between rigid official policies and rapid socioeconomic change in the country, that is, from the limits and the failure of the reform strategy followed by the leadership since 1978.

Most observers, as well as many actors and victims of the crisis in China, agree that the dominant factor in the Chinese modernisation is and will be the articulation of socioeconomic and political change. My main concern will be a sober and not too optimistic evaluation of the prospects for political reforms in the PRC. Leaving aside the reactionary options of those who would re-establish central controls and ideological mobilisation, the solutions that have been suggested for this complex problem of articulation are four, ranging from Deng Xiaoping's decentralised economism to Zhao Ziyang's 'neo'-authoritarian statism, and from Hu Yaobang's pre-Gorbachevian controlled pluralism to democracy.

However, in order to examine these options a preliminary assessment of the socioeconomic crisis and of the political stalemate is necessary. Thus, I will try to evaluate:

- how and why Deng's initial economic and social success (prior to 1985) led to an overheated, unbalanced and inflationary growth, which in turn disintegrated Chinese society;
- how the political crisis emerged from confrontations in 1987–88, marking China's (or rather, Deng's) refusal to enter the new era of political reforms.

THE FAILED MODERNISATION: ECONOMIC-SOCIAL DISINTEGRATION AND THE COLLAPSE OF THE STATE AS REGULATOR

China's economic crisis is twofold. Overheated, unbalanced and inflationary growth is a *structural* phenomenon that began surfacing in 1985. In addition to this, government policies since autumn 1988 have generated a downward cycle, that is a *conjunctural* adjustment resulting in industrial depression and lower inflation rates. In this section the long-term, structural aspects of the crisis will be examined.

It is advisable to start with economic and geographical factors. Inherited scarcities (consumer goods, services, protein products, etc.) translated as a structural quantitative and qualitative excess of demand over supplies in underdeveloped sectors, both in industry and agriculture, when readjustment policies inaugurated in 1978–9 increased urban and rural incomes, i.e. created a consumer market. The consequence – unbalanced sectoral growth – is compounded by high relative-price differentials between basic sectors (energy, steel, or grains, cotton) and transformation industries (consumer goods) or vegetable, fruit, dairy and meat products. Furthermore, these distortions have been aggravated by geographical factors. Coastal regions, that were traditionally more developed and the kernel of light industries, have received the biggest part of foreign investments and technology. They are also the prime location for urban and rural collective and private enterprises, whose rapid increase exploits (and at the same time indicates) the unequal opportunities fostered by China's new growth over the last ten years.

Inflationary pressures are also due to the lack of macro-economic equilibrium. The high rate of personal savings is counterbalanced by increasing trade and budget deficits, and by a sustained increase in money supplies. Adjustment policies are at best short-lived (e.g. 1980, 1985). When inflation crept ahead of foreign trade deficits as the major sign of crisis (after 1985), a crisis of confidence developed and savings were spent (in a panic during the summer of 1988) on personal stocks and consumer goods.

Inflationary pressures also stem from the incomplete restructuring of the state industrial sector, where the dual price system has pushed input prices and costs upward. Permanent pressures for higher wages and bonuses in state enterprises - another sign of piecemeal, irrational reforms - concur to the same effect.

With the dislocation of the (relatively) integrated Maoist economic system, and with the evils of rapid, unchecked and unbalanced growth, China clearly displays a Third World identity. Another feature of the last decade contributes to this new picture, as well as to the dislocation of the economic and social system. The salient component of Deng's reforms, implemented step by step in the countryside and in the cities, has been the decentralisation of investment decisions, resource allocation and of the authority to manage farms and firms. Far from curtailing bureaucratic power, these policies strengthen local power networks and lobbies, which still control crucial inputs (energy, construction materials) and use bureaucratic privileges (as members of the local party-state *nomenklatura*) to squeeze autonomous and private economic agents (decentralised state enterprises, rural households, *getihu*, etc.). The deconstruction of central planning and controls does not result in a market economy, but in the confusion of bureaucratic power and economic management, that is in the emergence of a localist and bureaucratic competition for economic advantages between units, localities, provinces, ministries, etc.

Marked by the rapid increase in extra-budgetary funds and

parallel financial channels, the emergence of these 'small societies' or '2000 feudal powers' is responsible for runaway investments, that are in turn a prime factor of inflation and unbalanced growth. Because of the weakness of the fiscal, banking and legal systems (that are either underdeveloped or dominated by local influence), the erosion of central state controls due to the end of the command economy has not been counterbalanced by an 'indirect' macroeconomic regulation. Although the goal of 'indirect' regulation has been repeatedly stressed as central to modernisation policies, the state's ability to check, balance and 'moralise' economic growth is severely impaired for want of proper instruments. The ideal of the state as regulator is in sharp contrast with the reality of the decentralised state as predator. Chinese society, on the other hand, is too weak (as a result of the absence of any central state protection through a working legal system) to operate without local protection or to withstand bureaucratic squeeze. It is also weakened by traditional sociocultural patterns (such as interpersonal relations or *guanxi*), that is, by the non-emergence of a modern social order in accordance with economic and technological modernisation.[1]

In sum, the rise of corruption, while it is related to the growing commercialisation of the economy, stems from an acute *crisis of the state*: collapse of the archaic command structure, inability to institutionalise a modern state structure (as regulator), expansion of bureaucratic interests and influence at the expense both of the (central) state and of independent economic and technical elites. A bureaucracy without a state, official corruption, disorganised competition, inefficient authoritarian rule: the descending phase of Deng's decade is not unlike the end of the Ming and Qing dynastic cycles.

Altogether, the dislocation of the economy, the disintegration of state controls and the inability of the new economic and professional elites to resist bureaucratic pressures, have resulted in what Hirshman calls a 'conflictual growth'. If we turn to social aspects, the dislocation of the Maoist economic order and status framework has increased disparities between regions, units and individuals, resulting in aggravated frustrations and tensions: northerners against southerners, urban wage-earners (*zhigong*) against peasants, poor farmers against wealthy 'specialised households', intellectuals against private business owners, etc.

The general consequence – a rapid disintegration of the Chinese social body – is compounded by several factors, that are also symptoms of a deep, and deepening crisis: a greater geographical mobility of the people (including peasants), a better access to information through the diffusion of electronic devices, the rise of crime and the erosion of social discipline, and finally the tension - the clash - of values. Modern, individualistic cultural and social patterns must share with traditional structures, religions, and behaviours the ground liberated by the collapse of socialist values and controls over daily life. The immemorial city–countryside contrast is no longer an absolutely discriminating factor, if only because the rapid development of family farming and collective enterprises in rural districts and small towns is really modernising some coastal areas, while cities, notwithstanding their new, Western-oriented and individualistic values, are still organised on the collective (or should we say communal) basis of the *danwei*.

Since 1985–6, the dominant impression, when one looks at the contradictory movements in Chinese society, is that of a Brownian agitation dominated by particularistic patterns.

However detrimental to the success of modernisation, and to national unity, this process of disintegration was an important asset for an authoritarian political system. 'Divide and rule' was Deng's golden maxim, and to many observers the actual state of Chinese society seemed to verify his strategy of economic movement and political status quo. Yet, since 1985 it has also become clear that every segment of Chinese society has lost confidence about its economic gains or status. As contractual (negotiated) prices lag behind market prices and costs, farmers have become losers; industrial workers find it more difficult to fight higher prices for consumer goods by increasing bonuses, and fear for their *danwei* privileges if state enterprises can fire them, close, sell housing facilities and rent them at higher costs. With the freeze on investments and extra-budgetary projects, contractual workers and business owners in the non-state sector discover their high vulnerability for want of any organised social protection. All attributed their fears or hardships to inflation, and all resented bureaucratic profiteering and corruption as a functional evil and, above all, as a moral failure.

Conditions were ripe, then, at least in urban China, for the political emergence of collective frustrations, when the leadership launched a drastic economic freeze in the autumn of 1988, after closing to political reforms in 1987. Such reforms could – perhaps – have avoided an open split in the leadership and put popular support if not behind the austerity programme, at least not against it. Whereas the long-term efficiency of political reforms for solving economic problems is highly debatable, their short-term efficiency for solving political problems is certain. The articulation of the democratic movement on the coalition of popular fears, frustrations and hopes is problematic. For all its actual or potential political novelty, however, the spring crisis followed the recurrent pattern of social movements in China since 1949. The voice of urban China would not have been heard so forcefully if the power structure had not given signs that some of its components were ready to listen to it. In other words, if Deng Xiaoping's coalition, sealed in 1978, had not been split, and if his strategy of turning social divisions into political domination had not been undermined – not by the emergence of an organised civil society, but by unmanageable divisions in the political structure. That is to say, if Deng had not lost his mandate as a reform leader.

FROM DIMINISHING RETURNS TO BLINDNESS: DENG'S FAILED LEADERSHIP AND THE ROOTS OF THE POLITICAL CRISIS

The rape of Tiananmen Square has darkened Deng's image to a point where many observers forget his past accomplishments, namely that he led China far ahead on the road of Socialist reforms before the emergence of Gorbachev's 'new deal'. These merits should be acknowledged, even by those who never entertained any hope that Deng could go much farther. His rejection of a 'new deal' for China, essentially, has not come as a surprise. Yet, this rejection – this refusal of being the Mainland's Jiang Jingguo – can be seen as a capital sin. He could have initiated a transition to more liberal politics that would have suited China's needs, the actual stage of development of the Chinese society, and its prevalent cultural patterns, without neglecting the bureaucracy's vested interests. Deng will enter history as a traditional reformer (that is, in the Chinese way, as a decentraliser) and as the man who only knew how to deconstruct Maoism.

As Mao's Nemesis, Deng was successful insofar as he made use of a margin of flexibility in China's political and social system – unreformed but degraded and ready to harbour, without much political discomfort, a carefully limited and shaped set of non-political reforms. It is hardly possible to characterise this margin of flexibility in the system without a thorough investigation of the latter's degradation since the 1950s. The problem is too complex to be examined in detail here.[2] I shall only list five main points:

1 Deng broke with Mao's politics by ideologically separating the party's monopoly (over politics and ideology) from an autonomised economic sphere. He therefore liberated social energies for economic growth without altering the power structure or antagonising bureaucratic vested interests.

2 From 1978 to 1984, he established himself at the centre of the political system, by checking the more reformist elements in his coalition (after crushing the democratic movement in 1979), as well as conservative and reactionary hardliners who repeatedly tried to launch ideological counteroffensives against the new social deal, thus endangering the basic standstill of 1978. His main achievement in this respect was probably to put an end to the campaign against 'spiritual pollution' in 1984, and to give the 'go' signal for more reforms. The result, indeed, has been a political–economic 'stop-and-go', with Deng moving from one front to the other and acting as the charismatic crisis manager. Even after his status was undermined by the student political demonstrations at the end of 1986 and by Hu Yaobang's dismissal in January 1987, he made sure that the campaign against 'bourgeois liberalism' would be restricted to the party. And he is presently striving to maintain this basic principle from a position of greater weakness, as he had to side with the hardliners in the decisive crisis of April–June 1989.

With these two points, the profile of Deng's strategy appears clearly: structural reforms in the economic and social field, no innovations in the political system (sheltered by the 'Four Principles'), and institutionalisation of 'socialist' law to regulate interactions between the two sectors; and, above all, no aggression of one against the other, no expansion of one at the expense of the other. In many ways, Deng's 'pragmatic' management of the party's revolutionary legacy in the new perspective of economic modernisation, with his skilful balancing of 'movement' and 'resistance', is not unlike Louis-Philippe's *juste milieu* in France during the 1840s.

3   Structural economic reforms succeded where they were profitable on a short-term basis and politically less sensitive, that is, in the countryside. After a first attempt at industrial reforms met (albeit on a small scale) with the usual, structural consequences of urban restructuring (in China as in other socialist countries, e.g.: chaotic overinvestment, budget deficit, inflationary pressures) that led to a first readjustment of readjustment policies at the end of 1980, Deng's NEP was the masterstroke of his career as a reformer. Although short-lived and soon crippled by the distortions analysed above, the agricultural bonanza helped the reformers to eliminate the last Maoist remnants in the leadership and to weather the ideological counterattack launched by the hardliners in 1983.

4   Deng's NEP was paralleled by another proof of pragmatic (if short-sighted) skill: his decentralisation policies, that mellowed bureaucratic resistance and developed strong vested interests in the reform, notably in open-door policies.

5   At the same time, Deng capitalised on the lasting segmentation of Chinese society. He therefore did not fear the re-emergence of non-party elites (economic and professional elites) as long as they would not move towards the political centre of the system. His strategy was to confine them to a horizontal, economic articulation, not leading to a vertical, political construction.

Neo-capitalist structures were thus welcome, but as peripheral pockets. A similar logic informed the 'one-country, two systems' strategy for the reunification of Hong Kong and even Taiwan. Ad hoc neo-United Front policies were not meant as initiating a political pluralism. They were the standard nationalist trick used by statism to lure patriotic elites and deprive them of further political aspirations. The single political door opened to the new elite was the party itself. Hence, Deng's support of its restructuring (with the campaign to recruit 'intellectuals', that is professionals and experts, launched in 1984–5) and, conversely, his constant support of policies aiming at strengthening party structures and ethos against 'evil tendencies' and corruption, that is, against the new economic, social and cultural trends stemming from the reforms.

Allowing social and economic change while striving to make the bureaucratic structure impervious to change had been the dilemmas of past dynasties. Failure had meant corruption and dynastic decline. The Deng leadership found itself caught in the same dilemma. As it was unwilling to use the ideological weapons suggested by the hardliners, it could only rely on the traditional devices of party homeostasis (purification and rectification). The fact that those devices were restricted to the party while society at large was developing new ways and new values made them largely inefficient. This was the other factor in the rise of corruption (in addition to the economic factors).

Deng had enough wisdom to realise that his initial success would be short-lived and that he had to move forward. Capitalising on the renewed ideological standstill in the first months of 1984 (that ended the campaign against 'spiritual pollution') and on the exceptional crop of the same year, he supported an extension of the reforms to urban areas and to the industrial system (with a Central Committee decision of October 1984). He therefore increased difficulties and resistances, while his room for manoeuvre and easy gains was narrowing. In sum, while Deng's reforms had the initial advantage of deconstructing Maoist structures and propelling economic growth before they unhinged it, their basic flaw was that they did not reform or rebuild in the areas (legal system and culture, instruments of macroeconomic regulation) that were crucial for actually severing the economic sphere from the bureaucratic world (and sheltering the former from the latter), and essential for checking and balancing economic growth when the first signs of crisis appeared (in 1985).

These difficulties, as we saw, were not the trivial problems generated by industrial–urban reforms in Socialist economies, and requiring more reforms (prices, labour allocation) as a cure. The crisis of the state in the transition from socialist mobilisation and command economy to a market economy with social pluralism demanded strong, coherent *state-building* policies. The diagnosis was as clear as the symptoms of crisis already since 1986. And the politics of the Chinese leadership in 1985–6 seemed to indicate a fresh awareness of the necessity of political reforms. The October 1984 decision on urban economic reforms indicated that the 'party must reform itself in order to help the reforms', which was done in 1985 in traditional party style, with a rectification–consolidation campaign (the co-optation of 'intellectuals' into party cells was one aspect of this campaign). In 1986, in spite of the economic freeze decided in the summer of 1985 (that preceded a conservative offensive and the launching of an anti-corruption campaign), the political articulation of the theme of political reforms progressed significantly along two main lines.

One current of thought (later articulated as 'neo-authoritarian' by members of Zhao Ziyang's think-tank) proposed standard statist-authoritarian state-building policies. The party and the state would have to be clearly separated, but the new state structures, as well as the remodelling of Chinese society and mentalities for the sake of modernisation would be decided, built and engineered on the state's sole strength and authority. Authoritarian statism, that is political reforms as technocratic measures, was to be better articulated and officialised by the Thirteenth Party Congress in October 1987. China's unmanageable size, the economic chaos, and clear threats on national unity made a good case for it. But how could state building under authoritarian statism work with few civil servants and professionals to run state agencies? And how could the technocrats count on the party-state bureaucracy's good will for reforming itself, since a younger and better trained elite reflecting China's modernisation will not take over, in the best of cases, before at least one or two generations?

The other trend, that Hu Yaobang's think-tank strove to explore and formalise, suggested to match the economic and social pluralism developed by the reforms with a genuine political pluralism, allowing the political articulation of different and admittedly contradictory 'interests'. The assumption was that pluralist politics would serve as a counterweight to the authoritarian and communal structures stifling Chinese society and perverting economic growth. The advocates of pluralism did not go beyond the Gorbachevian scheme (still to be unveiled at the time). They suggested a plurality of candidates for party and state elections, not free elections. It is not clear whether they perceived the ultimate consequences and requirements of political pluralism, namely the development of new habits and the establishment of a sphere of political debate related to independently organised social groups, but well above the particularistic and interpersonal ties which, so far, add up to make Chinese politics. The evolution of a new political culture goes hand in hand with the institutionalisation of these 'interest groups' through the cultivation and legalisation of individualistic values and civil rights. With democracy in the background, both developments contribute to, but also require, the emergence of a modern civil society. Again, it is not clear whether the advocates of political pluralism realised that they would have to break the traditional dependency of the intellectuals in their relation to political power, even when they moved from speculating on pluralism to demanding democracy.[3]

If political pluralism is a necessary transition to a democratic political culture and institutions, their absence or weakness makes it highly vulnerable. Because it should legitimise opposition (where opposition is usually not voiced, or perceived as illegitimate), an effective pluralism could easily be misrepresented as anti-national and chaos-creating. One related area of vulnerability is that, while a majority of the population may not be interested in modernised politics, some narrow segments (students, intellectuals) may not be willing to suffer further delays in establishing a democratic order. During the last weeks of 1986, student demands for a genuine liberalisation overflooded in this way Hu Yaobang's moderate intentions. Both – demands and intentions – were rejected and criticised by conservatives and authoritarian statists.

By the latter, I mean Zhao Ziyang and Deng Xiaoping, who could still count on the wide gap isolating the intellectuals from the economic interests of the vast majority of the population and, therefore, had no use for genuine political reforms. Deng stuck to his own programme by supporting Zhao's at the Party Congress in October 1987; sharper economic reforms (prices, labour allocation, housing, etc.) were to be supported by a technocratic restructuration of the state, so as to bring the economy and the bureaucracy under control. In fact, Zhao's scheme increased fears and precipitated a crisis of confidence that led to the panic of the following summer (1988). Deng only hastened the social crisis, then, by breaking with Zhao's programme for growth and condoning Li Peng's austerity measures, without the slightest popular support. He had by then exhausted not only the system's margin of flexibility, but the immense capital of confidence and expectations invested in his leadership by the Chinese people in the early 1980s.

King Louis-Philippe's 'juste milieu' was legitimated by La Fayette in July 1830 as the 'best of republics'. Deng Xiaoping proved for a while that the best reform could be no political reform, and just like the July Monarchy in France, his unreformed pragmatic leadership fell from grace with History. Yet, from rejection to political reconstruction the transition may be long and convulsive, as it was in France down to the conflictual rise of republican radicalism in the last decades of the nineteenth century. What are the prospects for a Chinese 'republic'?

POLITICAL CHANGE: CONSTRAINTS AND PROSPECTS

This section will be primarily problematic, as we are dealing with facts and variable parameters that are not completely known or understood. These problems boil down to a few main questions. Is China's political system weakened enough – by the spring 1989 crisis, by the protracted power struggle for Deng's succession – that a new political deal will emerge from the ruins of Deng's failed leadership? What could be the political profile of a post-pragmatic China: a new Emperor or a new political order? Which amounts to asking whether China's society and culture contain seeds of political modernisation (be it authoritarian or democratic) in sufficient quantity. Last but not least, what will be the role of the pressing economic and social crisis, that political reforms would cure no more in China than in the USSR and Eastern Europe?

The spring 1989 crisis made clear that the crisis of the state as regulator was compounded by a crisis of the central power structure, which probably contributed to make anti-government demonstrations more daring and to increase the number of declared opponents. Yet, the expected collapse did not occur. The power structure has been able to maintain a modicum of cohesion, while organising a selective repression that has frozen the seeds of democracy and civil society grown in the spring 1989 over Tiananmen Square and elsewhere in urban China. The evaluation of the potential for future divisions contained in today's alliances and compromises (e.g., around Jiang Zemin's promotion) is at best speculative.

The paralysis of the political system is a clearer fact. Reports agree that the crisis of confidence is striking within party ranks, in spite of the terror and renewed ideological controls and training. At the top, Deng's charisma and strategy of 'stop-and-go' have collapsed. The 'stop' phase was too conflictual and too brutal to allow any rebound towards a 'go' phase in the near future without drastic changes in policies and personalities. As already stated, Deng is cornered into rear-guard actions in order to preserve – from a weakened position – the ideological separation of ideology and economics that has been the foundation of China's reforms since 1978. In a paradoxical way, the strongest bulwark of the fundamental standstill is the practical confusion of bureaucratic power and economic management; that is, state, army and party vested interests in reform and open door policies. The *de facto* economic and social segmentation of China also prevents hard-line ideological or austerity policies decreed in Beijing from freezing initiatives at provincial and local levels. When involution is an asset, the dynastic cycle comes to a close. But how near is the end?

In the wake of the spring crisis, gloomy economic forecasts predicted a speedy collapse. Yet, the conjunctural cycle started in the autumn of 1989 seems to show that results will be less negative than expected (for instance, there has been an increase in the 1989 crop). Subsidies to urban consumers have also increased and retail prices seem somewhat less unstable than in 1988.[4] Industrial runaway growth has been checked by a brutal investment squeeze and forced taxation. Although sizable chunks of the economy in the south and along the coast ignored the freeze for a while, the depression or downward slope of the cycle (some observers speak of 'stagflation') is now more pronounced and more generalised than in 1985–6, with chain bankruptcies in the private sector and growing urban and small town unemployment. As economic sanctions will not be felt before 1990, foreign borrowing remains high. Trade deficits are higher. In sum, inflation is somewhat checked and peace is bought in urban and rural areas at the expense of greater budget deficits and future borrowings on foreign financial markets. Wholly aware that they are only buying time, Beijing authorities are already signalling their willingness to do business as usual in spite of Western sanction policies.

Whether these signals will be heard or not, money can be obtained in the meantime from private banking, but at higher costs (reflecting China's degraded status as an international borrower), while the servicing of foreign debt is no longer negligible in state budgetary expenditures. In addition to these constraints, central authorities will have to inject liquidities in the economy before their goal of industrial restructuration (mainly at the expense of the private sector in light industry) is reached. With the present emphasis on centralisation and on the state sector (where plans for closing non-profitable enterprises and opening a labour market are shelved), the economy jumped from chaos to near death (to borrow a Chinese saying). To be sure, state-building policies are stressed with the present emphasis on the reform of the taxation system. We may observe, however, that taxation reforms have surfaced in the official discourse, without much practical effect, in the wake of the successive readjustments since 1980–81. How, then, can a new inflationary cycle – from near death to chaos – be avoided.

Some observers would claim that, economically, China is doing better than many Third World countries, or Poland. However, economic problems in China cannot be assessed on the sole merit of relative economic performances, and will probably not be solved on the sole economic strength of the country. Managing China through economic cycles will soon prove a short-term solution when recent conflicts show the collapse of the state as regulator and make political solutions unavoidable. Far from fostering an economic 'miracle', Deng's policies have introduced politics in the Chinese equation. It would be tempting to go from this statement to the conclusion that China is ripe for democracy: democracy forced by politics, not obtained, as in Taiwan, as the crowning achievement of decades of economic growth and social change marked by the emergence of an urbanised, educated population around the new pole of a fledging middle class. Indeed, we should be aware that rather than providing solutions, a working democracy requires that basic issues be solved. I shall only name three.

State-building policies should be well advanced. Pre-modern

social structures dominated by rural values and fragmentation should be steadily replaced by urbanisation, education and middle-class development. And if one claims that democracy can be learned and shaped in the making, as it was in France under the Third Republic, we may observe that the long French apprenticeship depended on democratic institutions and education, and that we witnessed the incremental diffusion of the republican political culture through the electoral process, public school system and military conscription. Through these structures, the sustained action of the sizable radical–republican elite was felt, as well as the pedagogical influence of recurrent crises (e.g. the Dreyfus case).

China's society is in a state of flux, but as it was analysed above, its evolution clearly does not meet these requirements (or those for a transition to political pluralism). The coalition of fears and frustrations that opposed the government from April to June 1989, and the universal call for democracy do not indicate that the prevalent patterns of social fragmentation and political alienation have been significantly altered. To be sure, some new articulations emerged during the spring, and before, in urban China: 'salons' regrouped intellectuals, politicians and professionals; semi-official professional associations (e.g. associations of managers) tried to organise and protect sectoral interests through the legal and representative process. In May, autonomous organisations (worker and student unions) were created. But for a vast majority of the government's opponents, it seems that 'democracy' was viewed in the traditional, moral and personal perspective, as the means to obtain a better yet identical order. Democracy is an ideal not formulated in a positive way. It mainly echoes what people reject. And as soon as it went beyond the consensual rejection of inflation and corruption, the echo was quite contradictory: from the workers who displayed Mao badges for fear of the reforms, to *getihu* participation for more reforms.

In other words, conditions for the articulation of opposition politics on a political debate are not ripe. Even among the radical students, the prevalent attitude seemed to amount to a moral-activist vision mixing calls to the Emperor to 'purify' the state (including by stepping down), the exaltation of self-sacrifice in the tradition of revolutionary heroism, and practical signs that here and there the apprenticeship of opposition politics was under way. To be sure, democratic aspirations in Eastern Europe meet with all the difficulties of the so-called 'transition'. Yet, bridges to democracy exist, thanks to the presence of civil societies and to an ad hoc political culture. Can we, for instance, compare China after Tiananmen to Czechoslovakia – not the Czechoslovakia of 1989, but the society that froze under Warsaw Pact occupation and seemed to lose sight of its intellectual vanguard in 1968?

Notwithstanding recurrent economic problems, a Chinese democratic breakthrough under the present circumstances would be a short-term solution, one that could well endanger the future prospects of democracy in China. Although circumstances are quite different in Eastern Europe, many observers formulate a similar analysis. For all its cultural and historical idiosyncrasies, China does fall under a general law. How, then, should we formulate it?

China may not be fit for an immediate democracy, but – leaving aside the arguable case for protracted 'dynastic' decline and/or possible partition – I do not see any long-term solution without a better political articulation of social and economic change. Mainland China's path will not be Taiwan's. Allowing for cultural differences, can we foresee for post-revolutionary China a future akin to the pattern followed by post-revolutionary France during the nineteenth century? Although I use the example of post-revolutionary France as a heuristic device, my essay ends up in question marks. I realise, of course, that my title contains some wishful thinking. If Deng's capital sin was to miss clear opportunities for political reforms in 1986–7 and 1989, it was not only because a radical revision of his pragmatism could have avoided bloodshed. A political move initiated by him could have started the process of incremental political modernisation, perhaps just like he initiated the process of economic modernisation. Perhaps. . . . And if China's path may be similar to the French one, how long and how convulsive will the Chinese apprenticeship of the modern *res publica* be?

NOTES

1 The collapse of the state as regulator and the 'weakness' of the economic and professional elites against bureaucratic privilege also generate crippling consequences at microeconomic levels: financial constraints, permanent bureaucratic encroachments upon firm management (autonomous in prin-

ciple) in state enterprises, arbitrary fees and fines extorted from private farms and businesses, etc.

2 I have tried elsewhere to study these dynamics and how Deng's reforms found convenient 'ecological' niches by selecting areas of relative systemic weakness and avoiding or encircling its areas of strength. See notably Y. Chevrier, 'Une société infirme: la société chinoise dans la transition modernisatrice', in Claude Aubert et al., *La société chinoise après Mao: entre autorité et modernité* (Paris: Fayard, 1986).

3 I should add here that the dependency of the intellectuals could stem from several factors: historical legacy, absence of a modern society in the twentieth century while the Chinese intelligentsia reached ideological maturity, which left the intellectuals prisoners of a solitary dialogue with state authority and under nationalist pressure to approve statism; finally, manipulation of the intellectuals as alienated, activist, critical and obedient elements by Maoist system.

4 I am indebted for these observations to Claude Aubert, who recently conducted a field survey in the PRC.

5

TIANANMEN 1989: BACKGROUND AND CONSEQUENCES

Marie-Claire Bergère

The Tiananmen movement in the spring of 1989 fascinated Western public opinion; in the same way, the brutal repression of the Chinese students and citizens on 4 June putting a tragic end to the movement that had roused so many hopes, provoked a cry of outrage. Yet, sympathy and compassion are not always conducive to a real understanding of events. While the French were celebrating the bicentennial of their revolution, many observers yielded to the temptation to analyse the events in Tiananmen by using the standard of Western democratic traditions and the ideology of human rights. But China has its own idiosyncrasies, its own political culture, its own geographic characteristics and its own historical and demographic peculiarities. This is not to say that China cannot aspire to the freedom and democracy that Western societies enjoy. But historians must put emotions aside and be as objective as possible in their analyses. The opportunity for more detached thought offered by the relative indifference towards China of public opinion today, captivated by the downfall of the Communist regimes in Eastern Europe and the changes in the Soviet Union, must not be lost. Otherwise, the events in Tiananmen Square risk being seen merely as a reference point for Western debate on Socialism and post-Socialism, with the consequence that Western-liberal perceptions remain as distant from Chinese reality as European and American perceptions of the Cultural Revolution were during the 1960s and 1970s.

The most important question is about the *nature* of the Tiananmen movement. From a Western perspective, the movement has frequently been perceived as the rejection of Communism by the Chinese people, tired of the failures of the regime and

132

stripped of all faith in Marxist–Leninist ideology. On the other hand, a few experts see it as just another wave of popular protest (previous waves were in 1976, 1978–9, 1985–6), the periodical recurrence of which is facilitated by conflicts within the leadership group, particularly during periods of succession. In their view, the explosion in Beijing in the spring of 1989 coincided with the exacerbation of the political conflict and the struggle among factions for succession to Deng Xiaoping: above all, the struggle between the then General Secretary of the CCP, reformist Zhao Ziyang, and the Prime Minister Li Peng, who had the support of the conservatives and the veterans. Moreover, the spring movement would not have differed from previous protests if it had not been for the exceptional presence of the media, involving the world in the demonstrators' hopes and frustrations.

Avoiding both enthusiastic approval and simplistic analysis, this essay attempts a detached study of the following issues: the importance of popular mobilisation, the ideological orientations given to the movement by students and intellectuals, the strength drawn by the protest movement from the hesitations of, and the divisions within the leadership.

THE MOBILISATION OF THE URBAN POPULATION

From the beginning of the 1980s, latent student unrest flared a number of times into large demonstrations: in September–November 1985 against the new Japanese economic imperialism and in November–December 1986 in support of the reformist policy of Hu Yaobang. But on those occasions, the urban population did not unite with the students. In May 1989, on the other hand, blue- and white-collar workers, small entrepreneurs and even some members of the police and the army mobilised en masse in Beijing and in a number of other large cities in support of the student demonstrations.[1] Why the change?

Stressing the rapid growth in the Chinese economy (approximately 11–12 per cent per annum between 1978 and 1988) and the improvement in the standard of living of most of the urban population, many observers conclude that the crisis was caused by the contrast between the success of economic reform and the lack of political reform. Referring to the instability marking the recent evolution of the newly industrialising countries in

Asia, these observers feel that after ten years of economic reform, China is as ready for democracy as Taiwan and South Korea are after four decades of 'miraculous' growth. They feel that the Chinese protest movement has the same motivations as the discontent of the new Taiwanese and Korean middle classes: economic growth. But this kind of analysis raises a number of doubts.

After considerable success in the early 1980s, the economic reform undertaken by Deng Xiaoping came up against a series of difficulties in 1984 and 1985, that is, when it was extended to the urban/industrial sector; *de facto*, the reform generated excessive growth, instability and inflation. In 1988, investments constituted 39 per cent of the GNP. Moreover, it should be pointed out that, despite greater autonomy, firms did not operate according to market laws, while the loosening of controls on monetary policy and loans forced local authorities to increase financing. In this way, the pressures exerted on the economy spurred inflation, which rose to over 20 per cent in 1987–8. The austerity programme and the new centralisation decided upon in September 1988 did not yield the desired results: they led to stagflation rather than stabilisation. Thus, besides being deprived of the security and guarantees they had enjoyed under central planning, the urban blue- and white-collar workers now also saw the benefits they had received from the economic reform (higher salaries and more bonuses) threatened. Discontent and unrest spread. Each group advanced specific demands that were often divergent from or contradictory to others. Social envy of the *nouveau riche* was also a factor.

The students appealed to their compatriots to mobilise by demonstrating above all against the corruption and the rapid accumulation of wealth by public officials exploiting their positions for personal gain. In this the students hit the mark: the city dwellers were more concerned about inflation and its consequences than about democracy. The consensus between students and the population was based on the shared indignation at the personal increase in wealth of corrupt party officials. That is why it is argued here that the equation *economic prosperity + political immobility = popular mobilisation* does not apply to the Tiananmen protest movement. Mobilisation was the result of economic instability and of uncertainty about future prospects. In brief, it was the result of the shortcomings of the economic reforms rather than of their success. The main obstacle to the economic reforms was not the lack of political liberalisation, but the way in which the reforms were managed: alternate acceleration and braking. These cycles were more indicative of the inexperience and the infighting among political leaders than of a lack of democracy. Unity of direction, bureaucratic competence and popular support – indispensable ingredients for any balanced economic growth – are not characteristics peculiar to, and not even always characteristics *tout court* of, democratic regimes. Viewed in this light, the Tiananmen movement seems radically different from the movements that have arisen in the newly industrialised countries of Asia. Tiananmen was not the result of successful modernisation, because modernisation has not yet been achieved in China and may not be for many years. Yet, while being exposed to all the inconveniences of a modernisation process, the people were still far from enjoying its benefits and demanding the transformation of an economic power over which they did not have political control. This does not rule out the fact, however, that the leaders of the movement, both the students and the intellectuals that inspired it, aspired to changing the political system.

THE ROLE OF THE STUDENTS AND THE INTELLECTUALS

The students who demonstrated in Tiananmen were not merely seeking to improve their own lot, although the corporative difficulties they face (deterioration of campus life, employment uncertainty) were not totally unrelated to their mobilisation.[2] Their slogans and their banners demanded mainly democracy, freedom – of the press and of the judicial system – and the defence of human rights.

These demands sprang from a line of thought developed during the 1980s in the ever more numerous and explicit debates published in newspapers and magazines and in discussions in the so-called 'democratic salons' and on university campuses. These debates vitalised the activity of cultural groups which, in the summer of 1986 with the so-called 'double 100 flowers movement', reached a level of freedom and intensity close to that of 4 May 1919. The students drew their ideas from the protagonists of these debates: men like physicist Fang Lizhi,

135

writer and journalist Liu Binyan, theorist Yan Yiaqi, reformers Bao Tong and Gao Shan, economist Chen Yizi, novelist Zhang Xianliang and many others.

The transformation of the Chinese political system into a Western-type democracy was not the main subject of these debates (even though some intellectuals, such as Zhang Xianliang explicitly called for it). Emerging after decades of silence and oppression, many Chinese intellectuals spontaneously returned to the traditional attitude of Confucian scholars, associated for centuries with the dominant ideological and political structures of imperial power. They called for a reform of the CCP that would bring people of quality to power, whom they, as intellectuals, could serve as advisers. Very few of them were actually concerned with the problem of creating new institutions or modifying the structure of the state. According to men like Fang Lizhi or Liu Binyan, all problems, including those of economic modernisation and political reform, could be solved by good leaders and honest administrators.

Thus, the students found inspiration in these ideas. Their aspirations to democracy and freedom were expressed in slogans like 'Down with Deng Xiaoping' and 'Down with Li Peng', while their hopes were concentrated on the 'good' Zhao Ziyang. Instead of trying to channel their opposition into an institutional framework, all hopes were placed in one man. Only at the end of May was a fleeting attempt (which ended in failure) made to turn to the NPC, whose president Wan Li was said to be a reformist. This non-institutionalisation of the conflict proved to be fatal for the movement, in that there were no political alternatives to the intervention of the army. In fact, at the end of May, the army appeared to be the only part of the old state structure still on its feet.

Yet, the intellectuals and their student spokesmen were not the only ones responsible for the failure to translate the popular power gained at Tiananmen into political leverage. The persistence of traditional moral and political values was not the only obstacle to the institutionalisation of the opposition; it was also paralysed by the absence of support for the demonstrators from civilian society and autonomous structures. Checked by those in power and rejected by the people, who did not identify with them, the mass organisations (the youth league, the student federations and the trade unions) had no political weight. And the associations created by the students (the Beijing Students' Autonomous Federation, founded on 20 April, the Dialogue Delegation for College Students, founded on 5 May, the Hunger Strikers Delegation established on 13 May, the Federation for students coming from the provinces) and by the intellectuals (the Beijing Association of Intellectuals, headed by Yan Yiaqi) and by the workers (the Capital Workers' Autonomous Federation) remained at an embryonic stage, lacking any real representative capacity.[3] In this sense, the situation in China was quite different from those in countries like Poland or Eastern Germany, where the churches, active despite persecution, provided material support and an organisational framework for the protest movements.

While ideological weakness and the lack of a civil society (that is, an organised social structure with autonomous institutions) may be considered as reasons for the final failure of the movement, how can its extraordinarily wide-ranging initial success be explained? Enthusiasm, patriotism and the courage of the student demonstrators were definitely factors. But perhaps most important of all was the students' extremely skilful and intelligent strategy. Through strict respect of the precepts of non-violence, using the funeral (22 April) of a respected party leader (Hu Yaobang) as a pretext, and the visit of Gorbachev to Beijing (16–17 May) as a political platform, declaring their loyalty to the country and the party, the students managed to avoid open conflict and repression for many weeks. When time started working against them – as of 13 May – they resorted to a hunger strike. Although borrowed from the Western protest repertoire, this new strategy was well suited to the Confucian contest between the demonstrators who were eager to appear as the champions of virtue and truth and the oligarchy which, in the name of the same Confucian political moral, declared itself open to their criticism. In fact, according to traditional concepts, the use of violence reduces the legitimacy of the authorities who are to blame for it. Thus, the hunger strike threatened to throw discredit on the regime by making it responsible for the martyrdom which it had scrupulously tried to avoid up to that time. The hunger strike forced the regime to put an end to hesitations and to set a deadline: that of the physical limit of the strikers.

The political acumen of the young demonstrators and the

rigid discipline they observed were indeed so remarkable that they authorise conjecture of expert political help or guidance from members of government and mass organisations or party officials sharing some of the students' ideas and hoping to be able to exploit the popular mobilisation to further their own power. Recognition of the role of these advisers in no way denies the existence of a spontaneous student movement or suggests that the students blindly followed the directives of some figures working behind the scenes. It merely means that the protest movement would not have enjoyed its initial success without the help of numerous powerful allies in the party and state apparatus.

GOVERNMENT DIVISIONS AND HESITATIONS

The rivalries among the various factions of the CCP, the generation struggle and the political and personal conflicts among the leaders played an important role in the events in Tiananmen. They paralysed the ruling group from day to day, keeping it silent from 16 May to 9 June 1989. The consensus between moderate and radical reformers, upon the support of which Deng Xiaoping had relied for his return to power in 1978, disintegrated in 1985. From that date, the moderate reformers – defined as 'conservatives' – continued to express their opposition to the evolution of the reform. In September 1985, at the Party's Conference on Labour, Chen Yun made a solemn appeal for prudence. In autumn 1986, Peng Zhen, then Chairman of the NPC, headed an offensive against the CCP General Secretary, Hu Yaobang, who was finally removed in January 1987. After the victorious counteroffensive of Zhao Ziyang at the Thirteenth Party Congress (October 1987), violent inflationary pressure again swung the internal balance of the leadership group towards conservative Prime Minister Li Peng and central planner Yao Yilin.

Conservatives and reformers did not agree on the extent of economic and political changes. According to the conservatives, the reforms had been carried out too quickly and had gone too far; it was imperative to reestablish the control of the state (that is, of the central government) over the economy. For the reformers, the reforms had not been completed; it was important to push ahead to allow a real market economy to develop.

These political divergences were exacerbated by the generational conflict between the veterans, deprived of their power and positions – but not their privileges – and given honorary functions as advisers at the Thirteenth Party Congress, and the fifty to sixty year-old party officials, more receptive to technical requirements and the need for change and eager to assert their authority.

Deng Xiaoping tried to manage these contrasts in the leadership group by alternately supporting one faction and then the other. But as the crisis and the conflicts deepened, this oscillatory tactic lost much of its efficacy. And since the old guard seemed unable to choose an heir that was acceptable to both the party and Deng himself, the rivalry became fiercer. Compromises between the factions became more difficult, making the oligarchy appear more undecided, impotent, lacking any strategy for the future and unable to come to an agreement on the present.

While Li Peng and Yao Yilin implemented the 'adjustment' policy officially adopted by the party in September 1988, Zhao Ziyang and his allies openly expressed their opinion that it should be abandoned as soon as possible. Li Peng and the conservatives had the support of the veteran advisers in the Central Committee of the CCP. Zhao Ziyang and the reformers sought the support of the intellectuals, the students and public opinion, exactly as Deng Xiaoping had done during a previous 'spring' in November–December 1978, in order to get rid of his rival Hua Guofeng (the successor designated by Mao Zedong) and to consolidate his power.

But in 1989, the spread of popular mobilisation and the weakening of the leadership apparatus upset the rules of the game. Internal conflicts in the ruling group could no longer be settled by negotiation. On 19 May, Zhao Ziyang was not able to prevent the declaration of martial law. But at the same time, the conservatives were not able to form a majority to condemn Zhao Ziyang during the Politburo meeting of 23–4 May, a meeting which had been expressly expanded to include representatives from the Central Advisory Commission, i.e. the veterans. So, when the protest movement threatened the very existence of the regime, Deng Xioaping reacted in the same way as his predecessors, Mao Zedong and the imperial dynasties had done. He called in the army.

The recourse to the use of the armed forces started with the declaration of martial law. Initially, however, it failed: the citizens of Beijing physically opposed the entry of troops into the city and some officers hesitated to use force against the people. These divisions in the army between the moderates and the advocates of brutal repression evoked images of civil war and chaos. The urgency of the situation triggered a reaction by the government. There can be no doubt about the fact that the military leaders played an active part in the negotiations that finally concluded in the bloody repression of 4 June and the reunification of the political leadership of the party under Deng Xiaoping and the new General Secretary of the Party, Jiang Zemin.

TIANANMEN: A 'CHINESE' FAILURE

After this brief reconstruction, it is clear that the Liberal–Western interpretation of the Chinese crisis must be discarded. The Tiananmen movement was not an expression of protest by a society anxious for political change, whose aspirations are interpreted by a democratic vanguard. In spite of the diversification and dynamism introduced by the reforms, the Chinese (urban) society was still fragmented and cellular. The convergence of the discontent of various sectors that occurred during the course of the Tiananmen movement was not enough to unify and orient the social drive. In the absence of institutional structures and guiding ideologies, the popular mobilisation did not turn into a political movement: it remained the expression of a generalised feeling of discontent.

The strength and duration of the popular mobilisation was strongly affected by the internal divisions of the goverment. Its democratic prestige was, to a large extent, conferred on it by foreign observers and media, misled by the vocabulary used by the intellectual vanguard. Actually, the words 'freedom' and 'democracy' seem to have been used as 'fetish words'; the young demonstrators were unable to give them any meaning other than their own immolation. The intellectuals and the reformist party members with whom the students were allied tried above all to use the impulse of the popular protest to reform the party rather than change the regime. But has democracy ever been known to be 'good government' by a 'good party'? One is tempted to conclude that the immaturity of a society corresponds to the shortcomings of its elites.

But it is obvious that the key to the events in Tiananmen must not be sought in the West, even though the country's opening to foreign technology, capital and influences somehow precipitated the crisis. Evaluation is required of the internal contradictions of the Socialist post-Stalinist regime and, above all, the Chinese political culture – a culture that is still profoundly rooted in Confucianism and that gives priority to the role and the responsibility of the elites and that mediates relations between the government and the people through an almost autonomous bureacracy. The tragedy of Tiananmen is not so much the substantiation of the failure of a democratic revolution as that of the antiquatedness of a state unable to undertake modernisation, of the backwardness of a fragmented society and of the decomposition of a system stripped of its 'heavenly mandate'. In fact, the meaning of the word 'virtue' underlying the words 'freedom' and 'democracy' has to be understood, and the persistence of a Confucian moral regulating the reciprocal rights and duties of the governors and the governed in the common interest recognised. It was, in fact, in the name of virtue that the honest critics, the generous students and the indignant population arose. In the same way, the recourse to brutal force was part of a tradition that has always, throughout the centuries, been able to combine moral imperatives with the constraints of power. The conservative reaction underway since June 1989 is presented as a restoration of the virtue (meaning orthodoxy) jeopardized by the disorders in the streets and the dangerous influences of the outside world.

This kind of analysis, which deliberately gives priority to cultural and specific features of the Tiananmen movement that are systematically concealed, should make it possible to see the failure of the Chinese protest as insignificant with respect to the experiences of Socialism and post-Socialism in Eastern Europe. Then again, very recent history has belied the pertinency of the Chinese model in this field. But it does beg another question: what will be the fate of the conservative restoration underway in China since June 1989, given the general downfall of the European and Soviet socialist systems?

After the repression of 4 June, the government regained control of public activity and consolidated its political and ideological power through arrests, purges and propaganda campaigns. Deng Xiaoping, the target of student protests, maintained his pre-eminent role. On 9 November 1989 he resigned from his last official position as Chair of the party's Military Affairs Commission, but most observers feel that, like Empress Cixi, he is still behind the scenes guiding and checking on his appointed successor, the new General Secretary of the CCP, Jiang Zemin. This recovery of power was officially announced as a mere restoration of the status quo. On his first return to public view on 9 June 1989, Deng Xiaoping stated that the 'open-door policy' and the reforms would continue. Therefore, the first problem to be examined is whether the centralisation currently underway is still a part of the reform process or whether it constitutes a return to a centrally planned economy and a state-dominated society.

ECONOMIC REFORM OR COUNTER-REFORM?

This question may come as a surprise. At first glance, the violence of the repression suggests that the counter-revolution won and throws doubt on the credibility of the official reform plans. Nevertheless, on an economic plane, this would not be the first time that a reform has been slowed down by a phase of stabilisation and consolidation which does not, however, stop the course of the reform. In 1981–2 and again in 1986–7, measures reintroducing central control helped combat the distortions of an essentially pragmatic policy, the accelerations and slowdowns of which responded to the economic priorities of the moment. It can also be claimed that the current policy of a return to centralisation was not caused by Tiananmen, since it was introduced in the summer-autumn of 1988. Finally, it should be pointed out that it partly corresponds to recommendations made at that time by some foreign experts concerned about the excesses of decentralisation and runaway inflation. In its report on China in autumn 1989, the World Bank gave its cautious and conditional approval of this policy: the report recognised the usefulness in the short term of the new centralisation (in order to re-establish the economic balance), but added that prolonged application would have negative effects.

After the Fifth Plenum of the Thirteenth Central Committee (November 1989) – the resolutions of which were only pub-

lished on 17 January 1990 – it is difficult to consider the current
policy a mere extension of the adjustments undertaken a year
earlier. The text of the adopted 'Decision'[4] distributed to the
main central and provincial officials at the end of the plenum,
established the terms of implementation of a clearly conservative political line; the line advocated by Li Peng and Jiang Zemin
in October 1989 during the celebrations of the fortieth anniversary of the foundation of the PRC. Distinguishing between 'two
kinds of reforms and openings', one of which upholds the
priorities of Socialism and the other of which paves the way for
capitalism and 'bourgeois liberalisation', this new line calls for
a limitation of the activities of the collective and private sectors,
a strengthening of command planning, restoration of the state
monopoly for the marketing of essential raw materials (starting
with coal) and abolition of the 'double' price system by eliminating fluctuating prices and returning to official fixed prices. The
managers of public enterprises will once again have to reckon
with the authority of the party committee; while foreign trade
will be channelled through resuscitated state companies. The
new three-year adjustment plan (1989–90), prepared by the state
planning commission under the direction of Yao Yilin, goes far
beyond the austerity plan adopted in September 1988. In order
to acquire the instruments for this new policy, the government
has sought to increase its resources by imposing the purchase
of treasury bonds on administrations, enterprises and the
public, and by reassessing remittals when the contracts for the
provincial budgets are reviewed.

Yet, the new policy does not imply abolition of the reform:
the decisions on rural decollectivisation and family farming have
not been reneged. The collective/private sector in the country
and in the cities is still acknowledged, but its activities have
been limited by higher taxation, new credit restrictions and the
rationing of raw materials and energy supply. Its growth should
not exceed 15–20 per cent per year (against the 30–40 per cent
recorded in 1987–8). The autonomy of public enterprise has not
been abolished, only strongly restricted. The production quota
provided for by the plan has been increased to 80 per cent. The
decline of production beyond that quota (limited to 20 per cent)
and new central controls on raw materials and prices have
shifted the role of the market into a secondary position. Public
enterprises have once again been subjugated to the state, but

to a poorer state, ready to cut credit and fire workers. Thus, the return has not been to the pre-reform era prior to 1978, but to an era of limited reform experienced between 1978 and 1984 – the period in which the influence of Chen Yun was felt and in which the large public enterprises in the cities dominated the small business and tertiary sector left open to private and collective activity.[5]

The government's primary economic objective was to curb inflation and bring it below a 10 per cent ceiling. In fact, the inflation rate fell in 1989 to around 20 per cent. But the austerity policy implemented through a return to central controls, seriously limited production. In October 1989, for the first time after many years, China recorded negative industrial growth (−2.1 percent as compared to 10.6 per cent in October 1988). The enterprises hardest hit were obviously those in the private and collective sector, in both the countryside and the cities. But even the public enterprises were obliged to lay off workers (15 to 20 million workers and employees out of a total of 135 million), to lower wages (as of September 1989), to eliminate production prices and increase wage deductions through the acquisition (of up to 10 per cent of the salary) of state treasury bonds. Unemployment estimates vary between 4 and 5 per cent, with tens of millions of uprooted farmers and workers roaming the countryside and the cities in search of work.[6]

But is there no risk that the high price of economic stabilisation and the authoritarian methods adopted to implement it will rekindle the protest movement? It seems unlikely. Left on its own, social pressure seems to be neither strong enough nor, above all, consistent enough to generate a protest movement. In the rural areas, the regime does not have much to fear from the hundreds of millions of farmer families broken up and subjugated to the tyranny of the local party officials charged with administering collective property. It is in the cities that the situation could become explosive. In January 1990, workers demonstrated against worse work conditions in Wuhan, Tianjin and Chongqing. To counter this risk, the regime again embraced the theory of the leading role of the proletariat and revived the alliance which was so strong in the 1950s between the CCP and the workers owning nationalised companies, seen as the worker elite. Obliged by the economic austerity programme to cut back the public sector activity, the government guaranteed laid off workers 70 per cent of their salary (aiming for 100 per cent by December 1989). The municipality of Beijing recommended that laid off workers replace workers under contract, who will simply be sent to the countryside or out onto the streets.

Undoubtedly, the participation of the Beijing workers in the Tiananmen demonstrations came as a shock to political leaders. Had the 'noble' working-class of the cities not always been a privileged ally of the regime? But the reform and the resulting inflation threatened this privileged status. The counter-reform and above all the austerity programme has hit the workers a second time. As a result, the regime has taken the necessary precautions. They may not be sufficient and there may be new urban protests, but the social discontent will only be forceful enough if it coincides with a crisis of succession or the overturning of the balance of power within the leadership group. Otherwise, it will not, for the reasons mentioned above, be able to provoke significant political changes. It is more likely, that the counter-reform will aggravate the conflict – potentially very dangerous for the regime – between the central power and regional authorities.

STATE POWER AND REGIONAL AUTHORITIES

The place in which the demonstrations took place – the large square in the centre of the capital, the place of all official ceremonies – gave the Tiananmen demonstration an exceptional symbolic force. Thousands of provincials stormed the trains to join the demonstrators in Beijing. Many cities throughout the country were inspired by the capital to launch their own movements. But not all made the same effort. The reticence of the cities in the south, especially Canton, was particularly evident. It was as if the political pressures originating in the centre – both the protests against central power and the recovery of control by the power structure – ran up against the primary concern shared by all in the south of preserving the wealth attained and not jeopardising the development underway.

The economic separatism of the southern provinces was based on the actions of the local bureaucracy, the main beneficiary of the reforms and the prosperity deriving from them in these regions. In the autumn of 1988, Guangdong refused to implement the slowdown ordered by Beijing and to put a brake on the economic growth which peaked at 33 per cent between January and September of that year. The collective and private enterprises to which the government threatened to cut credit resorted to their own reserves and appealed to the participation of the workers and local credit co-operatives. Political and economic interests allied to exert pressure on the central government or to circumvent the directives. In fact, these interests were often interwoven, since the decentralisation of power in the period from 1984 to 1989 mainly benefited local officials. Using various legal and illegal means, these officials financed, exploited and controlled the enterprises, exercising an authority that the Chinese compare to the traditional power of the 'mother-in-law'. When the regime tried to regain control over this sector, it came up against the opposition of the local patrons, that is, the bureaucrats, more than that of the entrepreneurs or the managers. Thus, the government ran the risk of conflict with its own administration. The new centralisation of the economy decided upon by the government required a parallel centralisation of the bureacracy to regain control of command.

The recovery of control over the bureaucracy was pursued by means of an ideological campaign. The fight against corruption in the party is a popular subject (the slogans used in Tiananmen prove it) and at the same time constituted an effective way to strike at members that were too independent and often the most enterprising in business. In 1989, 12,500 members were expelled from the party. The purge was especially strong in the southern provinces. The Governor of Hainan, Liang Xiang, was removed in September 1989 and replaced by a bureaucrat from Beijing. The accusations of corruption against Liang Xiang (exorbitant expenses for banquets, private speculation) actually disguised other motivations: he was guilty of having tried to modernise Hainan through its link with Hong Kong, opening it to foreign capital and transforming it into a free port. The province bordering on Guangdong was also a target: the person mainly responsible for foreign trade, Xu Yunian, was removed. The positions of the Guangdong provincial Governor, Ye Xuanping, and the Vice-Governor, Yu Fei, seem uncertain.

Yet, this regional bureaucracy was not without its supporters at the centre. Zhao Ziyang, close to men like Liang Xiang and Yu Fei, was its principal patron. After his downfall, the coastal provinces were not as effectively safeguarded. But the appointment to the Politburo of the former Mayor of Tianjin, Li Ruihuan, and the former Mayor of Shanghai, Jiang Zemin, made the new General Secretary, suggest that regional interests continue to be taken into account in CCP internal debates. Some political scientists have pointed to a 'regionalist' faction besides the conservative and reformist ones in the party.

Thus, it is quite likely that the new centralisation policy, reinforced after Tiananmen, will come into more or less open conflict with an important part of the high-ranking regional bureaucracy. The outcome of that conflict is not yet clear. During the agricultural reform of 1950, the central government was forced to intervene brutally, sending ten thousand administrators from the north to quell the autonomy of the Cantonese apparatus. Since then, this autonomy has been frequently reasserted, but never as forcefully as in the 1980s. It should not be forgotten, in this context, that the first attempts at modernisation in China made by the central, authoritarian and reformist government at the beginning of this century, came up against the opposition of the local administrations, supported by the local elites, who wanted to implement their own reform, not one imposed on them by the central government and one that was more in keeping with their own interests. As is known, this conflict led to the downfall of the last imperial dynasty with the revolution of 1911 and the establishment of a regime that was a republic in name only.

THE RETURN OF THE ARMY

The decisive role played by the army in the outcome of the crisis of June 1989 has already been mentioned. Before that date, the last spectacular intervention of the army in Chinese political life dated back to the Cultural Revolution in 1967-8, when Mao Zedong asked the PLA to support him and later to eliminate the Red Guards. At the CCP's Ninth Congress in 1969, Mao designated Field Marshall Lin Biao as his heir. At the time, generals and officers controlled the regional apparatus of the revolutionary committees and held numerous positions in the party leadership. It took fifteen years – from 1970 to 1985, first under Mao and later under Deng Xiaoping – to confine the military to their barracks and to limit their influence. But the appeal to them in May 1989 to suppress the protest movement brought the army back to the centre of the political stage. It is clear that in the case of crisis – whether or not it be linked to Deng's succession – its weight will be decisive.

Its influence is already demonstrated by the increasingly important role played by the Military Affairs Commission in the party, not only in guaranteeing domestic and foreign security but also in managing political life.[7] The dominant figure in the Commission is General Yang Shangkun, the main advocate of the declaration of martial law (19 May 1989) and the subsequent suppression. Although Deng Xiaoping was succeeded in November 1989 by Jiang Zemin as Chair of the Commission and Yang Shangkun had to settle for the position of first Vice-Chairman, the decision-making power seems to rest in the general's hands. This is thanks to a strong network of personal contacts in the army and in the party; within the Commission, Yang Shangkun can rely on the support of his brother-in-law Yang Baibing.

Yang Shangkun and his clan exert a strictly conservative influence; the army is interested in regaining ideological and political control throughout the country. An investigation has been opened into 3,500 officers, suspected of having actively participated in the May–June protest movement. The highest ranking officer is General Xu Qinxian, commander of the Thirty-eighth Army, who refused to open fire on the demonstrators and is supposedly in prison now.

As in the other socialist regimes of Eastern Europe and the Soviet Union, the power of the military is limited by other institutions, in particular, by the forces of law and order. But the Chinese people's police force, while 500,000 strong and adequately equipped, did not play the role the regime expected of it in May 1989 and rapidly let the situation slip out of control. Today, the body seems weakened with respect to the PLA. Its commander has been replaced by an army general, Zhou Yushu, and after the abolition of martial law (11 January 1990), a certain number of PLA contingents that had been moved to Beijing to enforce martial law have been integrated into the force.

In essence, the PLA has strengthened its role and a conservative tendency has taken the upper hand within it. This tendency is not monolithic, however. There continue to be divisions in the army, as in the party. 'Moderates' and 'professionals' (the group to which the Minister of Defence, Qin Jiwei, seems to belong) have not been eliminated. And the purges underway, while striking open and active sympathies for the protest movement, do not impede hidden sympathies. In case of crisis, the army has a number of options open to it. This is confirmed by the extreme nervousness of the Chinese leaders, who put the armed forces in Beijing and Shenyang on maximum alert after the downfall of the Rumanian dictator Nicolae Ceausescu (26 November 1989).

Whatever the scenarios for the future, one thing is certain: it will not be easy to reduce the army's role. It is unlikely that the successors to Deng Xioaping, given their minor prestige, will be able to do what Mao and he managed to do after 1970 and after 1978. And it is very probable that the political choices of the army will be decisive. Although a prospect of this kind does not rule out the possibility of a transition to a pluralist political regime, as proven by the East European countries, it does suggest some kind of Bonapartist or authoritarian-reformist solution, if, that is, the regional trends within the military and civilian apparatus do not lead to a return to a regime of warlords!

NOTES

1   For a description of the events of Tiananmen and a more detailed analysis of the economic, social and political evolution in the previous months, see M.C. Bergère, *Histoire de la République populaire de Chine* (History of the PRC) (Paris: Colin, 2nd edition, 1989), Chapter 2.
2   See the analysis by Jacques Andrieu, 'La mobilisation des intellectuels et des étudiants' ('The Mobilisation of the Intellectuals and the Students'), *Où va la Chine?* (Whither China?), texts from a colloquium organised at the Senate, 2 February 1990 (Paris: IFRI/INALCO, 1990).
3   See, the chapter in this volume by Tony Saich and more particularly Tony Saich, 'The Beijing People's Movement, Spring 1989', *The Australian Journal of Chinese Affairs*, July 1990.
4   A Translation of 'Decision on Further Improving the Economic Environment, Straightening Out the Economic Order, and Deepening the Reforms (Excerpts)' can be found in *Beijing Review*, Vol. 33, No. 7, 12–18 February 1990.
5   See Yves Chevrier, 'Les nouvelles classes urbaines après la repression de Tiananmen' ('The New Urban Classes After the Suppression of Tiananmen'), *Où va la Chine?*
6   See Claude Aubert, 'The Agricultural Crisis in China at the end of the 1980s', report presented to the European Conference on 'Agriculture and Rural Development in China', Sandbjerg, Denmark, 18–20 November 1990; and

by Claude Aubert, 'Le poids de la paysannerie' ('The Weight of the Peasantry'), *Où va la Chine?*

7   See Jean-Pierre Cabestan, 'Le facteur militaire et ses implications politiques' ('The Military Factor and Its Political Implications'), *Où va la Chine?*

6

TO REFORM CHINA

Su Shaozhi

THE STRUCTURE AND SHORTCOMINGS OF CHINA'S PRESENT SYSTEM

The Socialist phenomenon as it appeared in China is quite different from that envisaged by Marx. The Socialist society Marx envisaged was to have been the product of the internal contradictions of a highly developed capitalist society. This new Socialist society was to have drawn upon all of the accomplishments of capitalist society, have overcome different kinds of alienation within the old system and have promoted the emancipation of man to a higher level.

Correspondingly, the emergence of Socialist revolutions required the simultaneous presence of three basic conditions: the development of a revolutionary situation in the principal industrial countries; the emergence of a high level of socialised production; and the existence of an advanced culture among the people. Logically, the new society would be qualitatively superior to the old one.

However, the existing Socialist societies do not belong to the phase of post-capitalist society. On the contrary, to a great extent, they still belong to the pre-capitalist epoch either in terms of the extent of their economic development or the cultural and educational levels of the people. There has been no possibility for them to abolish all the contradictions of the capitalist societies. In fact, the existing Socialist societies still contain many of the remnants of pre-capitalist ones, remnants that are no longer present in capitalist societies.

As far as China is concerned, the feudal despotism and egalitarianism of the small peasantry that have existed for thousands

151

of years, still hamper contemporary China. This is because, in our present society, although some elements of Socialism have been introduced, the old traditions stubbornly remain. Moreover, the old traditions were very closely connected to the so-called 'neo-tradition' – Stalinism. In fact, Stalinism is the continuation of the extreme, forced and militarised Bolshevik policies of the period of 'War Communism'.

The personlity cult, the practice of personal arbitrariness as well as highly centralised and unified economic and political management are similar to a type of state monopoly. Under the control of a certain kind of seemingly sacred totalitarian ideology, the state interferes and controls every aspect of social life, even including the behaviour and thoughts of the people. By employing the concept of 'socialist primary accumulation', the state limits the people's consumption to a low level, and it deprives them of the freedom of management, initiative and self-development. Under the 'command economy', the social economy lost its automatic mechanism. As Moshe Levin has noted, under Stalin's control two triads emerged: 'party–state–economy' and 'power–ideolgy–culture'.

Under such conditions, party control and the state mechanism expanded; the legislative and judicial organs became but empty shells and the independence of the mass media was completely eliminated. Under the concept of 'unified politics', society and the masses were over-managed. During decades of long-term transformation, the spirit of state-worship infiltrated the human mind and into every corner of society. Of course, these factors have greatly influenced China. Without exaggeration, feudal-despotiam and Stalinism are the two big mountians that have rested as a dead weight upon the Chinese people. In order genuinely to implement reform and modernisation, we must throw them off.

TWO TASKS OF REFORM

Since 1978 China has been implementing an historic reform programme. The success of this ten-year-old reform programme cannot be denied. Principally, it has shown that the process of China's modernisation should not slip backward. This modernisation not only involves the economy but also both politics and man himself.

On the other hand, the progress of the reforms shows that the measures which we have used to date and with which we are familar are limited in scope and have shortcomings.

Many of the ideas and reasons behind the reform with which we are familar should be reassessed and revised. For example, we lack reform of the system itself. Also, the position of the monopoly of state ownership has been preserved, though it has been criticised. Power is still highly centralised and even monopolised. The rights bestowed upon the people by laws and by the constitution receive only lip service. Cultural despotism in the ideological sphere, though weakened, has not yet been completely abolished. The out-of-date 'management' and monolithic control of public opinion still prevail.

Generally speaking, the reform process in China has entered a stage where, if it does not transcend further the trammels of the old theory, the old system (i.e. the system of the combination of feudal despotism and Stalinism), and the old ideas, it may be trapped by the past, may suffer delays or may even retrogress.

How can the reforms be deepened

From the macro point of view, we face two major tasks:

1   to establish a real market-oriented economy; and
2   to establish democratic political pluralism.

Introduction of these will decide the future and fate of China.

Full development of the functions of the highly competitive market mechanism is the most decisive lever to increase quickly economic efficiency and develop similarly science and technology. In addition, establishment of a market economy would be helpful in limiting the functions of the party and the government as well as depriving the state monopoly of its economic base. A socialised commodity economy is the necessary form for implementing economic and social modernisation. Experience proves that the market is the summation and pivot of commodity–money relations. Also, the marklet mechanism is the most effective form for the reasonable allocation of resources by competitive mechanisms.

The market economy based upon 'the laws of elimination through competition', forces the law of value to assume the decisive role in the allocation of resources and distribution of income. The role of the competitive mechanism cannot be replaced by any administrative measures. In any country, any district and under any social system, if we want to develop commodity production and modernise the economy, we can efficiently attain these objectives only through the use of the market. Without a market economy, the scope and degree of commodity production and exchange will be seriously limited. China's experience in recent years has proved that without a healthy and competitive type of market economy, it is very hard to force the state to give up its excessive administrative interference, and the enterprises and the entreprenuers find it very hard to realise their true potential.

To put this historic task into practice, we must first explain several problems:

1   A modern market economy can run parallel with the government's directive role. The report at the CCP's Thirteenth Congress put forward a new formula: 'The state regulates the market, and the market guides the enterprises.' This means that the market is the link connecting the state with the enterprises. It reflects the measures the state uses to direct the enterprises under its jurisdiction. It causes the state to express its demands indirectly to enterprises by using the market as an economic lever. At the same time, it gives enterprises the power to make their own decisions and the right to select their own policies.

History repeatedly proves that without the active role of the commodity and money relationship, the 'planned economy' is inefficient. Planning that does not take into consideration the market amounts at best to wishful thinking.

Our suggested reform does not call for the abolition of planning. Rather, it asks for the revision of the traditional forms and concept of planning in order to establish planning as the basis of market forces and conditions.

2   Marketisation does not only entail advantages, there are also disadvantages. The market economy also has its negative side. Just as traditional planning has its own superior features (i.e. the power to mobilise and concentrate existing resources), the market economy has its own specific problems. For example, the role of the market's competitive mechanism is, in principle,

a type of ex-post facto regulative one. Also, the behaviour of the market's economic participants unavoidably has some tendency towards spontaneity and blindness.

The formation of the market widens the difference in monetary income among the people. This happens explicitly in the early stage of marketisation and thus worries the public. The 'fetish of commodity' phenomenon dispels the feudal relationship as well as corroding the people's spirits. Development of inflation and unemployment during the process of achieving marketisation increases instability. We must be mentally prepared to deal with these problems. Otherwise, when difficulties arise, they may terrorise us and raise considerable doubts about the necessity of establishing a market economy.

3   The monopoly of state ownership should be abolished. The state worship of Stalinism brought about the control of a social economy through state ownership.

The monopoly position and economic strength resulting from state ownership supports policies of arbitrariness and corruption in the political sphere. Reform of the old structure of ownership pertains not only to the abolition of this monoploy, but also to reform of the highly centralised and unified system. Multiple ownership can and must be the goal of reforms of the ownership structure. Alternatives include an increase in cooperative ownership and other forms of non-state ownership as well as the development to the optimum level of privatisation and the introduction of share capitalisation in certain state-owned enterprises. The abolition of the state's monopoly position and the promotion of competition should be the general requirement of economic life. The abolition of the monopoly of state ownership is the most important and decisive step towards realising the reform measure of marketisation.

It is insufficient if we only have economic reform. Both experience and logic prove that without thoroughgoing and powerful political reform, economic reform can neither last nor be deepened. The military crackdown of the 1989 democratic movement in China and the following retrogression of reform was an example.

The essence of political reform is democratisation of society, which at present can be achieved by putting into practice provisions in the state constitution. A basic requirement for a country that wants reform is the establishment of a social system that has as its goal realisation of 'Man's free and comprehensive development'.

The political system should aim to produce a democratic form for social management. The concept of pluralism is very important if the goal of democratisation is to be realised. In contemporary democratic political systems, recognition of the importance of pluralism (including pluralism of economic, social, political and ideological interests) is the important symbol of a modern society. We must give up the out-of-date and orthodox concept of monism. The development of pluralism should progress from first ideological pluralism to organisational pluralism and finally to pluralism of political power, i.e. the ending of the monopolistic power of the CCP.

Reform should establish the authority of the constitution in a society guaranteed by law. The practice of 'rule by man' should be replaced by the principle of 'rule by law'. Within the authority of the constitution, both the peoples and parties of China have a system of norms to be observed by everyone.

As political reform in other socialist countries has demonstrated, when a certain degree of reform has been achieved, amendment of the constitution should be put on the agenda. In contemporary China, a broad discussion of the 1982 state constitution and preparation for its eventual amendment are required. The new constitution should recognise the existence of the principle of the market economy, pluralism, separation of the party and the government etc. The adoption of a new constitution will open a new page of Chinese history.

At the core of democracy are such concepts as the operation of a system of checks and balances on power to prevent the development of any personality cult or the personal use of arbitrariness. All forms of the monopolisation of power and interests by any organisation or individual should be repudiated. Modern democracy is established upon the principles of decentralisation, termination of single party monopoly, checks and balances, general elections, rotation of leadership, and the leaderships' supervision by the masses. The prerequisite of democracy is the ability of people to make free choices. These include their free choice of the form of management, political leadership, system of values and lifestyle. Democracy should recognise freedom and pluralism.

Democracy does not negate authority and discipline. This should be established on the basis of democratic principles and a system of law. Authority and discipline should be exercised within the framework of the rights and obligations contained in the constitution and according to fixed procedures and principles. In order to guarantee that authority and discipline respect the prerequisites of democracy, we must prevent the tendency towards anarchy from developing, and we must oppose any kind of behaviour and speech transcending legal procedure.

We emphasise the authority of the government. But authority requires supervision as well as checks and balances. Authority is not equivalent to authoritarianism. In the final analysis, authority is the authority of the constitution and the rule of law, not individual arbitrariness. History proves that such individual arbitrariness will bring about dictatorship and corruption, not democracy. In this sense, we completely oppose the idea of so-called 'neo-authoritarianism', that represents a noteworthy tendency towards anti-democratic thought. This runs counter to the tide of our times.

REFORM OF THE PARTY IS THE KEY TO REFORM

All of the existing Socialist countries face similar difficulties (which are very hard to solve) as they attempt to introduce reforms. We can mention different reasons, but the key problem is that the Communist party – in its role as the ruling political party – has not reformed itself. This has been proved by the tremendous changes in East Europen countries in late 1989.

As far as China is concerned, it is no wonder, since among the forty-eight million CCP members, there are a large number of ranking officials and special-interest groups.

The position of the CCP has been shaped by history. Thus far, no other party has been able to replace it. But, we cannot deny that the CCP has been in power for too long a period. It cannot and does not put forward policies for self-renewal and self-reform in line with developments in society.

Bureaucratism easily develops. A part of the CCP leadership takes advantage of its position and power. These individuals integrate their power and money to grab illegally high profits. The corruption and degeneration existing within the party provokes protests from the people and prevents the deepening of reforms. It was one of the direct causes of the 1989 democratic movement in China.

If there is no serious reform of the Communist party itself, other reforms in different fields might be in vain. Reform of the party is the core and the key to all other reforms. The abolition of the monoploy position of the Communist party in the Soviet Union and East European countries opened up the way to a bright future.

Reforming the party: where and how to start?

Analysis reveals that the theory of party construction, its organisational principles, its work methods and its work style, etc. contain remnants of some traditions that contradict the contents and requirements of modern democracy. For example, the party still preserves some traditions dating from its period as an underground organisation and from during the revolutionary war. It still maintains some ideas and organs that took shape under the direction of Stalin and the Comintern. And it still retains some policies that date from the 'transitional period'. Since the implementation of reforms, we have made a preliminary reconsideration of party history between the late 1950s and the end of the Cultural Revolution. But we have not yet been able to reconsider and reassess the entire history of the CCP. Therefore, while our reform programme has corrected some 'ultra-left' policies and ideas, we have not fundamentally overcome certain antiquated elements with respect to the party itself. These include totalitarianism, the tendency of state-worship, the tendency towards being anti-democratic and opposed to openness, the emphasis upon the two triads of 'party–state–economy' and 'power–ideology–culture', etc.

'Absolute power corrupts absolutely.' This truism is the basic reason for the emergence of bureaucratism, the personality cult, personal arbitrariness, and corruption and degeneration in the party.

The party's reform of itself should be built around its modernisation and democratisation. Its principle elements will include the following:

1 We must thoroughly reject dogmatism, emancipate our minds and fully understand the necessity for the party to reform itself.

It will be essential to have a major debate about the problems concerning its position, role, and structure during the new period of history. Different organisations, cadres of various ranks, ordinary CCP members from within the party should be joined by representatives of special-interest groups and social forces from outside the party (especially the media) in this wide-ranging debate.

Through such a procedure, people will be able to arrive at a common understanding of the defects and the harmfulness of the old system, its organisation and its traditions so as to be able to apply pressure for reform.

2 The first step in the reform of the party should be its demo-cratisation.

This should include the real implementation of the principles of rejuvenation and specialistion of cadres; and the implementation of the principles of democratic elections with more than one candidate for each post and a system whereby those chosen serve for a specific term of office. The reforms should also include the strengthening of the power of the Central Committee and the Party Congress and the effective supervision of the Politburo and Secretariat.

Particularly essential would be the establishment and recognition of such concepts as:

- Party members should not violate either the national constitution nor the party's own constitution.
- Cadres should not act arbitrarily.
- Anyone violating established democratic procedures should be condemned and punished in order to avoid repetition and dangers of extra-legal political procedures.

We should carefully absorb the lessons the country learned as a result of the reliance upon arbitrariness and the personality cult during the Mao Zedong era so that there are guarantees that neither will re-appear in the system.

3 Modernisation of the party should especially emphasise its decentralisation, the end of its monopoly position, the termin-

ation of its identification with the state, and the introduction of safeguards against totalitarianism. This means:

- There should be clear separation of party and government. Party members should take part in the government only if elected and should leave office when defeated. The party should no longer exercise direct control over the government.
- A similar separation should exist between the party and the army. 'The party commands the gun' was one of the basic CCP principles during the war. Now, we are in the period of peaceful construction. As a result of the separation of the party and government, relations between the party and the army should change. Because of the very nature of the army's role in national defence, it must be loyal to the state and obey the government. The army must no longer be controlled by the party.
- Separation between the party and finances. We should recognise that the party's massive organisation is not only supported by membership dues and other voluntary contributions, but also that the CCP obtains funds from the treasury for which it does not have to account. This is not in keeping with the party's nature and is not helpful in establishing a good image among the people. A reformed party should cut off the flow of funds from the treasury and other outside financial resources. It should strive to organise a small but highly trained adminstrative group paid from membership dues and other contributions.
- Separation between the party and the legislature and the judiciary. The party should recognise the independence of the legislature and the judiciary and not interfere in their operations.
- The party should give up control over ideology. It is no surprise that every Communist party takes Marx as its source of ideological inspiration. But the party does not have the right to ask members of non-Communist organisations or groups as well as the whole of society to accept Marxism.

In a modern society, no party has the right to compel a whole country to accept its theory. The Communist party can prove the correctness of its ideology by the model behaviour of its members and their persuasive implementation of its policies.

It cannot and should not use administrative measures to force the masses to accept its ideas. From the first day of its establishment the Communist party declared the interests of the Chinese people to be the highest interest of the party itself.

There is nothing more important than the establishment of a humanistic, democratic, rational, free and pluralistic society.

7

THE CHALLENGES TO CHINESE FOREIGN POLICY

Gerald Segal

The Beijing massacre seared the psyche of Chinese and China-watchers alike. And yet those who watch Chinese foreign policy more than domestic events are also struck by the ironies of the crisis. The events of May 1989 just preceding the massacre demonstrated that Chinese foreign policy, certainly in the Communist era, had never been more successful. Indeed, it is several hundred years since China has been so secure from external threat.

Of course, the triumphs of Chinese foreign policy as seen in the meeting of the Asian Development Bank and then the Sino-Soviet summit in Beijing (May 1989) also allowed the student protests to gather momentum under the 'protection' of the Western media. Nevertheless, the two events also demonstrated two of the major reforms of recent Chinese foreign policy: greater integration with the international economy and detente with the Soviet Union. While there has sometimes been a close connection between China's domestic and foreign policy reforms, the two seem set to diverge more distinctly than at any time since the early 1970s. Then, as now, China seems able to open up (or stay opened up) to the outside world, despite a closing of doors at home.[1]

This concept of 'opening up' is, in fact, crucial to any discussion of recent Chinese foreign policy. If one assumes reform Communism to be centrally concerned with opening up at home and abroad, it has become clear that there must be at least a minimal link between the two reforms. As China saw in the early 1970s, without more far-reaching domestic reform, there was a limit to how much Chinese foreign policy could be opened up in either ideological or economic terms.[2]

Such limitations have long been recognised by China's leaders and the struggle to find an answer to the question about how wide the open door should be has never been adequately answered. Modernisation of China and its foreign policy has always been hampered by the unwillingness of China's proud leaders to admit just how little they know and how much less they have achieved for their people. While some Chinese leaders hoped that the revolution and Communism would soon provide many of the answers and much of the growth necessary to raise China from the bottom ranks of world wealth, Beijing has watched with dismay as much of the world, and most of their own home region have pulled further ahead.

Thus China faces several key challenges, many of which link domestic and foreign politics. After briefly reviewing the nature of these challenges, China's reactions will be assessed. While it is true that much of the reform of Chinese foreign policy has contributed to international stability, there are some disturbing signs that China, as an irridentist power, is determined to reform the international system as much as the system forces reform on China.

THE MAOIST LEGACY

Before turning to the challenges facing Chinese foreign policy, some scene-setting is required. December 1978 is usually taken as the starting point for the decade of reforms in China. In internal politics this division makes much sense, but it is far less useful as a dividing line in Chinese foreign policy. In the way we have defined reform – openness – it is clear that Mao began the reform of foreign policy.

It was Mao who took the view that the United States should be encouraged to open contacts with China and that an open-door economic policy could be contemplated. It was Mao who took China into the United Nations and began opening China to other international institutions. It was Mao who shifted Chinese foreign policy away from support for revolutionary movements and put more stress on state-to-state relations.

These basic elements of what would become known as Chinese foreign policy reform had complex roots. In part, they were merely the result of reform in United States policy that had it been adopted earlier, might even have received an earlier welcome from Mao (but probably not). Of course, there is also a difference between the extent of openness in Mao's time and that pursued by Deng. But certainly nearly all the tough decisions about opening to the capitalist system were taken by Mao. Thus foreign policy reform pre-dates domestic reform, and so foreign policy reform might even outlive a curtailment of domestic reform.

The most serious unreformed legacy left by Mao in foreign policy was the attitude towards the Soviet Union. Openness is not merely about opening doors to the West, but it is about the multiplicity of options. It is notable that the most difficult reform for Deng to achieve in foreign policy concerned the Soviet Union, and it was not until after a decade of domestic reforms that relations with Moscow could be normalised.

It is interesting and important to speculate on the extent to which reforms in foreign policy have been related to domestic reforms and domestic debates. This question is far too complex to be assessed here, but suffice it to say there is no clear connection between debates in domestic politics affecting foreign policy. To be sure, there have been times, as in the run-up to the Cultural Revolution, where domestic opponents of Mao seemed to have a different foreign policy agenda. The same could be said for Lin Biao and his defeat in 1971. In each case, Mao's triumph determined a specific foreign as well as domestic policy.[3] But there is no solid evidence of debates taking place primarily about foreign policy.

This is not to suggest that differences on foreign policy are unimportant. As the following analysis will make clear, there are differences in China about foreign policy and they do affect the policies chosen. But the debates are always much more complex interminglings of domestic factors, making analysis of positions hard to document. What is most striking is the extent to which foreign policy can be largely isolated from domestic debates. Thus the decision to continue with a mostly open-door policy after the events of June 1989 is credible, even though some aspects of the retrenchment in domestic reforms does affect the open-door policy. But the effects are secondary, and do not necessarily cripple the reform programme. Thus, unlike other chapters in this book, less attention will be devoted to the impact of policy debates.

THE CHALLENGES TO CHINA

Of the four major challenges to Chinese foreign policy, the first and most important one comes from internal politics. To say that China chose the path to reform is to suggest more coherence to the change than was actually the case. But it was undoubtedly true that Chinese leaders recognised, even in the dying days of Mao Zedong in the mid-1970s, that domestic reform was necessary. After leadership struggles and false starts, the much-hyped 'Four Modernisations' was put into gear.

Although the gears ground, sometimes loudly, and direction was sometimes shifted, it was recognised that China was embarked on a process of reform that included ideology and economics. The Chinese system opened up to more professionalism and decentralisation. China's leaders never really had a clear sense of where they were going, but as long as they were getting growth out of the economy with a reasonable degree of political stability, the reform coalition could hold together.

It was only when the needs of professionalism came into conflict with the outdated certainties of ideology that political instability emerged. So long as economic growth continued, the crisis of political legitimacy could be staved off. But when even the economic reforms staggered into the roadblocks of inflation and corruption in late 1988, the real crisis could be clearly seen. Reform of Communism has, so far at least, never been achieved without such far-reaching political change that the system can no longer be properly described as Communist. Arguably, China learned this lesson before any of the other reform Communist regimes, and like any self-respecting authoritarian regime, it chose to preserve itself before it agreed to abolish its own power.

Therefore, any attempt to disentangle the political and economic elements of reform Communism is bound to be inadequate. China has apparently reached the limits of a 'mixed' economy of Communism and capitalism and moving back and forth in the middle of the spectrum will not solve the deeper, systemic problems. This is not to say that China must embrace the kind of radical political reforms seen in Eastern Europe, for all that they demonstrate is that one way out of the systemic crisis is to abandon the system. A much more difficult task, and one that is still open to China's leaders, is to focus on a political reform that is really professionalism but that is not political pluralism.[4]

This first challenge of reform Communism obviously goes to the heart of the existence of the regime in Beijing. But it also has major implications for Chinese foreign policy. More openness at home has usually meant more openness to foreign influences. More decentralisation has allowed for a wider range of foreign influences on China, and the tendency to pull China in different directions at the same time. And most pressing of all, reform Communism has put China back in touch with other parts of the Communist world and made events in Europe more important for China than at any time in the last thirty years. China's search for, and struggle with, models of reform from the outside world now focuses on the mild authoritarians in East Asia or the rapidly de-Communising comrades of Eastern Europe. Neither one offers an off-the-shelf model for China, and both suggest that Chinese reforms cannot simply remain on hold and hope there is a self-correcting mechanism around somewhere.

The second major challenge to Chinese foreign policy comes from the changing nature of great power politics. So much of Chinese foreign policy has been based on calculations of the superpower balance and the best way to manipulate this major 'contradiction' in international relations. More so than any other great power, China has changed sides in the superpower confrontation and thereby shifted the balance of power more decisively and disturbingly than anyone else.[5]

China has been this sort of restless great power because it has recognised its basic weakness in an age of superpower chauvinism. The further local conflicts were from Asia, the less able China was to play in the superpower league. And yet just because it was unable to act, this never meant China was unwilling to do so when it acquired the ability in the future. Despite its wounded protestations that it never sought to be a superpower, China never intended to remain second best.

As we shall see below, in the 1980s China eventually moved to a more equidistant position between the superpowers in an attempt to maximise its room for manoeuvre. But the real challenge to China has come from the fact that the two superpowers have seen their relative position decline, but for reasons that have little to do with China and in ways that China has so far been even less able to affect.[6] The move to more multipolarity in international relations is unevenly implemented around the world, but is seen most acutely in North-east Asia.[7]

The retreat of Soviet power was first seen in the disengagement from many regional conflicts in the developing world and was most recently and dramatically evident in the collapse of the Soviet empire in Europe (and even perhaps within its own borders). China, like other observers, could not have known that the collapse would be quite so rapid and peaceful (so far), but as we shall see, it has made possible many changes in Chinese foreign policy.

By contrast, the retreat of United States power took place much earlier, and was confined more to the military sphere. In relative terms, the United States remains more powerful. Because of its economic power, the United States is now the only power credibly able to claim genuine superpower status. Thus the Americans play on many fields of power, while the Soviet Union retreats from many areas. Others, such as Japan, are still sorting out which games they wish to play. China is potentially an 'incomplete' superpower like the Soviet Union, although at least in East Asian terms it will hope to be considered more complete.

The third challenge to Chinese foreign policy comes from the related question of the fate of Japan. Of course, Japan is living evidence to frustrated Chinese leaders of what might have been achieved if China had chosen the path of more wholesale learning from the West. The rise of Japan to the status of the world's second largest economy and third largest defence spender is a challenge that will only grow in years to come, especially as the Chinese economy stagnates.

As a result, and especially at a time when the Soviet Union is seen as much less threatening, China grows concerned about which way Japan will go in modernising its own foreign policy. Will regional interdependence develop in a way that reduces China to a pool of cheap labour but locked out of the higher, and more profitable reaches of the international economy? Will China find itself in greater military conflict or at least an arms race with Japan as Tokyo becomes a more complete great power? These questions comprise the most recent of the challenges to China, and perhaps the most potentially dangerous ones as well.

A final set of challenges to China has come from a new feature of the international system already alluded to, the growth of interdependence, especially economic. The image of ancient China isolated from international affairs has always been much overdrawn.[8] Yet it is true that China usually perceived itself as more important to the world outside than foreigners were to China. Indeed, this has been part of China's modern problem. In much of the past this sinocentrism was mostly accurate, but for several hundred years it has been wrong and harmful to Chinese growth.

It is easy to argue that modern Chinese leaders recognise that isolation from the international system is no longer an option. But measuring the extent of China's integration is more an art than a science. The ratio of China's trade to GDP has more than tripled in the decade of reforms. China now ranks in the top five of Pacific trading nations and is now dealing extensively with all its neighbours in the vital North-east Asian complex.

But interdependence is not merely a matter of trade flows and FDI. The challenge of interdependence means accepting that new ideas come in with joint ventures that require more professionalism and political reform. It also means company-to-company contacts that undermine the Victorian value of national sovereignty. Most recently of all, China also sees that interdependence means that China cannot dictate the basis on which foreigners will lend to or trade with China, and therefore there is an economic cost when deciding to ignore foreign protests about Chinese practices.

Interdependence also means that different parts of China will integrate at different speeds. It is already clear that different parts of China have very different trade patterns and are affected by changes in Chinese foreign policy in very different ways. As a result the shaping of Chinese development will be crucially affected by outsiders, but it becomes increasingly difficult to generalise about the patterns of development and the relationship with external affairs.[9] To some extent China risks becoming more than one state.

Needless to say, all these challenges to China are intercon-nected. It is less useful simply to elaborate the nature of these challenges, and more effective to focus on China's responses. As this is primarily a reflection on Chinese foreign policy, it is probably a better idea to assess Chinese foreign policy from the standpoint of the international system rather than to remain mired in the sinocentrism of 'the view from Beijing'. With such a more detached perspective, it is relatively clearer that China remains ambivalent about its new role and perhaps is best seen as posing more of a challenge to international stability than does any other great power.

CHINA'S REFORMED FOREIGN POLICY AS A FORCE FOR STABILITY

The Chinese would have us believe that changes in their foreign policy are the result of conscious decisions by well-informed leaders. The reality, as for most states, is that pressures from within and without create the conditions that limit the choice of leaders. The 'logic' of reform in foreign policy that is forced by the outside world is harder for China to admit than it is for those states more used to playing their part in the new complex interdependence. Thus China says that the new pragmatism in foreign policy and the detente with the Soviet Union were the result of 'free will', even though all but the most sinocentric analysts could see it coming a long way before the Chinese could admit it to themselves.

Sino-Soviet detente

The single most important reform in Chinese foreign policy, and the single most important bilateral relationship in East Asia is that between the region's two largest states – China and the Soviet Union. When the two giants fell out in the 1960s, the strategic balance in the region and around the globe shifted more noticeably than at any other time since 1945. By the 1980s, the two Communist powers were gradually repairing the rift and by May 1989, relations were normalised.[10] The original split had also affected a large number of states in the region and thus the healing of the split had a similar impact. For example, Vietnam and North Korea were both able to find more room for independent action by playing off one Communist superpower against the other, but the Sino-Soviet detente forced them to reassess policies and indeed alliances with Moscow and Beijing.

For both China and the Soviet Union, the normalisation of relations was of major strategic importance. Chinese defence planners could feel more confident than at any stage since the revolution in 1949 that China was at peace. To be sure, there were potential threats, but Chinese strategists ceased talking about tension along the Sino-Soviet border – the most vulnerable frontier.

For the Soviet Union, the improvement in its strategic position was even more important. The fear of having to wage a war on two fronts, which developed in the 1960s, was lessened. Just as the original split was the single greatest loss suffered by the Soviet Union since 1945, so the new detente with China was the single greatest improvement in the Soviet strategic position.

The upshot will be a virtual halving of Soviet troop numbers along the frontier with China, just as China had reduced the size of its armed forces by a million men by 1987. This *de facto* arms control is more sweeping than anything seen in Europe and suggests just how much military security can be improved without resort to formal arms control agreements. The key was resolving the political problems – military deployments were the effect rather than the cause of conflict.

The improvement in regional security is evident in a wide range of spheres. Tens of thousands of Chinese and Russians now cross the frontier on business and for tourism. Visas are no longer required for such travel – a requirement still in force for travel in Eastern Europe. Troops now fraternise in shooting competitions instead of taking pot-shots at each other in dangerous border skirmishes. Talks about border demarcation have made progress, and rail, road and air links across the frontier have been developed. Chinese workers have crossed into Soviet territory in their thousands to staff Soviet factories and farms and there is increasing talk of up to a million Chinese working in the Soviet Far East within the next ten years.[11] The Soviet Union now supplies electricity for Chinese towns as part of a boom in local trade.

In fact, the growing interdependence in trade had preceded the military detente. Confidence-building measures were defined more broadly than in the usual military sense. The reduction in the sense of threat was due to a perception on both sides that their rival was actually less interested in war and more concerned with national reconstruction. This appreciation was first reached by the Chinese in 1980 and by the Soviet

Union some two years later. Improvement in economic relations then followed as both sides tested the political waters. Leadership changes, especially in the Soviet Union, slowed the process of detente. But the coming to power of Mikhail Gorbachev led to a lurch forward in the relationship. The Soviet Union then showed itself willing to take the first steps in clearing away what China had set up as the 'three obstacles' to normalised relations.[12]

By 1989, the level of interdependence between China and the Soviet Union was higher than at any time in the last thirty years. Military security had been vastly enhanced and both sides were now discussing formal confidence-building measures as a way of codifying and strengthening the relationship. Unlike the European theatre, a sense of mutual security was far less dependent on formal agreements. Both sides understood that 'the correlation of forces' left no room for war as a useful instrument of policy.

In economic terms, by the late 1980s interdependence was returning to the levels last seen in the late 1950s. China is the Soviet Union's second largest trading partner in the Pacific (after Japan) and trade is increasing at a faster rate than in any other Soviet bilateral relationship. The Soviet Union is now China's fifth largest trading partner as China has opened a distinctive door to the East European world. Although detente with China was vital for a Soviet Union hoping for greater integration into the wider Pacific, the Soviet Union was merely useful as yet another door for a China already involved in many different trade relationships in the region. For China, improved trade relations with the Soviet Union offered a more balanced foreign policy and allowed China's northern provinces to feel happier about the strategy of an open door to the outside world. Especially after the Beijing massacre in June 1989, when Western states pressed China to change its domestic policies, China saw the open door to the Soviet Union as vital to ensuring independence in foreign and even domestic policy.

Finally, there was another, more distinctive form of integration that both sides minimised in public – party-to-party relations. Of course, the restoration of party ties in May 1989 did not mean a return to the 1950s, when a Soviet elder brother dictated terms to a younger Chinese brother. In fact there was no more potent symbol of the importance and dangers of this interaction than the millions of Chinese students demonstrating for Soviet-style political reforms at the time of the Sino-Soviet summit in May 1989. Although it was initially thought that the Soviet Union was less worried about the Beijing massacre than many Western states, the reality (albeit, unofficial) seems to be the precise opposite. For the Soviet Union, the failure of reform in China is a matter of political life and death if only because Soviet reformers are so anxious about the chances of their own reforms. Ideology has been crucial in the normalisation of Sino-Soviet relations and now it is central to the fundamental disagreement between the two parties. Moscow's most vivid response to the tactics of Tiananmen was to tell its East European allies that they would have no Soviet support for a similar crackdown. Chinese hardliners interpreted recent events as confirmation of their original judgement that to have failed to use the PLA in June would have meant the end of Communist power in China. While one can still not rule out a similar bloody decision in Moscow in the future, it is clear that the Chinese action was regretted in most of Eastern Europe and supported in most of Communist East Asia. But it is also clear that the latest Sino-Soviet honeymoon lasted barely hours between the time of Gorbachev's departure from Shanghai and the declaration of martial law in Beijing.

Nevertheless, by 1989, because the Sino-Soviet relationship was still closer than at any time in thirty years, the course of regional interdependence can still be said to have taken a major turn for the better. Although most of the causes of this change can be traced to bilateral relations, it was also assisted by superpower detente and indeed other trends in the region. There was also fall-out from the Sino-Soviet normalisation. As already suggested, North Korea and Vietnam were forced to reassess their policies because they could no longer play off one power against the other. While North Korea chose to wait for the death of Kim Il Sung for any real reform, Vietnam embarked on its own version of *perestroika* in order to strenghten itself.

Sino-Soviet detente also allowed China to use force in the South China Sea in March 1988 (see below) and made it easier for the Soviet Union to open new relations in East Asia, most notably with South Korea and Taiwan. Sino-Soviet and superpower detente also put pressure on Japan to improve relations with the Soviet Union and even made the United States more cautious about dismissing China's desire for real foreign policy independence. Sino-Soviet detente could also be said to have had an impact on superpower relations because it made the Soviet Union less jittery about such military cuts as ground forces or INF weapons in East Asia. In short, just as there was a vicious circle of conflict in previous decades, in the period of detente in East Asia there was a virtuous circle of detente in which Sino-Soviet relations was the most important part.

Maturing relations with the United States

Although Sino-Soviet relations have been the most dramatic new feature of Chinese foreign policy, it cannot be denied that the most important of the initial reforms of Chinese foreign policy was the detente with the United States in the 1970s. To some extent, if only because of the length of calm relations that followed the full normalisation of relations in 1979, Sino-American relations had become boring. Yet this is not to say they were unimportant, for as the recent downturn in relations has shown, deteriorating Sino-American relations can become a major problem for Chinese foreign policy. The importance of Sino-American detente is not to be measured in terms of trade. While it is true that bilateral trade has increased, it has not been steady and is far less important than Sino-EEC trade. Indeed, there were signs well before the events of June 1989 that trade relations had flattened out into a phase of regular problems and limited potential for growth.[13] The United States was useful as a trade partner, but more because it was yet another Western trade partner that improved China's bargaining hand.

To be sure, China understood that the United States was the leading Western trading nation and the key to a more general acceptance of China into the prosperous world of international trade. If China wanted to join the IMF or the World Bank, not to mention the GATT, it would need American support. If it wanted high technology and preferential treatment as a special kind of Communist trader, then it also needed American approval. Although other countries were more important trade partners, the United States was still the key to the wider network. Thus China's decision to improve relations with the United States, although not initially part of a decision to enter the global market economy, was a reform that made the reform in international economic policy possible.

The initial rationale for normalising Sino-American relations had far more to do with a shared concern about the Soviet 'threat'.[14] As it became clear that the threat was less serious than first thought, and that the United States under President Reagan was serious about re-building American strength, so China grew less interested in such strategic rationales. With superpower detente and then Sino-Soviet normalisation in the late 1980s, the United States was even less important in China's strategic calculations.

For a time, China seemed to be a supporter of the American military presence in Asia and Beijing even seemed to take the American side in assessing relative superpower responsibility for various conflicts. Gradually, China became more balanced and indeed objective in its analysis, and eventually it criticised each superpower as Beijing saw fit. The United States complained about the 'two Americas' policy whereby China sought special treatment from the United States, although Beijing felt free to denounce American policies. This was a more natural policy than the earlier phase of leaning too far to the American side, but it was bound to lead to a cooling in the Sino-American relationship.   The coming to power of the Bush administration might have been expected to lead to a revival in Sino-American relations. Indeed, President Bush's first stop in Asia was China and warm words were exchanged about his previous experience as head of mission in Beijing. And yet the extent to which the President was his own 'China desk' was not apparent until the events of June 1989. Despite a swift official condemnation and imposition of sanctions after the massacre, the President was determined to keep open the doors to dialogue. NSC chief Scowcroft was sent to Beijing twice in the last six months of 1989, including one trip in July. Chinese technicians were allowed back into the Gruman plant to work on re-furbishing Chinese fighter aircraft, despite a formal embargo on military contacts. Co-operation regarding a listening post in Xinjiang designed to monitor the Soviet military effort was also continued.

This was not quite business as usual, but it was close. It was also a policy that infuriated Congress and surprised American allies. At the same time as the United States praised the collapse of Communism in Europe, it was doing far less for the same cause in Asia. Under these circumstances, Sino-American relations were relatively insulated from domestic unrest in China. Although Sino-Soviet relations on the surface appeared to be better than Sino-American relations, the reality suggested the opposite.

Chinese pragmatism

Perhaps one of the most distinctive ways in which Sino-Soviet co-operation helped ease tensions elsewhere in the region has been in the way both Communist powers, but initially China, opened contacts with the NICs and the global market economy. So long as both Communist powers were dealing with the non-Communist world in similar ways, there was less price to pay, either in terms of domestic legitimacy or in rivalry for the friendship of other Communist states.

From the point of view of the NICs, there were certainly strong incentives to improve relations with the Communist states of east Asia. In the case of Hong Kong, the need to get on with China was most pressing and thus a form of normal relations has operated for much of the forty years since the revolution on the mainland. By 1984, Britain had agreed that Hong Kong would be returned to China and all the parties set about preparing for the formal handover in 1997. This was to be the ultimate in interdependence, for under the slogan of 'one country – two systems' the idea was sufficiently to blur the lines between China and Hong Kong until the two naturally merged.[15]

Yet it was also part of the essence of the 1984 agreement that the system in Hong Kong be maintained for as long as possible. This required a sense of confidence in China's good behaviour, something that became increasingly difficult to sustain after the events of June 1989. Until then, the creation of Special Economic Zones on the Chinese side of the border with Hong Kong, and the heavy investment in China by overseas Chinese, were intended to hasten the blurring of the lines.

Of course, it is clear that China will still take control of Hong Kong in 1997 and a form of unity will be achieved. But if it ends up as unity at the point of a bayonet, as seems increasingly likely, then this can hardly be a model for that other major case of Chinese irridentism, Taiwan. Unlike Hong Kong, Taiwan can stand on its own as an independent state if it so chooses. China could try to invade or blockade the island, but at a high cost in prestige and materiel.

Indeed, it can be argued that while Hong Kong slides inevitably into the grip of China, Taiwan is moving closer to *de facto* independence.[16]Of course, what is striking about this process is that it is achieved at a time of closer economic and person-to-person relations between Taiwan and China. But it is the very contacts that show the people of Taiwan that they are much better off without unification with the mainland. Events such as the Beijing massacre, just at the time of increasingly democratic elections in Taiwan, makes the incentives for *de facto* independence even greater.

While the case of Taiwan may appear to be against the grain of growing interdependence in East Asia, all is not what it may seem. Taiwan and, in a very different way, even Hong Kong, demonstrate a special meaning for sovereignty and independence in the region. Hong Kong, a colony of Britain, became *de facto* independent because of its close integration with the global economy. If it is to survive as a *de facto* independent state of China, it must become so closely involved (and successful) in the global economy that it cannot be sacrificed for political principle. Yet such involvement also requires that the Hong Kong authorities retain less control of their economy as decisions are taken in the international market-place and in the conclaves of the G–7. Formal sovereignty becomes a quaint Victorian value.

Taiwan seemed to lose sovereignty as China gained recognition in the 1970s, but looks like winning it back as an independent state because it has shown that the world can get on with more than one Chinese state. The more Taiwan demonstrates that it can trade with China and yet retain its independence, the better chance it stands of retaining its independence. The more Taiwan becomes involved in the global economy and loses control of its own economy to international market forces, the more important it becomes for the world at large, and the safer it is.

The case of South Korea shows similar calculations about how taking part in the global economy helps strengthen national independence.[17] Interdependence breeds independence of a kind. In fact, similar calculations seem to apply to South Korea's relations with China and the Soviet Union (although not yet to relations with North Korea). China and the Soviet Union had been seen as the main adversary because Chinese troops had fought alongside their North Korean comrades in the 1950s and it was Soviet weapons and aid that both comrades used to wage war. At least until the end of the Cultural Revolution, China was seen as the more extreme and dangerous of the Communist powers.

But Korea had traditionally close relations with China, and it was always artificial that only North Korea should embody this past in its post-war alliance with China. Of course, so long as South Korea saw China as the most active supporter of the belligerent North Korean enemy, then relations were unlikely to improve. Similar, but less intense hostility was expressed towards the Soviet Union.

The thaw in this cold war only came with reforms in China's domestic politics after the death of Mao. As part of this 'fifth modernisation' – in foreign policy – pragmatism was permitted in the cause of economic modernisation. All manner of countries, including Israel and Saudi Arabia, were able to open trade relations with China so long as they did not demand diplomatic relations. But it was South Korea that was the main beneficiary of the new Chinese policy. Seoul had grown increasingly confident as its economy went from strength to strength and trade problems with the United States encouraged a wider horizon for trade partners. At a time of East–West detente, the United States was happy to see South Korea improve relations with the communist world.

From the early 1980s China rapidly accepted South Korea as a trade partner, so that by the late eighties the annual turnover was reported to be nearly US $ 3 billion. This only constituted roughly 3 per cent of Chinese and South Korean trade. But it was at least five times the level of Sino-North Korean trade and appeared to have a far more substantial base. Chinese exports, such as agricultural products and coal, were more than matched by South Korean exports of steel and consumer goods.[18] China sought technology at a cheaper price than was available from more developed Western states.

South Korea was pleased to have a new market, but was equally interested in breaking out of its relative diplomatic isolation and forcing North Korea to be more reasonable. But, as Israel also discovered, China could hold off these demands for political payment so long as there was sufficient attraction in the economic relationship. Thus Sino-South Korean co-operation remained primarily economic.

However, the economic relationship could not have opened up in the first place if there had not been a new political attitude in Beijing that tolerated such an economics-in-command foreign policy. The result produced a political impact because North Korea received the message of Beijing's pragmatism loud and clear. With a new trade relationship with South Korea, China was not interested in supporting North Korean adventurism. China was determined to enhance its global position by attending the Seoul Olympiad, and so North Korea was told to behave itself and not terrorise the event. Thus China was responsible for helping push North Korea to the negotiating table with South Korea, even if the talks have so far still failed to reach any significant agreement.

Of course, the Chinese push would not have been nearly as effective if it were not for the fact that the Soviet Union was pushing with the same force, at the same time, and in the same direction. The Soviet Union had supported a peaceful settlement of the Korean question long before China, but so long as Sino-Soviet relations were bad, Pyongyang could play off one Communist ally against the other. As China and the Soviet Union became more friendly, they both could develop their interests in a more peaceful Korean peninsula.

The Soviet Union's interest in peace and quiet was initially due to a desire to avoid crises in Korea that would drag it into conflict with the United States. It was also hoped that in a more peaceful environment, American troops would leave South Korea. Although these policies did not disappear in the late 1980s, they became less central to the Soviet approach. With the positive example of Chinese trade with South Korea, and continuing problems in Soviet-Japanese relations, many in the more reforming Soviet Union saw relations with South Korea as a way to become more involved in regional integration and economic growth.[19]

Thus there is growing economic interaction in this part of East Asia, and Chinese reforms have played a vital role. In fact, China's overall foreign economic policy has undergone major reforms in the past decade. In the pre-Maoist period, China, as a continental economy, had rarely sought economic prosperity through close contact with the outside world. In the very distant past, before the coming of Western imperialism, China merely collected curiosities from as far afield as Africa. Even though China was ravaged by Western imperialists, it took centuries to accept the benefits of trade and it never fully adapted to the idea of modernity derived from openness.

In the 1950s, prosperity and modernity were sought by forming an alliance with the Soviet Union and adopting the Soviet model. The impact on China is impossible to quantify, but given the desperate state of the Chinese economy at the time, even the limited assistance was crucial to putting China back on its feet. The rapid Chinese growth had a great deal to do with simply taking up the slack from the past, but Soviet aid was vital to the speed and direction of modernisation.

The Sino-Soviet split and the ensuing Cultural Revolution did massive damage to Chinese foreign economic relations, as well as making a serious mess of the Chinese economy. It was only the Dengist reforms that changed the domestic base which in turn made real foreign economic policy reform possible. The major expansion in Chinese foreign trade is shown in Figure 7.1. The ratio of Chinese trade to GDP nearly quadrupled in that time, taking it to a level even above that in Japan. China became a major trading nation, and a new economic power in the booming Pacific economy. China was not yet in the league of Japan, but it was approaching the status of South Korea as a major trader in the region.[20]

Neither was the pattern of Chinese foreign trade a matter of disrespect. Unlike many developing states, China's exports were primarily manufactured goods and by 1988 primary goods accounted for 31 per cent of the value of exports. China's ability to adapt to the rapidly changing commodity prices was testament to the value of a command economy.

Imports were concentrated on two categories: machinery and equipment; and intermediate goods. The main partners, as with exports, were with the developed, industrialised world (see Figures 7.2 and 7.3). Import substitution was a specific aim of policy, and was aided by foreign firms. It has been relatively successful in that, for example, by 1989 China was satisfying some 80 per cent of the domestic demand for road vehicles.

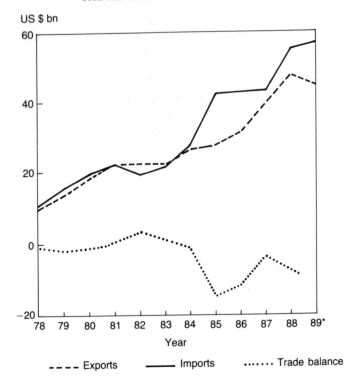

US $ bn

*Annual rate based on first six months.

Source: China's Customs Statistics.

Figure 7.1 China's foreign trade, 1978–89 (in US $ billions)

Once again, the command economy has proven its benefit in some respects, for example in clamping down on imports in 1989–90 when domestic retrenchment was necessary. When faced with a looming debt bill to pay in the early 1990s, China was able to order a trade surplus to help ease it through its problems. These were not perfect solutions, but the economic crises were far less serious than in domestic economic policy.

Indeed, China has been remarkably successful among command economies in its ability to obtain and sustain foreign investment (see Table 7.1). Of course, the FDI has not always been where China wanted, for example nearly half was in the service sector and only 10 per cent was in energy and resources and 30 per cent in productive projects. In 1988 some 58 per cent

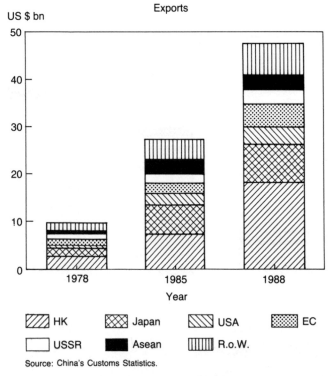

US $ bn
Exports

Figure 7.2 Direction of China's foreign trade, 1978–88 (in US $ billions)

HK Japan USA EC
USSR Asean R.o.W.

Source: China's Customs Statistics.

of all FDI went into productive projects, suggesting the trend was turning in the direction desired by the central authorities, even though much of the trade was handled by specific regional authorities. FDI had fallen in the last half of the decade of reforms and China was only using some half of the promised funds because of difficulties in running enterprises in the confusion of laws and authorities. Nevertheless, foreign debt which in 1980 had been 1.6 per cent of GNP, by 1988 stood at 10.5 per cent of GNP (see Figure 7.4). The crunch of payments in the first half of the 1990s has been part of the reason for economic retrenchment and early indications suggest the reform of the reforms is working.

But it is undoubtedly true that basic features of China's economic relations with the outside world have changed in the decade of reforms. It is not simply a matter of snazzy new

181

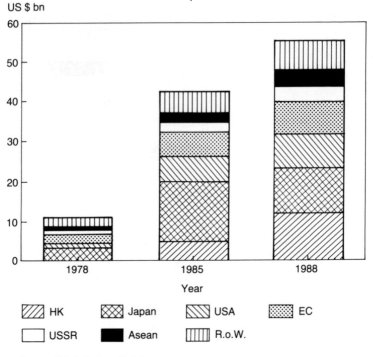

Source: China's Customs Statistics.

Figure 7.3 Direction of China's foreign trade, 1978–88 (in US $ billions)

Table 7.1 Composition of foreign investment in China, 1979–88 (in US $ billions)

	Amount contracted	Amount utilised	% spent
– Foreign loans	47.0	33.1	70.4
– Direct foreign investment	28.2	11.6	41.1
equity joint ventures	9.9	4.8	48.5
contractual joint ventures	13.9	4.0	28.8
wholly foreign-owned	1.5	0.3	20.0
offshore oil exploitation	2.9	2.5	86.2
– Barter trade and assembly operations	4.0	2.7	67.5
Total	79.2	47.4	59.8

Source: State Statistical Bureau, in *Beijing Review*, 6 March 1989

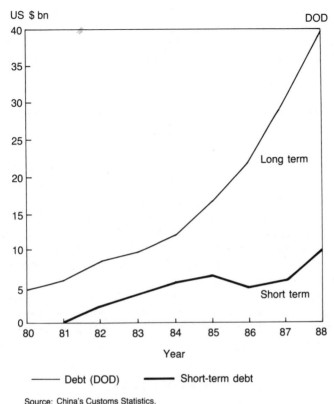

Source: China's Customs Statistics.

Figure 7.4 China's foreign debt, 1980–8 (in US $ billions)

hotels and advertising hoardings for Western consumer goods. Foreign technology and expertise has been brought in, along with the masses of tourists. Most interestingly, Special Economic Zones, built largely on domestic and overseas Chinese capital, have set up new experiments in foreign economic relations. Despite the serious problems with the SEZs, business is still being done.

China has also joined international economic institutions such as the IMF and World Bank and is seeking GATT membership. All of these actions have involved obligations to open China, at least to some extent, to foreign ideas and ways of doing business. Considerable sectors and regions of China now depend on this international business and often share vested

THE REFORM DECADE IN CHINA

interests with international actors who wish to see reforms in China. China may have begun to join the world, but the consequence is also that the world has begun to join in Chinese politics. That is, after all, the meaning of economic interdependence.

THE DANGERS OF THE NEW CHINESE FOREIGN POLICY

For all the evident detente and pragmatism in Chinese foreign policy, Beijing is also notable as an irridentist power. When coupled with the fact that the decline of the superpowers and the rise of Japanese influence creates a far more complex balance of power, it is clear there are perhaps more possibilities for China to think it can reshape the world around it. Although the superpowers seem to be growing out of this dangerous illusion, the Chinese are sometimes encouraged to believe this means their time has come. Certainly, if the Chinese, like the Europeans believe that the lifting of the superpower overlay means a reversion to old-style balance-of-power relations, then China can recall its previous domination of East Asian international affairs.

Wary of Japan

Perhaps the most disturbing cause of future instability is to be found in the relationship between Japan and China. Although there are supposedly bonds of a similar culture, there are major differences in ideology. Although both Japan and China are heavily populated, China remains a poor peasant society while Japan is one of the more developed, urban economies.

In the distant past there was rarely much regional interdependence. Although Japan borrowed many aspects of Chinese culture, the Japanese have always prided themselves on being adapters more than adopters of things foreign. In the more practical realms of military and economic affairs, China and Japan have an uneasy tradition.[21] Japan was never successfully invaded by China but tinier Japan did succeed in holding vast swathes of China for decades during living memory. Some of those parts of China, most notably Manchuria, were briefly integrated into the Japanese economy and war machine. The most enduring legacy of this experience is Chinese suspicion about Japanese motives, even when engaged in seemingly beneficial trade relations. Less openly stated, but no less real, is Japanese disdain for the once-revered Chinese elder brother who is now seen as having fallen on hard times. Japanese ambiguity about whether it is really a part of Asia is largely to do with the sneering attitude towards China behind the veneer of diplomatic equality.

To be sure, there have been great improvements in the Sino-Japanese relationship since the 1970s. In fact, trade between the two states is one of the few major bilateral patterns of trade in the Pacific to change dramatically in nature over the past forty years. China has emerged as Japan's third largest trading partner in the Pacific, now taking about 4 per cent of Japan's foreign trade.[22] Japan is an even more important trade partner for China, but the importance can be said to have declined as a percentage of the generally increasing total of Chinese trade. For much of the 1970s Japan was taking some 20–25 per cent of Chinese exports and it provided 27–30 per cent of Chinese imports. But by the late 1980s, as the size of Chinese trade increased, Japan accounted only for 16 per cent of Chinese exports and 23 per cent of Chinese imports. Overall, Hong Kong was a more important trading partner for China, but China imported more from Japan (23 per cent) than anywhere else.

But given all the bad blood in the relationship, simple trade or investment figures tell only a superficial story of integration. In fact, it is the very uneasiness of the way in which past and present coexist that makes Sino-Japanese relations so distinctive and unstable. Trade disputes have flared over the past decade due to a volatile mixture of Chinese domestic politics and Japanese trade practices. The pattern of trade has been uneven, with imports and exports often fluctuating wildly in response to noisy threats.

Yet the level of economic interdependence remains important, especially for China. The open door to Japan is, if one discounts the peculiarity of the Sino-Hong Kong relationship, China's most important portal. But China remains no less unhappy with Japan's economic power and the threat of Japanese domination of any possible East Asian trading system. As important as China may have become for Japan, Japan still remains more important for China as a source of aid and technology. Not surprisingly, Japan has also become a prime target of more xenophobic Chinese concerned about the perils of undue dependence on the outside world. That continues despite the fact that, in the aftermath of the Beijing massacre, Japan managed to contain the damage to its relations with China, in contrast to most other Western countries.

Ambiguity about economic interdependence is matched by ambiguity about regional security. The Sino-Soviet alliance of the 1950s was in part built on an anti-Japanese basis and China has never been quite happy with signs of a rearming Japan. Although the Sino-Soviet split and closer Sino-American relations led China to be less critical of Japanese defence spending and American pressure on Japan for greater sharing of defence burdens, by the mid-1980s China was changing its mind again.

In an age of declining superpower military power, China is more free to flex its own muscles. Operations, such as the defeat of Vietnamese forces in the South China Sea in March 1988, suggest just how much China is an irridentist power. Japan watches such Chinese action, and reads rumours of China's impending acquisition of an aircraft carrier with some alarm. Tokyo fears that its economic power might be vulnerable without military might to deter China at a time when the superpowers seem less inclined to do so. Japan is now the world's third largest defence spender, although it has so far avoided acquiring clearly offensive weaponry. Japan remains firmly under the American military umbrella and therefore sees no need to match China's growing nuclear arsenal.

Indeed, the American presence seems to be a crucial stabilising force, at least in this aspect of the East Asian calculation of security.[23] Deteriorating US-Japanese relations might lead to greater Japanese independence and therefore an open arms race with China. There is no question that Japan could soon deploy a more formidable armed force than China, even though, by virtue of its geography, Japan would remain so vulnerable as to make it a less than credible great military power.

A more optimistic discussion would stress that the winding down of regional conflict in East Asia makes military force a less useful instrument of policy in the region. But the decline of the perceived Soviet threat also provides less reason for at least tacit Sino-Japanese agreement on security matters. In an age of multipolarity, and multipolarity on the very different levels of economic and military power, Japan and China can be seen as more likely rivals than allies. It must be the hope of the optimists that economic interdependence will restrain the baser instincts of those more inclined to reach for their rifles.

Chinese irridentism

Nearly all unsettled territorial disputes in the region involve China. It is all too often forgotten that China is an irridentist power which has used military force outside its existing borders in more major conflicts more often than any other great power.[24] China has shown itself willing to act unilaterally and to be ruthless in pursuit of its objectives when it is able to do so. Therefore it is of great importance that China's military modernisation has not been neglected, even though it is not of the highest priority.

The nature of civil–military relations is too complex to be discussed at length, especially in the light of the events of 1989.[25] Suffice it to say that the PLA has only been called into politics in the past when the leadership has been divided. But it has always supported the largest faction of the civil leadership and did so again in 1989. The difference in 1989 was that the PLA had become a more professional body and therefore was reluctant to get drawn into politics on a long-term basis as in the Cultural Revolution.

This professionalism has clearly been manifest in the acquisition of new military equipment in recent years that allows its armed forces to operate further from its shores. The trend in the defence budget in the seven years following the war with Vietnam in 1979 was to cut the PLA budget as a percentage of the overall budget, although the real amount received was not always falling as well. In the past few years the rate of decline had slowed and the real defence spending was higher because of cuts in the number of soldiers, arms sales, and economies in such sectors as the defence industries. For the past two years the military budget has been increasing, well before the events of 1989. The massive increase in 1990 may have something to do with better rates of pay, but it has far more to do with keeping promises on re-equipment made to the PLA while the economy as a whole was booming. The year 1990 was not the time to disappoint the professional soldiers.

Naval operations have certainly been extended and even the airforce is making good progress. The rumours of China's acquisition of an aircraft carrier persist. China's military doctrine has been revamped and Chinese leaders make no secret of their desire to become a major power.[26] Unlike Japan, they will avoid 'mere' economic power and will acquire the ability to support territorial claims. China is therefore the power most likely to use force offensively in the region (even if China defines it as lawful acquisition of Chinese territory). Nowhere is this seen more clearly than in the South China Sea.[27]

Although the Sino-Vietnamese conflict is drifting towards detente, China still is willing and able to use force against Vietnam in the South China Sea.[28] When China is finished with Vietnamese claims in the region, it may well move on to challenge Philippine and then Malaysian and Taiwanese claims. The potential for conflict with south-east Asians is clear, and so the risks of tension and even war with Japan and the United States must also increase.

As the Soviet Union has shown by its unwillingness to defend Vietnamese claims in the region, when the superpowers are in decline, regional conflict may be made more likely. If the United States would provide strong deterrence of Chinese pressure on ASEAN allies or Taiwan, a larger war might be prevented. But that would certainly mean increased tension in the region. And if the United States is unwilling to take on such an assertive role, will Japan do it for them? It is unlikely that ASEAN states would be happy to see Japan defending their claims, but the Japanese may well decide for themselves that some sort of response is necessary. It does not take an unduly paranoid analyst to see that if China acquires an aircraft carrier in order to support its irridentist demands, then Japan is unlikely to sit idly by. An arms race and tension may well follow, especially in the new age of multipolarity and uncertainty in East Asia.[29]

There can be little doubt that China is determined to defend, and indeed extend its interests. China played an important role in the Gulf war (again outside East Asia) as a provider of arms to both sides and also to Saudi Arabia. It is no exaggeration to say that China prolonged the war, and its provision of *Silkworm* missiles clearly made the crisis more dangerous as the missiles were used to sink tankers that eventually resulted in super-power and European involvement. The sale of ballistic missiles (the Chinese C-SS2) to Saudi Arabia was made possible by American refusal to supply similar weapons, and like the *Silk-worm* and other arms transfers show, China is now able to act more independently as a great power, and is willing to antagon-ise friends in doing so. Japan was not pleased that its oil spilled into the Gulf because of Chinese missiles, and yet Japan was unable to play in that game of great power politics because of its refusal to have or deploy military power at long range. Japan could soon play that game if it so chose, and therefore Japan grew worried that China would once again drag it into longer range military engagements.

Of course, China is also a nuclear weapons power and it has been far less dangerous in its use of these forces than it has been with its conventional arsenal. China has not apparently transferred nuclear weapons or technology to other states despite its failure to join the Non-Proliferation Treaty. Neither has China threatened the use of its nuclear weapons against any other state. Despite the improvement in the quality of its nuclear arsenal, China has not deployed large numbers of weapons in any category.

But China's approach to arms control, despite its small num-bers of nuclear weapons, is not positive for international stab-ility. Failure to sign any major treaty that would constrain Chi-nese forces – such as the Non-Proliferation Treaty – is a cause of concern. Yet China does tacitly abide by the Non-Proliferation Treaty and the partial test ban treaties. It shows some signs of joining the follow-up process to the Non-Proliferation Treaty and does play an active role in United Nations disarmament efforts. So far, China has yet to be put to the real arms control test – weapons cuts – but then the superpowers have yet to make sufficiently sweeping cuts of their own. If, as seems increasingly likely, the superpowers do begin to engage in far more serious and far-reaching arms control, then China's nuclear component of military force will also be placed under sharper scrutiny. Japan, a non-nuclear power, would certainly have something (probably unpleasant) to say if it is clear that China refuses nuclear arms control.

CHINA'S CHOICE

The challenges of China's domestic politics are clearly far more serious than those in foreign policy. Despite the recent domestic set-backs and the mild cooling of Sino-Western relations, China's foreign policy remains in better shape than at any time in the forty years of Communist rule. There are certainly few real threats to Chinese security that require any major reaction from China.

Of course, the reality of threats is not always the same as the perception of those threats and it is in this respect that the instability in China's internal politics may well have an early impact on foreign relations. It has usually been the case that changes of China's leadership are related in some way to foreign policy change.[30] The era of Deng Xiaoping will soon be over, and as in 1976, a power struggle seems likely. This is not the place to try to predict the outcome of such a struggle, but it is important to stress that this is not a time for expressing long-term confidence in the stability of Chinese policies.

While it is true that so far China has managed to minimise the impact of recent domestic events on foreign relations, there should be no confidence that this can be sustained even in the medium term. As in the case of North Korea, observers will be waiting for leadership succession before making longer term judgements about China. Even though from the outside it seems clear that China needs to join the whirling pace of inter-dependence that is developing outside its doors, it is by no means certain that China will do so. Sadly, China shows many signs of remaining ambivalent about the extent to which its open doors will remain open, and any firmer decision is far too much tied up with the vicious domestic politics of China.

Of course, it is unlikely that China will become a Burma or Albania and close itself off from its region. If only because of the developing trends towards regionalism in China, different parts of the country will maintain some sort of contacts and interdependence. But it is by no means necessary that China as a continental economy will become a major force for regional stability and prosperity. Like the Soviet Union, China may go through phases of being a poor, dissatisfied great power that uses military power in pursuit of its desire to re-order international relations. But as the more recent experience of Soviet policy suggests, such dangerous activities can be contained. In the end, like the Turkish empire (and perhaps even the Soviet one), there is nothing inevitable about any great power remaining powerful forever. Nevertheless, even if the scenario turns out to be unduly pessimistic, the neighbours of China will face a new, and perhaps more dangerous future than the proponents of the Pacific Century would have us believe.

NOTES

1 Gerald Segal, 'Introduction' in Gerald Segal (ed.), *Chinese Politics and Foreign Policy Reform* (London: Kegan Paul International, 1990). For the purposes of the book, and indeed for this chapter, reform is defined as 'openness'. Openness includes more and wider trade and investment relations, more and wider international agreements and membership in international organisations. Needless to say, there is often a close relationship between internal and external openness.

2 Michael Yahuda, *China's Foreign Policy After Mao* (London: Macmillan, 1983).

3 Such links are assessed in Gerald Segal, *Defending China* (Oxford: Oxford University Press, 1985).

4 Simon Long, Barbara Krug, Gerald Segal, *China in Crisis* (London: RIIA Discussion Papers, 1989).

5 For a wider discussion see Gerald Segal, 'China, the Pacific and the Balance of Power', *Jerusalem Journal of International Affairs*, September 1989.

6 Michael Yahuda, 'The People's Republic of China at 40: Foreign Relations', *The China Quarterly*, No. 119, September 1989 and 'The Pacific Community: Not Yet', *The Pacific Review*, No. 2, 1988.

7 Gerald Segal, 'Northeast Asia: All Aboard the Detente Train?', *The World Today*, March 1990.

8 S.A.M. Adshead, *China: A History* (London: Macmillan, 1988).

9 This complex issue is discussed in parts of David Goodman (ed.), *China's Regional Development*, (London: Routledge for the RIIA, 1988), Peter Ferdinand, 'Regionalism' in Segal (ed.), *Chinese Politics* and Stephan Landsberger, *China's Provincial Trade*, (London: RIIA Discussion Papers, 1989).

10 Details on the process can be found in Gerald Segal, *Sino-Soviet Relations After Mao* (London: IISS, Adelphi Paper No. 202, 1985) and 'Taking Sino-Soviet Detente Seriously', *The Washington Quarterly*, Summer 1989. See also Steven Goldstein, 'Diplomacy Amid Protest', *Problems of Communism*, September–October 1989.

11 See *China Daily*, 2 June 1989 cited in *Beijing Review*, Vol. 32, No. 30, 24–30 July 1989, p. 30.

12 The 'three obstacles' were: the level of Soviet troops along the Sino-Soviet border; the presence of Soviet troops in Afghanistan; and the Soviet support for the Vietnamese occupation of Kampuchea.

13 See the lively discussion in Jim Mann, *Beijing Jeep* (New York: Simon & Schuster, 1989).

14 Seiichiro Takagi, 'From Anti-Soviet Coalition to Cooperation for Modernization', in Gerald Segal and Akihiko Tanaka (eds), *China's Reforms in Crisis* (London: RIIA, 1989).

15 For the best of the new wave of books on the subject see Kevin Rafferty, *City on the Rocks* (London: Viking, 1989).

16 Lillian Craig Harris, 'Towards Taiwan's Independence?', *The Pacific Review*, No. 1, 1988.

17 See a general discussion of the foreign relations impact in T.W. Kang, *Is Korea the Next Japan?* (New York: Macmillan, 1989).

18 Jao Ho Chung, 'South Korea-China Economic Relations', *Asian Survey*, October 1988.

19 This subject is discussed at length in Chapter 6 of the forthcoming RIIA book by Gerald Segal, *The Soviet Union and the Pacific* (London: Unwin/ Hyman for the RIIA, 1990).

20 Details can be found in Michele Ledic, 'Foreign Economic Relations' in Gerald Segal (ed.), *Chinese Politics and Foreign Policy Reform* (London: Kegan Paul International for the RIIA, 1990), and Gerald Segal, *Rethinking the Pacific* (Oxford: Oxford University Press, 1990).

21 For careful, albeit cautious analyses see Allan Whiting, *China Eyes Japan* (Berkeley: University of California Press, 1989) and Laura Newby, *Sino-Janapese Relations* (London: Chatham Papers, 1989).

22 South Korea and Australia take roughly the same proportion of Japanese trade as China by the late 1980s, with figures fluctuating yearly.

23 Robert O'Neill, 'The Balance of Naval Power in the Pacific', *The Pacific Review*, No. 2, 1988.

24 Gerald Segal, *Defending China* (Oxford: Oxford University Press, 1985) and 'As China Grows Strong', *International Affairs*, spring 1988.

25 Gerald Segal, 'The PLA and the Tiananmen Massacre', *The PLA and the Tiananmen Massacre* (Kaohsiung: SCPS Papers, 1989) and 'The Chances of a Coup D'Etat', *PLA Yearbook* (Kaohsiung: SCPS, 1990).

26 Ellis Joffe, *The Chinese Army After Mao* (London: Weidenfeld, 1988).

27 Chi-kin Lo, *China's Policy Towards Territorial Disputes* (London: Routledge, 1989).

28 Mark Valencia, 'The Spratly Islands: Dangerous Ground in the South China Sea', *The Pacific Review* No. 4, 1988.

29 China also has a simmering dispute with India (formally outside East Asia), and the Tibet problem is far from cooling down. This is not the place to discuss the dynamics of a possible conflict between India and China, and the role of Indian domestic politics is clearly a possible source of an unwanted war in the Himalayas. But China is determined to keep control of Tibet, just as the outside world is increasingly willing to denounce China for its brutality in the region. It is unlikely that Tibet will gain independence or that India will really go to war in the area, even if Tibet provides a convenient excuse as did the problems of East Pakistan nearly twenty years ago. But China will certainly become more jittery if Tibet does become a major international problem and may well drive Beijing to take an even more forthright approach to problems elsewhere, such as the South China Sea. For a more complete discussion see Gerald Segal, 'East Asia: The New Balances of Power', *World Policy Journal*, fall 1989.

30 This is not the place to explore the complex relationship between domestic and foreign policy debates. Suffice it to say that even though changes of leadership can lead to changes in foreign policy, such changes can also take place with the same leaders in place. Consider the range of changes in either the Maoist or Dengist periods.

8

CHINA'S OPEN-DOOR POLICY: RESULTS AND PERSPECTIVES

Roberto Bertinelli

The ten years of reform in the People's Republic of China have seen a three-fold increase in the contribution of foreign trade to the country's GNP. By 1989 this item alone had reached a flattering 28 per cent. This bare fact tells of the scale of the effort made by Chinese leaders to open up to other countries during the decade. Despite the many problems encountered and still to be dealt with, this sector has been witness to the most interesting successes of the reform. It has also laid the foundations for a pattern of economic growth technologically, qualitatively and managerially closer to that followed by other Asian Pacific countries, which China cannot help but refer to. The foreign economic affairs (FEA) sector has been the subject of much government action aimed at increasing the dynamism and efficiency of its functioning, though such action has at times been scarcely coherent. An example is decentralisation, one of the crucial aspects of reform in this sector. It has been pursued along many different and often contradictory lines. The same may be said of the role played by Special Economic Zones (SEZ) and by enterprises with foreign investment.

A piecemeal approach and a lack of co-ordination have, in general, characterised the entire reform policy, in its various aspects. This is partly due to the effective complexity and novelty of the changes to be accomplished, but partly also to the compromises and concessions made to the political system. In any case, aside from the many uncertainties and hesitations, the growth and expansion of the FEA sector has demonstrated the validity of the reformers' efforts.

For almost thirty years this sector had functioned at very low levels. Reformatory measures have thus been taken within a rather rigid system, leading to some negative effects. In the early 1980s, China faced two strategic 'challenges': (1) through the FEA sector it could be possible to fill the technology gap created over the preceding thirty years; (2) it was important not to miss the unique chance to join in the tumultuous development of the entire geographical area and to take part in the economic relations of a market that was becoming ever more important.

The data below gives some idea of the FEA sector's increasing importance in the development of the Chinese economy and in meeting the demands of the population. The figures confirm the reformers' success in moving the country some way towards recovery from technological backwardness and insertion within the Asian Pacific economy.

The following pages examine some of the characteristic features of this economic opening. An 'external' approach is used: the reform, that is, is examined from the point of view of foreign transactors. We have attempted to understand to what degree the policy has been successful externally, trying to measure the impact and response it has had in terms of flows of trade, investments and capital receptivity. 'Internal' questions such as the coherence and compatibility of the economic opening with the rest of the Chinese reform process are overlooked. These problems are better dealt with in the other essays.

THE MAOIST LEGACY

In a system such as the Chinese, where ideology is dominant, changes are legitimised through their incorporation into the body of doctrines elaborated by the party. The various aspects of economic reform, preceded and accompanied by an intense process of ideological elaboration, are a case in point. The major product of this ideological work is the concept of an initial phase of socialism.[1]

The FEA sector, on the other hand, was not the subject of much doctrinal action aimed at justifying the changes about to take place. Little ideological importance was given to foreign trade; it was thought that this activity could not produce qualitative changes in the 'socialist system'. To find the point of departure from the Maoist legacy, it may be useful to refer to the debate on the productive forces. This has been perhaps the most important and rich in implications to be held in the years following the death of Mao.[2]

The revolutionary strategy followed by the Chinese for over thirty years and Mao's personal contribution advocated a weak link between the development of the productive forces and the construction of socialism. An opposite conclusion was reached by the Chinese debate of the early 1980s: the development of the productive forces is the basis for the construction of socialism. But the most interesting and memorable aspect of the debate is the fact that it introduced a new and much wider concept of productive forces. Thus technological aspects and economic management systems[3] were considered together with other aspects more traditionally associated with this concept.[4] It was established that the productive forces should be understood as a system of interrelated elements that interact in various ways,[5] and are not reducible to merely short-term production capacities.[6]

The new and widened interpretation of the notion of productive forces responded to a changed attitude in doctrine. Evidence for this new attitude may be found for instance in some articles which appeared during the celebrations for the centenary of Marx's death.[7] The articles, it would seem, were written bearing in mind the most immediate needs at that moment, such as responding elastically and within a reasonable period of time to the country's growing demand for consumer goods.

The 'open door' economic policy was seen as one of the roads towards this idea of Socialism, which relies heavily on productive force development.[8] This was especially true of Deng, who was the policy's most important and influential promoter. The Chinese leader stated clearly that one of the reasons for China's backwardness was its isolation, due both to some 'leftist' policies and to the (Western) world's closed-up attitude towards China. This was, of course, a political position, though it borrowed on preceding economic and theoretical analyses and works.

The circle is closed by noting that the degree to which productive forces are developed is certainly linked with the particular conditions of the country (and in this sense it is common to speak of 'Chinese-style socialism'), but it must also necessarily be related to events in other countries. This is true particularly

for technology and science, where a purely indigenous development would have little if any sense.

On this theoretical basis, together with other political considerations, the reformist leadership has gone beyond the
Maoist legacy. Now, it has often been said that commercial
relations between China and other countries had remained open
even during the preceding thirty years. This is, in fact, true,
as Gerard Segal points out in Chapter 7. During the Cultural
Revolution, foreign trade actually grew faster than GNP. But it
must be kept in mind, when considering this data, that trade
during the years from 1949 to 1979 answered immediate, pressing needs. It did not have the strategic value that it took on,
together with the rest of the FEA sector, during the reform
years. In this latter period, the country's modernisation has
been strongly linked, if not directly connected, to relations with
foreign trading partners. The opening up to foreign trade is
also seen by many Chinese studies[9] as a means to maintaining
internal balance, as it allows importation of products necessary
to the economic system while permitting the export of surplus
goods. The FEA sector has the advantage of helping further
development in those areas where China is strongest with
respect to other countries, thus allowing profit-making and favouring the readjustment and rationalisation of the country's
economic structure.[10]

THE CONCEPTION AND ROLE OF THE OPEN-DOOR POLICY

From the late 1970s it seemed that the possible short term role
and effects of an open-door policy were clear to the Chinese
leadership. There was a general agreement of opinion regarding
the beneficial effects of economic opening. Things were less
clear, though, as regards the long-term role of the policy.

To understand the nature of the internal debate, it may be
useful to compare (without going too far off the mark) with the
case of the 'Four Modernisations'. To some Chinese leaders this
was merely a technical expedient to 'increase the level of the
productive forces' and hence improve, through a stricter adherence to Marxist orthodoxy, the mechanisms of transition to
Socialism by laying the ground for the so-called objective conditions. As mentioned earlier, this has entailed a substantial

move in theoretical work from the maximalist subjectivism of the Maoist era to a conception of Socialism more deeply influenced by the 'objective conditions'.

Another segment of the leadership considered the 'Four Modernizations' as part of a more complex political project, with vaguer outlines and, most significantly, with a hazier horizon. This second position formally accepted the Socialist horizon, but in practice there was a constant drive to improve the functioning of so-called market categories, widening their role and field of action.[11]

This double interpretation may also be observed to some extent within the debate on the role of the open-door policy. A part of the leadership deemed the opening of China to the international economy necessary to guarantee the successful construction, in a relatively brief period, of a Socialist economy. Thus the open-door policy was interpreted as a limited tactical retreat from the concept of self-reliance which would strengthen the country and its Socialist system. Others, on the contrary, thought that the open door could lead to a more organic incorporation of China into the international economy, and that mechanisms favouring development of the FEA sector should be allowed to function freely without fear of endangering the system's socialist nature. The Chinese approach has constantly oscillated between these two attitudes. Perhaps the most significant example of this is the case of the special economic zones (discussed in detail below) where the two views clashed.

Yet there was initially a fair amount of agreement among Chinese leaders on the following two points:

1 the conviction that the open-door policy and the FEA sector in general are not independent variables but are functions of internal and international policy;
2 the certainty that the role, size and mechanisms related to the open-door policy are easily controllable and definable factors.

This mentality derives from years of planned and centralised management of the economy at large and particularly of the foreign trade sector. The new policy was thus to be implemented within the traditional state-planned scenario dear to the Chinese leadership. As it turned out, though, the opening to foreign trade came about in the rather more fluid context of the reform period, difficult to manage and control centrally. Considering, in fact, that reforms tended to reduce the role of the Plan, allowing more space for decision-making by single enterprises and increasing the effective number of economically productive entities, it is clear that the actual backdrop to the open-door policy was profoundly different from that envisaged by the leadership. As a result, FEA have been difficult to control and this again has led to a number of negative consequences.

To clarify further the Chinese approach to FEA, we should add that a preponderant role was assigned to economic aspects. It was thought that the opening to FEA would hardly influence Chinese culture and society. Thus Chinese authorities were unprepared to face the problem posed by the introduction of values that inevitably accompany new technology. The response has come as a series of campaigns launched by the Party against the spread of so-called 'bourgeois liberalisation' and warnings against 'spiritual pollution'.

These characteristics of the Chinese approach to FEA have proved inadequate to deal with the changes entailed by the reform. The approach suffers from its over-simplified view of a process that is broader and more complex than foreseen (especially considering the system of interrelations it implies).

The first aspect mentioned – that is, the dependence of FEA on Chinese internal and international policy – has turned out, after 1979, to be only partially true. Though the Chinese government has often asserted the principle of 'political control' over FEA, during the past decade the actual contents of FEA, formerly limited almost exclusively to commercial exchanges, have broadened to include financial relations and investments. These two characteristic elements of the open-door policy in the 1980s have substantially modified the issue of 'dependence'.

Doubtless the decision to allow investment and access to the international financial market was initially strongly connected to internal policy needs, while at the international policy level it went with the downfall of the 'theory of the three worlds'. Yet the very nature of investment and international finance make it impossible to define them as purely dependent variables, as they inevitably end up influencing internal and international decision-making. The foreign investments sector, for instance, requires some necessary internal economic conditions: a price system, transport, management and raw materials distribution systems and currency regulations, all of which should not only exist but should be adjusted and perfected in the wake of variations in the international market. The above is even truer of export-oriented foreign-invested enterprises. Moreover, China's new presence as borrower on the capital market requires it to maintain a high economic standing, a good standard in information and a solid political stability.

The second assumption – the possibility of maintaining centrally planned management – has also turned out to be partly mistaken. Trade flows in particular, and especially imports, have had a rather discontinuous performance. Globally it may be said that importation has exceeded the level foreseen by planners. This may be ascribed to the sum of two different processes: the decreasing influence of the Plan, resulting in wider decision-making capacities for enterprises, and the decentralisation of the foreign trade structure, which, launched in 1978, made its effects felt especially from 1980 onwards. The opening to FEA came at a crucial stage of the transition from a highly centralized to a mixed system. The opening was thus simultaneously cause and effect of some of the difficulties arising over the decade.

The difficulty in maintaining efficient control over aggregates resulting from foreign trade has especially affected the foreign debt. The banking and finance structure that supported commercial relations prior to 1978 was rather simple and consisted almost exclusively of the Bank of China. Possible operations with foreign counterparts were very limited in type and the banking system had no problem in controlling foreign exchange and visible items on the balance of payments.[12]

Economic decentralization, increasing numbers of Chinese transactors interested in foreign trade and an international banking system manifestly disposed to become involved in China have led to a significant increase in the country's debt. The most worrying aspect is not so much the size of the debt (around 40 billion US dollars) as its structure (which includes a slowly growing short-term debt) and above all the difficulties in its management.[13] There lacks in particular, a sound technical and data-management supporting system, which would permit adequate control of indebtment and optimization of the system of payments.

Finally, it has proved impossible to introduce foreign goods and capital into the country while avoiding their sociocultural effects. The interest shown by large sections of the population for foreign products and the first cultural expressions of foreign derivation have seriously embarrassed the Party.

The opening up to foreign trade has also, on the other hand, produced what may be defined an intangible asset for the country. It consists of the changed mentality of enterprises which, stimulated economically by the introduction of a flexible price system and hence by the possibility of raising profitability by employing adequate technology, have turned to the international market when dissatisfied by the products on offer nationally. Chinese operators, ranging from small to large state-run enterprises, now feel inserted into the network of international economic relations, though they do not always have easy access to markets. This feeling of being potentially an element of a vast network of economic relations is one of the greatest cultural changes arising out of this decade. A final point is that, besides the changes which have come about within China itself, it is beyond doubt that the country's internationalisation has also been made possible by a change in the attitude on the part of major countries towards Beijing, though this change has been pressed by a number of different motivations.

As for other aspects of Chinese politics in the 1980s, the opening to FEA may globally be seen to be a complex and multifaceted process that is not easily reduced to a series of items on the trade balance. In order to understand the economic consistency of the opening it is helpful to focus attention on three main aspects: the trade, financial and foreign investments sectors.

TRADE

As mentioned above, China has kept its commercial channels open, though with fluctuating intensity, even during the years of ideological rigidity and tense diplomatic relations. Yet the rate at which these trade flows have increased has been generally lower than the rate of growth of internal production.

The figures in Table 8.1 follow this trend with the marked exception of the period corresponding to the 3rd and 4th Five Year Plans. This deviation has been convincingly explained by some[14] by attributing the high rate of growth of foreign trade

Table 8.1 Percentage growth rate of foreign trade

Period	Gross social product	Import/export
1st FYP (1952–7)	11.3	9.8
2nd FYP (1958–62)	−0.4	−3.0
1963–5	15.5	16.8
3rd FYP (1966–70)	9.3	1.6
4th FYP (1971–5)	7.3	26.3
5th FYP (1976–80)	8.3	20.7
6th FYP (1981–5)	11	9.8

FYP = Five Year Plan

Source: 1987 Almanac of China's Foreign Economic Relations and Trade. Beijing 1986; 'Communiqué of the State Statistical Bureau' – Various years.

to increasing exports of raw materials (especially oil). Thus the anomalous growth rate would not be the result of a global turn in the Chinese economy towards increased foreign trade relations.

Qualitative changes may be noted from the start of the reform, which coincides with the beginning of an effective internationalization process in China. Evidence for this process, in terms of conventional economic indicators, may be obtained

Table 8.2 Position of the PRC in international trade

	1966	1976	1979	1980	1981	1982	1983
Export (world)	189.5	942.5	1,576.7	1,897.6	1,865.1	1,733.5	1,681.9
% Export (China)	1.41	0.007	0.086	0.954	1.151	1.262	1.318
Import (world)	199.9	946.8	1,582.1	1,945.1	1,930.0	1,803.0	1,748.3
%Import (China)	1.242	0.700	0.987	1.025	1.121	1.018	1.220

	1984	1985	1986	1987	1988
Export (world)	1,783.5	1,808.1	1,990.6	2,342.1	2,694.1
% Export (China)	1.392	1.551	1.565	1.688	1.764
Import (world)	1,862.8	1,878.3	2,056.1	2,408.0	2,787.3
%Import (China)	1.393	2.264	2.100	1.802	1.983

World import and export in billions of US$

Source: International Financial Statistics – 1989 Yearbook

considering the position held by inward and outward flows of goods within the world economy and by comparing such flows with the national income.

Two facts may be evinced from Table 8.2. The first is that China did not keep pace with the expansion of international trade during the Cultural Revolution. Import and export figures, in fact, taken as percentages of world trade, drop consistently throughout the period. This is especially noticeable for exports, which collapse from 1.41 per cent in 1966 (the first year of the Cultural Revolution) to 0.007 per cent in 1976, the year that marks (if only officially) the end of the Cultural Revolution. Yet Table 8.3 shows that trade flows during this period become increasingly important within the country, a trend which affirms itself during the 1980s.

Table 8.3 Foreign trade and national income

	1966	1976	1979	1980	1981	1982	1983
1: National income	148.7	242.7	335.0	368.8	394.0	426.1	473.0
2: Import + export	12.71	26.41	45.46	56	73.53	77.2	86.01
3: % 2/1	8.5	10.9	13.6	15.2	18.7	18.2	18.2

	1984	1985	1986	1987	1988
1 :National income	565.0	703.1	788.7	932.1	1,177.0
2: Import + export	119.4	206.89	258.47	308.49	381.85
3: % 2/1	21.1	29.4	32.8	33.1	32.5

1 and 2 in billions of current *renminbi*
Source: see Table 8.1.

These figures should be readjusted to take into account fluctuations of the *renminbi* with respect to other convertible currencies, especially the US$ whose rating in the period under consideration moved from 2.4618 *yuan* to the dollar (1966) to 1.5550 (1979) and 3.7221 (1988).

The global picture that emerges from these two groups of data is that of a country effectively opening up to foreign trade. To remain within the context of an economic approach, this opening up is also indicated by the diversification of China's trading partners. As regards exports, it is interesting to note a partial redefinition of target areas, with a significant shift towards LDCs and especially Asian countries, which took up 36 per cent of total exports in 1979 and 46 per cent in 1988. There is a drop, on the other hand, in the presence of Chinese goods on the markets of industrialised countries: by 1988, after a decade of economic reform, the market quota for Chinese exports had fallen by around 10 percentage points in developed countries (see Table 8.4). This fact, which taken alone would appear negative in the eyes of Chinese leaders, has a rather more complex interpretation. It should be considered together with corresponding figures for imports: in 1979, 78.4 per cent of China's imports came from industrialised countries while by 1988 this figure had dropped to 55.1 per cent.

Table 8.4 Percentage distribution of Chinese exports

	1976	1979	1980	1981	1982	1983	1984	1985	1986	1987	1988
Industrialised countries	44.3	46.5	44.7	44.0	42.9	42.2	41.9	41.7	40.1	36.8	36.5
LCDs	55.7	52.5	49.5	52.8	53.9	53.8	53.5	51.8	53.2	57.5	57.5
of which:											
Africa	n.d.	n.d.	2.7	3.2	3.5	2.4	2.2	1.5	1.8	3.1	3.4
Asia	n.d.	n.d.	36.0	34.6	33.0	34.6	37.7	39.2	40.2	43.6	46.9
W. Europe	n.d.	n.d.	4.2	2.7	2.5	2.4	2.0	2.8	3.3	3.0	2.3
Mid. East	n.d.	n.d.	4.4	9.9	12.5	12.4	9.8	6.5	6.7	6.7	4.4
Others	n.d.	n.d.	2.2	2.5	2.4	2.0	1.8	1.8	1.2	1.0	0.5
USSR	n.d.	n.d.	5.8	3.3	3.2	3.9	4.5	6.5	6.7	5.6	5.8

Source: Directorate of Trade Statistics 1987 and 1989 Yearbooks

The growing importance of Asian countries as recipients of exports, climbing from 36 per cent in 1980 to almost 47 per cent in 1989, should be observed. A crucial role is played by Hong Kong, China's most widely used market, as part of the goods imported into Hong Kong are re-exported to other parts of the world. This goods transit through Hong Kong creates problems in analysing the origin and destination of goods traded by the PRC. Thus it seems likely that the drop in trade with industrialised countries shown by the tables should be corrected upwards to allow for the Chinese goods that reach these countries through Hong Kong.

Japan has always been an important trading partner with China, and this was particularly true during the first five years of China's opening to foreign trade. This importance diminished, however, during the second half of the 1980s: the percentage of total trade between China and industrialised countries taken up by Japan fell from 45.20 per cent in 1976 to 39.89 per cent in 1988, as may be seen in Table 8.5.

Table 8.5 Trade between China and Japan

	1976	1979	1980	1981	1982	1983	1984
A	27.41	25.53	24.44	25.35	21.35	23.06	26.02
B	45.20	40.00	40.95	42.82	38.87	42.02	46.65

	1985	1986	1987	1988
A	30.47	23.51	19.93	18.55
B	51.59	42.32	40.20	39.89

A = % Japan/World total with China.
B = % Japan/Industrialise countries with China.

Source: DOTS, various years.

Thus a double process is revealed during the reform years, becoming more pronounced in the latter half of the 1980s. We have on the one hand a global drop in trade between China and industrialised countries, even allowing for the corrections due to the role of Hong Kong; on the other, it is the Japanese market quota that decreases, in absolute and relative terms.

The process is even more evident for imports (see Table 8.6). Between 1979 and 1988 China reduced the value of its imports from industrialised countries by 23 percentage points, from 78.4 per cent to 55.1 per cent. This enormous drop is balanced almost

Table 8.6 Percentage distribution of Chinese imports

	1976	1979	1980	1981	1982	1983	1984	1985	1986	1987	1988
IC	79.7	78.4	73.6	74.4	68.9	68.1	69.0	70.2	66.8	61.2	55.1
PVS	20.2	21.6	20.7	19.7	22.9	24.6	24.7	25.2	27.2	32.2	36.1
of which:											
Africa	n.d.	n.d.	1.5	1.1	1.4	1.5	1.2	0.7	0.6	0.4	0.4
Asia	n.d.	n.d.	8.7	10.9	13.4	12.7	16.0	16.7	19.0	25.3	28.4
Europe	n.d.	n.d.	5.1	3.4	3.5	3.0	3.1	3.0	3.8	3.2	2.8
Mid. East	n.d.	n.d.	1.8	1.0	1.4	1.4	1.1	0.5	0.3	0.6	1.0
USSR	n.d.	n.d.	5.7	3.4	6.3	5.9	5.4	4.5	5.9	5.4	6.0
Others	0.1	–	–	2.5	1.9	1.4	0.9	0.1	0.1	1.2	2.8

Sources: see Table 8.3

entirely by importation from Asian countries, especially Hong Kong, whose volume grew from 8.7 per cent (1980) to 28.4 per cent in 1988.

The type of goods involved in foreign trade has partially changed over the decade. Variations have particularly affected export goods. At an early stage export goods consisted mainly of raw materials, oil and products with a very low technological content. After the mid-1980s, there was a change in this composition, with manufactured products, textiles, toys, electronic and mechanical products taking on more importance. The value of manufactured products grew from 46 per cent in 1979 to 69 per cent in 1988.

Oil still occupies an important position, though less so than in the past. It is sold mainly to Japan and also, in much smaller quantities, to the Philippines, Brazil and Rumania. During the first half of the decade, oil accounted for around 20 to 25 per cent of the value of Chinese exports; after 1985 there was a gradual drop from 24.4 per cent in 1985 to 10.4 per cent (1986), 10.0 per cent (1987) and 7.15 per cent (1988). This change is due partly to the decrease in oil prices but most of all to the growth in internal requirements sparked off by the accelerated industrial development. Since 1986, China has had to deal with energy supply problems caused by economic growth and by the localisation (and concentration) of productive activities and of energy production. The most promising road to follow for China's export sector seems inevitably to involve a diversification of goods, and in particular a move away from raw materials. Such a strategy could help diminish the relative vulnerability of China's foreign currency income, which presently is dangerously connected to the erratic prices of raw materials.

As for imports, China buys mainly machinery, equipment and medium- and high-technology products; cereals and special steels still hold an important position. Thus while the structure of imports has not significantly changed, a positive result of the reform decade has been the change in the structure of exports, which reflects a dynamic response to the requirements of the international market. The Chinese government has on several occasions demonstrated its interest in changing the structure of foreign trade, putting emphasis on the export of machinery, electrical material and partly-finished products. At the same time there has been a reduction in the foreign sales of primary products, the internal demand for which has grown during the reform period.

China's effort during the ten-year period 1979–88 to increase the volume of its foreign trade had two main goals. In the short run, there was the question of responding to the internal demand for durable consumer goods such as television sets, refrigerators and air-conditioning systems. It was also hoped that, in the medium term, foreign trade would give impulse to the modernisation of the country's productive sector through the introduction of advanced means of production. Both aims have been achieved to some extent, though it is difficult to measure their economic impact. The most important difficulties have been encountered at the organisational level. This is due at least partly to the diverging views held by members of the administration as regards the strategic role of foreign trade.

The same ten-year period has seen an interesting change in the management of foreign trade. In particular there has been a certain amount of decentralisation both at the local level, with larger powers and functions granted to provincial and to large municipal administrations, and at the microeconomic level, where enterprises have been offered the possibility of accessing the international market directly. Administrative decentralisation has been put into effect concretely, as far as currency handling is concerned, by allowing local authorities to retain a part of the foreign currency obtained from exports. A further step has been taken by introducing a contract system in foreign trade.

Yet the effective enactment of decentralisation has been hindered by a number of factors. The resistance of the bureaucracy, conflicts of interest and overlapping functions, the excessive interference of the political sphere in the administration of the economy and so on, have all damaged the efficiency of the sector. A typical example is the scarce capacity of the system to gather quickly data concerning the formation of international credits and debits, which has made it impossible to manage foreign currency flows in a correct and economically sound manner.

Though decentralisation appears to be the only fruitful and possible road to increased competitiveness of Chinese goods and higher effectiveness of imports, it must be said that the progress made in the short term (such as an effective increase in the competitiveness of exports) is conditioned by negative effects on the balance of payments. The problem, to be sure, is not only the matching of imports and exports, though a balanced management of trade flows could constitute an important stabilising factor. It would be necessary to complement decentralisation with a fast and efficient system for the gathering of statistical data concerning these flows. Otherwise, in a country such as China, decentralisation would become an ungovernable process.[15]

FINANCIAL PRESENCE

It is widely known that until the early 1980s the Chinese government showed little inclination to propel internal economic growth by resorting to foreign credit. Foreign indebtment was considered the most evident and dangerous sign of dependence on other countries. Since then, two elements have helped change this attitude: (1) the realisation that it was necessary to import technology and machinery and that this inevitably implied, in the medium term at least, recourse to foreign credit; (2) the possibility for Beijing to exploit the favourable situation in international finance created by the Third World's debt crisis, which had led to increased international liquidity and a rather positive attitude on the part of industrialised nations (brought on in part by 'strategic' considerations) towards China's attempts at modernisation and reform.

China could, moreover, exploit the 'soft' credit offered by Western countries and Japan. Only later and very cautiously did China turn to commercial credits. Since 1982 the Chinese government has passed laws to discipline relations with foreign countries, particularly as regards capital flows. The branch of the administration that is operatively concerned with currency flows is the State Administration for the Control of Exchange.[16]

The particularly favourable conditions obtained by China include payment periods of on average fifteen years for loans obtained in the years between 1981 and 1988. The most advantageous conditions (that is, the longest payment periods) were granted by official creditors, though private creditors conceded periods of around seven years on average. It is interesting to note the sensitivity of the Chinese government for the debt structure and the efforts made constantly to adjust it. Short-

Table 8.7 Chinese foreign debt

	1979	1980	1981	1982	1983	1984
1 Public debt (of which with	2,183	4,504	4,913	5,221	5,301	6,179
commercial banks:)	131	1,514	632	369	405	546
2 Recourse to IMF			884	838	324	303
3 Short-term debts				2,300	3,984	5,600
Total	2,183	4,504	5,798	8,359	9,609	12,082

	1985	1986	1987	1988
1 Public debt (of which with	9,963	16,598	26,051	32,196
commercial banks:)	444	1,843	6,338	10,061
2 Recourse to IMF	430	1,072	1,155	1,013
3 Short-term debts	6,419	6,076	8,221	8,806
Total	16,722	23,746	35,428	42,015

Billions of US$

Source: World Bank.

term indebtment has been reduced, dropping from 27 per cent in 1982 to 20.9 per cent in 1988, after reaching percentages as high as 40 per cent during the three-year period from 1983 to 1985. (See Table 8.7.)

The sources of these capital flows are governments, commercial banks and international financial agencies such as the World Bank (which with its present 8.6 billion US$ on loan is one of China's biggest creditors), the International Monetary Fund and other regional development banks.[17]

From the financial point of view, China has diversified its capital supply channels as a function of the projects to which the capital was destined. The size of many projects was such as to suggest recourse to the bond and joint-loan market. Though far from being among the largest borrowers on these markets, China's presence in them has important implications. By their very nature, in fact, the monetary, financial and especially the bond markets require regular intervention. Above all, they require the maintenance of a high standing to prevent loan conditions from becoming excessively unfavourable. In July 1988, for instance, in the face of a deteriorating internal economic situation, Moody's Investment Services downgraded a 300 million mark issue to China which obtained A3 rating instead of the usual AAA. The same occurred after the Tiananmen crisis.

China's presence on the exclusive bond market is a fairly new phenomenon which has almost only involved official bodies, principally the CITIC and the Bank of China. From 1982 to 1988, China has issued bonds for a total of 4.25 billion US$ of which 1.01 in 1988 alone. The technical characteristics of these issues indicate a desire on the part of the Chinese to exploit as far as possible the general decrease in spreads observed in the sector.

China began issuing international debentures in 1982, with a CITIC issue in Tokyo for 100 million yen with an AA rating. From 1985 onwards, recourse to this channel become enormous, jumping from 83.17 million US$ in 1984 to 786.46 in 1985:

1982	43.58 (millions of US$)
1983	20.23
1984	83.17
1985	786.46
1986	1255.53
1987	978.97
1988	718.46

Recourse to joint loans is equally consistent. The above remarks concerning the international bond market are true also of this form of finance: funds may be obtained only if the country is capable of maintaining a good international image. Applications encountered no problems until 1988 and investors' portfolios did not appear excessively laden. The following figures illustrate the size of the involvement in this sector:

1982	333.95 (millions of US$)
1983	190.26
1984	152.95
1985	3409.15
1986	2157.45
1987	5235.01
1988	3771.76

One of the problems with bonds and loans is their denomination. While foreign currency income is mainly in US$, bonds and joint loans are generally in yen. Considering the rise of the yen against the US$, this could worsen the effective terms of payment and the global cost of the debt. This consideration would be less important if the above debts had been drawn with corresponding swap operations in mind; we do not know, however, if this is the case.

THE OECD AID POLICY

As mentioned above, one of the fundamental issues in the opening of China to foreign trade is the newly acquired view of this country as a trading partner necessary to industrialised nations. This attitude is evident from a number of events in international politics and also – this is the aspect we wish to underline-in economic co-operation policy.

From the first years of the open-door policy, that is since the early 1980s, it was clear that China could not undertake the modernisation of its productive (especially industrial) and services infrastructure without the concrete help of the industrialised countries. Besides albeit important political motivations traceable to a desire to support the reformist position, the aid given to China (and to other countries) forms part of a financial and commercial package used to sustain and promote the economic presence of DCs and to favour the initiatives of national transactors.

During most of the reform period, China has received a growing amount, in relative and absolute terms, of aid (see Table 8.8). This responds to both 'strategic' interests and to the promising economic perspectives the country offers to foreign transactors. The concession of this form of aid grew significantly after 1985, when China obtained bilateral and multilateral aid amounting to around 5 per cent of the total granted by OECD countries. This fact alone leads to two conclusions: (1) the Chinese government was by then firmly set upon the decision to open up to foreign trade, to the point of negotiating and obtaining large amounts of aid; (2) China had understood that economic penetration on the part of DCs could be negotiated; in this sense the aid obtained was intended in some way to offset China's opening to individual countries.

Of course it should be borne in mind that not all the aid mentioned above is granted on the basis of bilateral agreements: a part of it is supplied autonomously by international agencies, that is, it is supplied by OECD countries through such organisations. In the years from 1985 to 1988, bilateral aid (calculated

Table 8.8 OECD financial aid to China

	1981	1982	1983	1984	1985	1986	1987	1988
Net total granted of which:	99,533	86,071	71,326	80,507	47,060	72,052	67,399	82,326
Asia	27,189	21,459	22,179	26,522	16,798	20,864	24,853	30,637
China	1,888	678	748	938	2,297	3,479	4,363	5,276
China/total %	1.9	0.8	1.0	1.0	4.9	4.8	6.5	6.4

All data in millions of US$ unless otherwise specified.

Source: 1981–84: OECD, Geographical distribution of financial flow to developing countries, (Paris, 1989); 1985–1988: OECD, Geographical distribution . . ., Paris, 1990.

as total net receipts) has evolved as follows: 68.5 per cent (1985); 77.2 per cent (1986); 81.6 per cent (1987); 74.7 per cent (1988), where the figures are percentages of the total aid granted to China. this data shows the increasing interest of individual countries for China (see Table 8.9). Study of the following table reveals that the major donors are China's most important trading partners:

Table 8.9 Percentage breakdown of donor countries

	1985	1986	1987	1988
Australia	2.9	3.0	1.1	1.2
Canada	3.5	2.7	10.9	5.0
Denmark	1.8	2.1	2.2	1.1
GFR	18.7	9.4	6.0	5.4
Italy	3.9	2.7	7.9	6.3
Japan	62.2	74.6	62.7	61.6
Sweden	2.7	3.2	0.4	1.1
USA	0.8	0.2	1.4	3.3
UK	0.2	0.3	0.5	2.7
France	0.9	0.8	3.4	7.2
Others	2.3	1	3.5	5.1

Source: see Table 8.8. Data considered: Total Official Gross DAC Countries.

The data above and the entire issue of economic co-operation with China shows how much this country has become integrated into one of the most important mechanisms in international economic policy. This additional aspect of China's rich and complex internationalisation process sheds a particularly favourable light on the process itself. Many aspects of economic (and especially multilateral) co-operation imply, in fact, a relationship in which the parts come to know and collaborate with each other technically and in other ways. Thus it betrays a global inclination towards openness which results from a number of political decisions and which in turn promotes a culture better disposed to collaboration with other countries.

FOREIGN INVESTMENT

The most evident and tangible aspect of China's opening to international co-operation is no doubt the decision to allow foreign investment on Chinese territory. Great clamour was understandably raised when in 1979 the Chinese congress passed the first law on the subject.[18] It signalled unmistakeably the decision on the part of the Chinese leadership to resort to foreign and in particular Western countries in order to close the productive and technological gap that separated China from the rest of the world.

Another important motivation for resorting to foreign investment concerned the role of China in the Asian area.[19] Given the generally fast pace of development in the area, a failure to modernise on the part of China would have entailed a considerable reduction in its role, even politically. The good economic results obtained by Hong Kong, Singapore, Taiwan and South Korea, not to mention the leading role played by Japan in the world economy, and the perspectives for growth in the whole Asia–Pacific area have heavily influenced the decision to open China to foreign investment.

Allowing investment on Chinese territory was a sure method to attract foreign capital and above all to absorb foreign technology. But a number of problems had to be faced. Once past the traditional ideological obstacle, which viewed foreign investment as a threat to socialism and a limitation of the country's sovereignty, there was the problem posed by the lack of a suitable set of regulations to guarantee foreign interests and to discipline the management of investments.[20] It was in fact unthinkable for foreign investors, even if convinced of the fundamental soundness of China's opening to trade, to risk capital without legal guarantees. When the law was passed in 1979, China had only recently embarked on a complex and laborious revision of the preceding legislation which would lead to the passing of new laws better aligned to the new political climate. This work is still in progress and is not free from

212

contradictions and gaps, and it is one of the hardest but perhaps most valuable efforts undertaken by the Chinese leadership during the reform years.

One branch of the projected new legal and legislative structure deals specifically with foreign investment enterprises. This sector, given the particular problems it poses (among which is that of following internationally established customs and conventions), has been given a special status and been made the object of specific legislation. This has proved important as it put China immediately in connection with international regulations, though with some limits. Beijing could not in fact offer, at least officially, conditions worse than those offered by competitor countries in the area.

Table 8.10 Trends in direct investment

	Direct investment			Other types of investment	
	Contracts signed	Global value	Amount used	Global value	Amount used
1979–82	992	6,010	1,166	989	601
1983	470	1,732	636	185	280
1984	1,856	2,651	1,258	224	161
1985	3,073	5,932	1,661	401	298
1986	1,498	2,834	1,874	496	370
1987	2,233	3,709	2,314	610	333
1988	5,945	5,297	3,193	894	546

All figures in millions of US$.
Source: *China Economic News*, 6, 1990.

Two striking features emerge from a study of the trends in direct investments (see Table 8.10). There is first of all a rapid growth from 1985 onwards, with the exception of the usual 'pause for thought' in 1986. Secondly, the mean value of individual contracts decreases with time. If in the period from 1979 to 1982 the mean value of a contract involving foreign investment was around 6 million US$, it had dropped to 1.9 in 1985, 1.8 in 1986, 1.6 in 1987 and was under 1 million US$ by the end of 1988. The interest of this fact is that it indicates a gradual diffusion of foreign investment towards small and medium-sized economic entities. It is worth mentioning that whereas in the period immediately following the 1979 law the Chinese government accepted and approved the constitution of foreign-invested enterprises in various sectors (particularly in service sectors such as the hotel industry), in the past few years it has taken on a more thought-out attitude, aimed at directing foreign investment in some determined productive sectors more directly connected with planned economic goals.[21]

Several phases may be identified in the process leading to the constitution of foreign-invested enterprises. These correspond to changes in government strategy as regards a number of aspects. One of these, perhaps the richest in implications, concerns the destination of the goods produced by this kind of enterprise. Two phases may be distinguished. The first begins in 1979 and proceeds, with some oscillations, until around 1987. In this phase the legislative power urged but did not force foreign-invested enterprises to export their goods, without banning them from the national market. Subsequently, the authorities have attempted in every way to direct the activities of joint-ventures towards exportation, and introduced specific legislation for this purpose.[22] The root of this change may be traced to the deficit in the Chinese balance of payments and the competition to which national industries were subjected on the part of joint-ventures. This phase continues to the present and has created many difficulties for international investors who had initially considered joint-ventures as a beach-head into the Chinese market. This example serves to illustrate the lack of a common direction within the Chinese leadership, which has persistently hampered this sector's take-off.

At present, a number of factors has reopened the debate regarding the role to be played by foreign-invested enterprises in the Chinese economy. The destiny of these enterprises clearly depends on the future configurations planned by the authorities for each of the geographical regions the country has been divided into. The 7th Five Year Plan (1986–1990),[23] in fact, divided China into three areas; the eastern or coastal area is to develop rapidly, at a faster rate than the rest of the country, with stress on the technological development of traditional and existing enterprises and the creation of new enterprises. These should help lift the technological level of the existing productive system. Great impulse is also to be given in this area to developing the service and tertiary industries. In practice, the intention of the Plan is to strengthen the existing industrial infrastructure in Shanghai, Tianjin, Shenyang and Dalian and to accentuate further the role played by the Special Economic Zones. Central China is to concentrate on the development of the energy production industry, and on the production of raw materials and partly finished goods, while Western China is to develop stock farming and industry. The Plan orients the Eastern zone towards exportation, a role evidently inspired by the example of the four Asian dragons (Singapore, Hong Kong, Taiwan and South Korea). In this context, the Economic Zones should constitute the first important focus points about which a larger area well integrated into the international economy should gradually come to being. The possible role and size of foreign-invested enterprises shall be determined by the specific way in which this Plan, which foresees the creation of economic areas, will be enacted.

Table 8.11 Percentage breakdown of foreign investment in China, 1979–87

Beijing	2.6	Shanghai	3.0
Tianjin	2.4	Hunan	1.0
Liaoning	2.2	Zhejiang	1.5
Shaanxi	1.1	Fujian	10.0
Shandong	1.4	Guangdong	61.0
Jiangsu	2.0	Guangxi	2.9

Source: *Intertrade*, August 1988.

A geographical breakdown with these characteristics inevitably induces the destiny of foreign-invested enterprises[24] to coincide with that of coastal regions (see Table 8.11). It is in this sector that some problems arise, as is most evident in the Special Economic Zones.[25]

Strongly contrasting evaluations have been made of actual experience with foreign-invested enterprises. Such variations often correspond to differences in the histories of specific enterprises. It may be said quite generally that foreign-invested enterprises indicate a possible way out of backwardness, and they could be useful in inserting sectors of the Chinese economy with characteristics similar to those of the 'four dragons' into the international division of labour. Yet the studies mentioned throw light on limitations and difficulties that cannot be overlooked. Aside from problems connected with the Chinese economy's negative situation in the period from 1988 to 1989, there are difficulties rooted in the structure of the country. Firstly, granted that these enterprises and the coastal region as a whole are oriented (willingly or forcefully) towards exportation, it is essential to establish conditions therein that meet the standards fixed by foreign competitors, in particular those of the Asia–Pacific region. Such conditions should involve three aspects: goods production, first of all, and hence the quality and supply of resources and raw materials; secondly, conditions on tax levels and on the management of financial resources and, lastly, conditions regarding the freedom of capital flows.

The Chinese government has to some extent considered the requirements of foreign investors and in many cases has granted conditions similar to those existing in competitor countries.[26] This, however, was only a first step that should have been followed by a more radical transformation of the areas where these enterprises are sited, creating a better integrated system that could have permitted full take-off for foreign-invested enterprises. In retrospect, this experiment shows many bright points, but also some very dark shadows, hard to dispel even if the Chinese government were to recover its credibility. Some major steps forward, however, have been taken as regards the creation of a new mentality. An example is the introduction of a relatively flexible legislation, a point which until recently had been entirely ignored by the Chinese government.

However, it cannot be said that the experiment has been a success. Many major foreign investors have adopted a wait-and-see attitude, some have drawn back and others remain in China for purely strategic reasons bearing no relation with the profitability of the investment. After an initial phase of great and overly optimistic expectations for the outcome of foreign-invested enterprises, it was realised that the advantages they offered the country were heavily conditioned by the economic structure. Their siting, moreover, concentrated in the regions indicated in Table 8.11, raised particular problems. An all-out programme for the establishment of foreign-invested enterprises, in fact, would have clashed with the still rigid planning and resources distribution system, while the particular structure of the labour market, for instance, did not favour the diffusion of accumulated managerial experience to other Chinese enterprises.

At this point the discussion must turn to the Special Economic

Zones. The following is a brief summary of the stages that have led to the creation of these particular areas, endowed with wider freedom for autonomous decision-making and destined to attract foreign investment through the introduction of preferential treatment and more flexible regulations.

1 In 1980 the central government grants Guangdong and Fujian provinces the power to pass more flexible regulations as regards foreign trade.
2 Four SEZs are created at Shenzhen, Zhuhai, Shantou and Xiamen between 1980 and 1981.
3 Fourteen coastal towns and Hainan Island are opened in 1984 to trade relations with other countries.
4 The Yangtse and Pearl River deltas are opened to trade in 1985.
5 In 1986 the Shandong and Liaoning peninsulae are further opened to trade.
6 In 1988 Hainan Island becomes the fifth and largest SEZ, with the administrative status of province.

The opening of the coastal area, involving over 100 million people, has spread from the SEZs to other regions, though in various ways. Heated debate has developed around the rate of development and goals to be achieved by SEZs, which as usual has found the Chinese leadership quite sharply divided.[27] There were those, on the one hand, who like former General Secretary of the CCP Zhao Ziyang maintained that the nature and functions of these areas implied the adoption of more advanced measures, especially concerning prices, in the absence of which it would not be possible to integrate fully these areas into the international economy and assure their take-off. Others countered that development of these areas should be compatible with the socialist nature of the system. Thus the case of the SEZs, with all its peculiar characteristics, is interesting in that we find a situation similar to that described in the opening pages: that of a sector of international relations closely linked to international customs and conventions and hence with an intrinsically high capacity to bring about changes in a system such as the Chinese. Its very functioning requires the establishment of conditions that inevitably lead to deep modifications in the current system: particular forms of management in joint-ventures enterprises, free capital flows in SEZs, free importation and exportation etc. These modifications have widened regional differences and would have led to the creation of non-Socialist areas. This would have added yet another contradiction to those already present in the country, and the SEZs' take-off would have made the limitations of traditional Socialism clear to all. Hence the political importance of the process and the desire on the part of the Party to contain drastically the introduction of structural modifications in these areas.

The investments sector and the development of coastal areas and particularly of SEZs remains one of the fundamental aspects of China's open-door policy. Only by permitting adequate growth of the above will it be possible to achieve a high level of integration and to exploit fully the driving force that investments have in the Socialist system.

For the moment, it has been shown that once investment had been encouraged, many other steps and measures were taken simply because the economic enclaves thus created required them. Thus it may be said that investments forced the hand of Chinese leaders, or, according to another interpretation, that they bolstered the arguments of those leaders who intended to proceed to deeper and wider changes.

CONCLUSIONS

In the aftermath of the events at Tiananmen, China has reconfirmed its intention to proceed with the opening to foreign trade and invited foreign transactors to remain in the country, possibly benefiting from the newly found 'stability'. The volume of FEA has none the less sharply decreased partly as a result of the internal recession and partly because of the country's international credibility crisis. Among the most important internal measures that have negatively influenced foreign trade we may mention the cutback on credit, the revision and check-up process on enterprises – leading thousands of them to close down or merge – and the steps taken to reduce imports. The interaction of these and other elements has entailed a dramatic drop in the export sector's productive capacity together, as mentioned with a strong decrease in imports (which, by the way, represent a high percentage of imports). Exports have picked up after the first quarter of 1990, following the authorities' relaxation of some of the more restrictive measures.

Two circumstances have been especially important at the international level: the first, which existed before June 1989, was China's increasing 'sovereign risk'. The persistent internal economic crisis, added to the many uncertainties as to the success of the reforms and to the evident clash among Party leaders had led analysts to consider China increasingly risky. Hence the international transactors' cautious attitude and, for example, the decrease in foreign capital flows to China. After the events of June 1989, things have been worsened by an uncertain political situation that made long-term operations unattractive. In order to reassure international investors, many of which (the Europeans especially) are now more interested in the opportunities offered by Eastern Europe, the Chinese government has made a point of fulfilling all promises made to foreign-investment enterprises and has revamped its policy for the support of SEZs (though in a form which is not yet altogether clear). Besides this attitude, there is the ever more frequent publication of news regarding gold production, to make evident the Chinese government's intention to meet foreign debt deadlines on time. These news are objectively reassuring, though they render still more uncertain the future of the gold market, already influenced by the South African situation and the Soviet government's sales policies.

The second international element leading to a reduction of FEA are sanctions. It is difficult to ascertain their impact on the Chinese government's decision-making. Chinese leaders, in fact, tend on the one hand to use them to rouse patriotic feeling and rally the 'home front'. On the other hand, they do seem to have had a role, though secondary, in containing political involution after June 1989. Sanctions have concretely affected the Chinese economy above all because it is by now moderately open to FEA that cannot be handled by internal financial resources alone, but rely on international credits. If the above measures were to be maintained, enterprises linked with foreign trade could find themselves in difficulty, and this would only add to the problems faced by the economy as a whole.

It remains to evaluate whether the balance of power within the CCP could be affected by a worsening of the economic situation, and whether there exists a possible new CCP leadership ready to supplant the present one, which is doubtless the worst ever produced by Communist China and not only as regards human rights.

It seems in fact improbable that a downturn in the economic situation could weaken the present leadership: it is an illusion of perspective similar to that which in 1989 led some observers to hold that the street demonstrations of that year could weaken and overthrow the conservative wing of the Party. In spite of leadership changes, the CCP 'system' has on the contrary shown a resistance and tenacity far higher than expected.

Notwithstanding official declarations to the contrary, since 1990 sanctions are de facto being gradually reduced. Examples are the the concession of MFC status to China on the part of the American administration, the more or less concealed reappearance of financing, especially on the part of Japan, and of insurance guarantees for commercial transactions.

With an eye to the future, it is however important to consider just how much assistance DCs should offer China. In the wake of internal and international (Eastern Europe and the USSR) events, the Chinese experiment has clearly lost much of the political appeal that it enjoyed in the early 1980s and justified the extremely favourable treatment received by the reformist programme. There is still interest for the economic opportunities that the country objectively offers, but a return to economic co-operation with China should be more sober and measured than it has been in the past. Greater attention, in particular, should be given to China's capacity to pay back loans so as to avoid 'doping' China's foreign trade reform with excessive doses of an assistance that often benefits only foreign transactors and local governments.

The Chinese economy appears set to maintain and consolidate the degree of openness achieved over the past decade. The increase in internal demand and the perspectives for growth of the economy at large appear in fact to be closely linked with the internationalisation of the economy. The pause for thought imposed by the events of June 1989 could be a good occasion to redesign and rationalise some sectors of FEA, especially the foreign currency and banking systems, which have not kept in pace with the growth of foreign trade. More in general, the prospects for the development of FEA shall depend on the revamping of the internal economic reform policy and on the quality of the leadership.

NOTES

1 Yu Guangyuan, 'The Economy of the Primary Stage of Socialism', in *Social Sciences in China* (*SSC*), No. 2, 1989, pp. 89ff.
2 For an evaluation, see Wang Shuwen, 'Yinian lai guanyu shengchanli wenti de taolon zongshu', ('Summary of a year's discussion on the Question of Production Forces') in *Jingji yanjiu* (*Economic Research, JJYJ*), No. 2, 1982, pp. 73–6. A good assortment of the essays is contained in the anthology *Lun shengchanli* (*On Productive Forces*), 2 vol., (Jilin, 1980).
3 Xu Dixin, *Zhengzhi jingjixue cidian* (*Dictionary for Political Economy*), (Beijing, 1980).
4 Xue Yongying, 'Shengchanli xitong lun' ('Factors in Productive Forces'), *JJYJ*, No. 8, 1984, pp. 64–70.
5 Xue Yongying, 'Shengchanli xitong lun' ('Discussion on the System of Productive Forces'), *JJYJ*, No. 9, 1981, pp. 56–63, and Wang Yong, 'Shilun shengchanli de gaocheng' ('Discussion of the Process of Productive Forces'), *JJYJ*, No. 12, 1981, pp. 57–80.
6 This is due especially to the work of Xue Yongying.
7 See Chen Zheng, 'Makesi Zai "Zibenlun" zbong dui gongchanzhuyi (shehuizhuyi) jingji de yushi, ('Economic Predictions by Marx in "Capital" About Communism (Socialism)'), *JJYJ*, No. 4, 1983 p. 15.
8 Deng Xiaoping, 'Edifier un socialisme à la chinoise' ('Build Socialism With Chinese Characteristics') (30/6/84) and 'Intervention à la troisième session plénière des Conseillers du Comité Central Du Parti' (speech to the Third Plenum of the CCP Central Advisory Commission'), pp. 92ff, in *Les questions fondamentales de la Chine aujourd'hui*, (*Fundamental Questions on Contemporary China*), (Beijing, 1987).
9 See Liu Guoguang, Liang Wensen et al., *China's economy in 2000* (Beijing, 1987), pp. 482–7. Ji Chongwei, 'Wo guo dui wai kaifang zhengce de lilun' ('Theory of Our Country's Open-Door Policy'), *JJYJ*, No. 11, 1984, pp. 34–42.
10 Yuan Wenqui et al., 'International Division of Labour and China's Economic Relations with Foreign Countries', SSC, No. 1, 1980, pp. 37ff.
11 The empirical–analytical expression of this attitude is the so-called socialist market economy. Ma Hong, 'Guanyu shehuizhuyi zhidu xia wo guo shang-pin jingji de zai tansuo' ('A Further Exploration Concerning Our Nation's Commodity Economy Under Socialism'), *JJYJ*, No. 12, 1984, pp. 3ff.
12 Various authors, *Jingrong gailun* (*Broad Account of Finance*), (Beijing, 1989(2)), pp. 220–5; K.N.Y. Huang Hsiao, *Banking and Money in the Chinese Mainland*, (Taipei, 1984), ch. 4.
13 Much more optimistic, as usual, is the World Bank report *China: Country Economic Memorandum Between Plan and Market* (8/5/1990), pp. 95–7.
14 Zhang Shuguang, 'Jingji fazhan ji jiegou zhuanhuanzhong de maoji wenti' ('Economic Development and Questions of Trade in a Time of Transition') in *Zhongguo shehui kexue* (*Social Sciences of China*), No. 5, 1988, p. 27.
15 The particular problem of measuring the foreign debt at the moment it is created through currency, trade and financial operations with non-resident counterparts has been disciplined, but not very effectively, by a 1987 regulation: 'Wai zhai tongji jiance zanxin guiding', in *Zhonghua renmin gongheguo guowuyuan gongbao* (*Bulletin of the State Council of the PRC*) (*GWYGB*), No.

20, 1987. For its effects see R. Bertinelli, 'Nuove norme sul controllo statistico del debito estero cinese', in *Gazzetta valutaria e del commercio internazionale*, No. 6, 1988.

16 For a general introduction to the argument see Zhu Xiyin, 'Zhong wai hezi qiye waihui guanli de falu guiding' ('Laws and Regulations on the Management of Foreign Currency in Chinese–Foreign Joint Ventures'), in Sun Yanhu, *Zhonghua renmin gongheguo shewai jingji fa jieshao (Introduction to Economic Laws of the PRC Concerning Foreign Affairs)*, (Beijing, 1986), pp. 68–75.

17 Since 1979 China has joined many important international financial organisations such as the World Bank, the IMF, UNIDO, FAO, UNPD, UNCTAD, ESCP, etc. As regards the use made by China of these organisations, see Shahid Javed Burki, 'Reform and growth in China', in *Finance and Development*, December 1988, pp. 48–9. The most important agreement with the IMF is dated 12 November 1986 and involves the introduction of more profound reforms (*IMF Survey*, 12.1.87, pp. 8–9). The first agreement dates from 1981 (*IMF Survey*, 9.3.81).

18 For a treatment of this aspect up until 1986 see Sun Yanhu, *op. cit.*; for subsequent developments see M.J. Moser (ed.), *Foreign Trade, Investment and the law in PRC*, 2nd edn, (Oxford, 1987).

19 Nicholas R. Lardy, *China's Entry into the World Economy*, (Lanham, 1987).

20 R. Bertinelli, *Verso lo stato di diritto in Cina*, (Milano 1988), pp. 11–20 and 75–81.

21 'China to Readjust Foreign Investment Structure', in *China Economic News*, No. 5, 1989.

22 A wide range of measures was passed after October 1986 with the aim of encouraging foreign investment and strengthening its export orientation.

23 In *GWYGB* No. 11, Ch. 3, paras 16–18.

24 For a brief anthology see Yeh Chang-Mei, 'The Three Kinds of Foreign-invested Enterprises in Mainland China', in *Issues and Studies (IS)*, pp. 58–79. It must be recalled that foreign investments in China take three main forms: the traditional equity joint-venture (*zhong wai hen qiye*); the contractual joint-venture (*zhong wai hezuo jingying qiye*) and the enterprise with exclusively foreign capital (*wai zi qiye*).

25 An interesting treatment of its nature and role is in Fang Zhuofen, 'Lun jingji tequ de zhingxi' ('A Discussion of the Economics of the SEZs'), in *JJYJ*, 1981, No. 8, pp. 54–8. Of the vast literature on the subject, the following are used: M. Oborne, *China's Special Economic Zones*, (Paris, 1986), and Gao Weiwu and Li Ganming, *An Exploration of the Economic Effects of the SEZs* (Dalian, 1986).

26 David K.W. Chu, 'Comparative Bargaining Powers and Strategies of Multilateral Investors in Mainland China's SEZs', *IS*, July 1988, pp. 86ff.

27 'Communist China's "Strategy" in Developing the Coastal Areas', *IS*, March 1988, pp. 1–4, and 'A Heated Debate on Coastal Areas' Development Strategy', ibid., June 1988, pp. 1–4.

CHRONOLOGY: MAJOR EVENTS, 1976–90

1976

8 January
Death of Premier Zhou Enlai.

5 April
Demonstrations in Tiananmen Square.

7 April
The demonstrations in Tiananmen, suppressed violently by 'Gang of Four' supporters, are labelled a 'counterrevolutionary political incident'. Deng Xiaoping is dismissed from his posts and Hua Guofeng is appointed acting Premier and First Vice-Chairman of the CCP, significantly Deng retains his party membership.

28 July
Earthquake in Tangshan.

9 September
Death of Mao Zedong.

6 October
The 'Gang of Four' are arrested. The following day Hua Guofeng is elected Chairman of the CCP.

1977

March
Articles begin to appear supporting the 1975 policy documents denounced by the 'Gang of Four' as the 'Three Poisonous

223

weeds'. The documents were closely associated with Deng Xiaoping.

16–21 July
The Third Plenum of the Tenth Central Committee restores
Deng Xiaoping in his functions of Vice-Premier and Vice-Chair-
man of the CCP. Hua Guofeng is confirmed as Premier and
Chair of the CCP. The 'Gang of Four' are expelled from the
party.

12–18 August
Eleventh Congress of the CCP. Hua Guofeng announces an
official end to the Cultural Revolution. The 'Gang of Four' are
denounced as 'ultra-rightist'.

1978

26 February
Meeting of the Fifth NPC opens. In his Work Report, Hua
Guofeng unveils a new economic programme based on the
ambitious 1976–85 Ten-Year Plan. The rhetoric resembles that
of the Great Leap Forward.

May
The slogan 'seek truth from facts' is launched, within a campaign of re-evaluation of Mao Zedong's Thought.

12 July
Signing of the Sino-Japanese Treaty of Friendship.

August
Visit of Hua Guofeng to Rumania and Yugoslavia signals
China's interest in developing links with those socialist states
thought to be the most independent from Moscow.

11–21 October
The All-China Federation of Trade Unions holds its first conference since 1957.

15 November
The Beijing Municipal Party Committee formally reverses the
verdict on the Tiananmen demonstrations of April 1976.

15–19 November
The first big-character posters appear at Xidan, Beijing, marking the beginning of the Democracy Wall movement.

27 November
Amnesty international publishes a report on political imprisonment in China.

16 December
Announcement of the normalisation of Sino-American relations (to start as from 1 January 1979)

12–18 December
The Third Plenum of the Eleventh Central Committee decides to make economic modernization the primary focus of party work. The plenum marks the beginning of economic reform starting with reform of the agricultural sector. The Tiananmen square demonstrations are recognised as 'entirely revolutionary actions'.

1979

1 January
US–China normalisation takes effect.

8 January
Peasant demonstrations in Beijing.

27 January
Peng Zhen, formerly Mayor of Beijing and later arrested during the Cultural Revolution, is rehabilitated. In the following February he is appointed Chair of a new legal commission of the standing committee of the NPC.

28 January
Deng Xiaoping leaves for his first visit to the United States.

17 February
China launches her military offensive against Vietnam, following the Vietnamese invasion of Kampuchea (December 1978).

29 March
Wei Jingsheng, leader of the Democracy Wall movement and author of the article 'The Fifth Modernization: Democracy' is

arrested as a 'counterrevolutionary'. It is the beginning of the suppression of the democratic movement.

30 March
Deng Xiaoping stresses adherence to the 'Four Basic Principles': Socialism, the dictatorship of the proletariat, party leadership, and Marxism–Leninism–Mao Zedong Thought. This sets limits to the parameters of debates about democratisation.

3 April
China denounces the Sino-Soviet Friendship Treaty of 1950.

April
The State Council decides to increase the quota procurement prices for the major rural products.

18 June–1 July
The Second Session of the Fifth NPC abolishes the revolutionary committees set up during the Cultural Revolution as organs of local government and replaces them by elected peoples's congresses. It also adopts a code of criminal law, the first since 1949. Chen Yun is appointed, with Bo Yibo and Yao Yilin, Vice-Premier. Peng Zhen is elected Vice-Chairman of the Standing Committee. The ambitious Ten-Year Plan is postponed and in its place a three-year programme of 'readjustment, restructuring, consolidating and improving the national economy' is introduced.

July
Creation of the four Special Economic Zones in Guangdong and Fujian. Joint-ventures with foreign partners are legalised.

16 October
Wei Jingsheng is sentenced to fifteen years' imprisonment.

October–November
Visit of Hua Guofeng to Western Europe. Sino-Soviet talks concerning the normalisation of diplomatic relations begin.

1980

16 January
Deng Xiaoping's speech to about ten thousand party and state officials in Beijing on the need for modernisation.

20 January
China breaks off talks with the Soviet Union following the Soviet invasion of Afghanistan (25 December 1979).

January–February
First major reshuffle of the PLA affecting eight of the military commanders and five political commissars.

23–29 February
Fifth Plenum of the Eleventh Central Committee. The Secretariat is reinstated under the leadership of Hu Yaobang. Both Hu Yaobang and Zhao Ziyang are appointed to the Standing Committee of the Politburo. The 'resignation' from top party and state posts of Beijing Mayor Wu De and various other members of the 'whatever' faction are accepted. Liu Shaoqi is rehabilitated.

April–May
The PRC gains membership of the IMF and the World Bank.

18 August
Deng Xiaoping delivers a speech to an Enlarged Session of the Politburo on the need to reform the party and state structure. It is Deng's most far-reaching criticism of the inadequacies of the political structure and appears to sanction major reforms.

30 August–10 September
The Third Session of the Fifth NPC accepts the resignation of Hua Guofeng as Premier and he is replaced by Zhao Ziyang. The Ten-Year Economic Plan is formally abandoned.

September
The document n.75 of the CC legalises the 'production responsibility system' in agriculture.

November
Trial of the 'Gang of Four' opens in Beijing.

December
A work conference of the Central Committee approves the first economic 'readjustment'.

1981

April

Mao supporters in the PLA begin a media attack on bourgeois liberalisation' through an attack on a story by the writer Bai Hua. The story 'unrequited love' is denounced as a reflection of 'anarchism, ultra-individualism and bourgeois liberalisation'.

27–29 June

The Sixth Plenum of the Eleventh Central Committee accepts Hua Guofeng's resignation from the post of Chairman and replaces him with Hu Yaobang. The session adopts the 'Resolution on Certain Questions in the History of our Party Since the Founding of the PRC', which contains the party's assessment of Mao Zedong's achievements and errors.

Summer

A campaign is launched against bureaucracy and corruption.

30 November

Fourth Session of the Fifth NPC opens. In his report, Zhao Zyiang states that the readjustment policy would be continued.

1982

17 August

Joint Sino-American communiqué on arms sales to Taiwan.

1–11 September

Twelfth Party Congress. Hua Guofeng is removed from the Politburo. Hu Yaobang is confirmed as Party General Secretary. A new constitution is adopted that eradicates the remnants of the radical rethoric of the Cultural Revolution. A Central Advisory Commission to the Central Committee is established to ease veteran cadres into retirement.

November

Huang Hua, the Foreign Minister, goes to Moscow for the funeral ceremony for Brezhnev.

November

The 'production responsibility system' already applied to agriculture is extended to industrial and other state-owned enterprises.

4 December
The Fifth NPC meeting approves a new state constitution. The Sixth Five-Year Plan is approved. Under the new constitution, the people's communes lose their political functions, being replaced by the township (*xiang*) as the administrative unit at local level.

1983

January
Document n.1 of the Central Committee officially endorses the 'responsibility system' for agriculture and stresses household contracting.

1 June
A new taxation system is introduced for enterprises.

18 June
The First Session of the Sixth NPC elects Li Xiannian President of the PRC. Zhao Ziyang is re-elected Premier.

11 October
The Second Plenum of the Twelfth Central Committee approves a three-year 'consolidation' campaign within the party.

November
A campaign is launched against 'spiritual pollution'.

1984

January
The campaign against 'spiritual pollution' begins to soften.

April
Fourteen coastal towns are opened to foreign investment.

26 September
Joint Sino-British declaration on Hong Kong is signed.

20 October
The Third Plenum of the Twelfth Central Committee approves the 'Decision of the Central Committee of the CCP on the Reform of the Economic Structure'. The decision chronicles the problems in the urban economy and proposes a more thorough-going reform than the piecemeal approach to date.

21 December
Visit to Beijing of the Soviet Vice-Premier Ivan Arkhipov and signing of a Sino-Soviet agreement on bilateral trade and economic, scientific and technical cooperation between the two countries.

31 December
The *People's Daily* announces the intention of the state to abolish its monopoly over purchase and marketing of major farm products. This is codified in the Central Committee Document n. 1 of January 1985

1985

January
Publication of Deng Xiaoping's speech advocating the 'open-door policy' for China.

19 April
Hu Yaobang announces that China is to reduce the strength of its armed forces by about 1 million by the end of 1986.

May
Rise of food prices in Chinese towns.

23 May
The Military Affairs Commission announces the reduction in number and reorganisation of military regions.

July
Vice-Premier Yao Yilin's visit to Moscow, where he signed a five-year trade agreement between China and USSR.

18–23 September
CCP Special Conference at which Chen Yun delivers a speech critical of the consequences of the reforms. The conference approves the guidelines for the Seventh Five-Year plan (1986–1990). Major personnel changes are agreed. Ye Jianying steps down from all his functions and ten members of the Politburo resign, six of whom are military figures. Chen Yun and Deng Xiaoping remain.

18 September
Students protests occur on the occasion of the fifty-fourth anni-

versary of the Japanese invasion of China. Now, they attack the new 'Japanese economic invasion' of China.

1986

January
Eight thousand party and state officials meet to discuss the need to improve party and state work-style. An anti-corruption drive is launched.

10 March
China is admitted to the Asian Development Bank.

16 March
Arkhipov visits Beijing again. The decision is taken to exchange Chinese and Soviet technicians.

25 March
Opening of the Fourth Session of the Sixth NPC. Zhao Ziyang outlines the objectives of the Seventh Five-Year plan.

May
Opening of the debate on the 'double hundred flowers', concerning intellectual freedoms.

26 July
Speech by Mikhail Gorbachev in Vladivostok, defining the new Soviet policy towards China.

28 September
The Sixth Plenum of the Twelfth Central Committee adopts a resolution stressing the need to improve work in the ideological and cultural spheres. This was adopted after stormy summer discussions in Beidahe about political reform.

29 September
Visit to Beijing of Polish leader General Jaruzelski.

11 October
New legislation on joint-ventures.

28 October
Peng Zhen makes a speech critical of reform at a Standing Committee meeting of the NPC.

25 November
Peng Zhen again attacks the reforms at a meeting of the Standing Committee of the NPC.

5–9 December
Students demonstrate at the China Science and Technology University in Hefei, Anhui province. The head of the University is astro-physicist Fang Lizhi. Demonstrations follow in Shenzhen and Kunming (14–17), and in Shanghai (19–24).

23 December
Students demonstrate in Beijing, calling for more freedom and better living conditions.

25 December
At a meeting some members of the Military Affairs Commission suggest introducing martial law.

26 December
A decree is issued banning unauthorised demonstrations.

29 December
New demonstrations in Beijing.

30 December
Deng Xiaoping supports the regulations to ban unauthorised demonstrations and suggests student leaders should be arrested.

31 December
The Chinese government announces that there is a plot to overthrow the government and places new limits on all demonstrations.

1987

1 January
Students demonstrate in Tiananmen in defiance of the new regulations.

5 January
The *People's Daily* condemns the student demonstrations.

6 January
A new campaign against 'bourgeois liberalisation' is launched.

12 January
Fang Lizhi is removed from his post as President of the China University of Science and Technology and, together with the writers Wang Ruowang and Liu Binyan, he is expelled from the party.

16 January
At an enlarged session of the Standing Committee of the Politburo the 'resignation' of Hu Yaobang as General Secretary is accepted. Zhao Ziyang is named acting General Secretary.

18–20 January
Zhao Ziyang underlines that the reform policy will continue. Zhao lays down limits to the campaign against 'bourgeois liberalisation'.

9–27 February
Border negotiations between China and the Soviet Union, suspended in 1979, take place.

16 February
Publication of Deng Xiaoping's 1962 speech on democratic centralism.

2–3 March
US Secretary of State, George Shultz visits Beijing.

15 March
In a speech to senior party leaders, Zhao Ziyang reasserts his determination that the campaign against 'bourgeois liberalisation' should remain within strictly defined limits and not impede the country's drive for economic reform.

25 March
Fifth session of the Sixth NPC. Zhao is forced to amend his report on the Seventh Five-Year Plan to take into account delegates' criticism, especially from those in grain-growing provinces. He stresses the problem of imbalance in the economy but underlines the need for 'structural economic reform'.

29 May
Deng Xiaoping supports Zhao Ziyang's attempts to limit the effects of the campaign against 'bourgeois liberalisation'.

1–7 October
Riots in Tibet are put down. The US Senate protests.

25 October
The Thirteenth Party Congress opens. Zhao confirms the need for economic reform and proposes the creation of a *de facto* civil service. The reformist line seems again to prevail. Chen Yun, Deng Xiaoping and Li Xiannian all stand down from the Standing Committee of the Politburo.

4 November
The Chinese Foreign Minister refutes American allegations concerning the sale to Iran of Chinese *Silkworm* missiles.

17 November
Li Peng is named acting Premier.

1988

23 January
Zhao outlines a strategy of economic growth based on accelerating the development of urban coastal areas.

25 March
The First Session of the Seventh NPC confirms the appointment of Li Peng as Premier. Deng Xiaoping is re-elected Chairman of the Military Affairs Committee. Yang Shangkun is elected President of the PRC and Wan Li is named Chairman of the Standing Committee of the NPC. After much delay, the Enterprise Law that reduces significantly the authority of the party at the workplace is passed.

March
Incidents between China and Vietnam over the Spratley Islands.

Summer
Unprecedented inflation begins. News about price reforms provoke panic among the urban population.

15–17 August
At a Politiburo meeting in Beidaihe Zhao unveils a 'tentative plan' on price and wage reforms. It is rumoured that a decision is taken to prevent Zhao speaking out on economic issues.

30 August
The State Council decides to freeze the price liberalisation and adopts anti-inflationary measures.

1 September
Following the meeting in Beijing between Soviet and Chinese vice-ministers, an agreement on the withdrawal of Vietnamese forces from Kampuchea is reached.

15–21 September
The Politburo decides to postpone price reform for at least two years.

26–30 September
Third Plenum of the Thirteenth Central Committee approves the launch of deflationary economic measures within a more general 'austerity' programme. The Central Committee supports Premier Li Peng's efforts to slow the pace of economic reforms and to force new administrative controls on economic activities. The plenum marks a backtrack on reform.

1–3 December
Foreign Minister Qian Qichen visits Moscow.

9–23 December
Visit to China of the Indian Prime Minister Rajiv Gandhi.

18–21 December
Meeting of CCP intellectuals to mark the tenth anniversary of reforms. Su Shaozi makes a critical speech attacking the lack of political reforms

1989
6 January
Fang Lizhi sends an open letter to Deng Xiaoping calling for the release of political prisoners.

28 January
The death of the Panchem-Lama is followed by new riots in Tibet.

2 February
Letter to Deng Xiaoping from forty intellectuals calling for press freedom, freedom of political prisoners and democracy.

25–26 February
Visit to Beijing of the American President George Bush. Fang Lizhi is barred from attending the reception at the US Embassy.

5–6 March
Riots in Lhasa cause the Chinese government to declare martial law.

21–27 March
Second Session of the Seventh NPC. Prime Minister Li Peng reaffirms the austerity programme and clear indications are made that political liberalisation will be curtailed.

15 April
Death of Hu Yaobang.

20 April
The Beijing Autonomous Students' Federation is founded.

25 April
Students demonstrate in Tiananmen Square to mourn Hu's death.

24–29 April
Zhao's visit to North Korea.

26 April
The *People's Daily* publishes a hard-line editorial condemning the student demonstrations and calls the movement a 'planned conspiracy' against the party.

27 April
Once again students in Beijing respond by taking to the streets.

3 May
Zhao Ziyang in a speech commemorating the May Fourth Movement although calling for political stability does not include the need 'to oppose bourgeois liberalisation'.

4 May
Meeting of the Asian Development Bank in Beijing where Zhao Ziyang gives a speech referring to the need to meet the 'reasonable demands' of the students through democratic and legal means.

13 May
Students begin a hunger strike in Tiananmen Square to press their demands for a dialogue with the authorities.

15–18 May
Gorbachev's visit to China marks the first Sino-Soviet summit meeting since 1959. The normalisation of relations is officially stated.

19 May
Li Peng declares that martial law will come into force in parts of Beijing the following day.

21 May
Beijing population joins the students to prevent the PLA occupying the city.

3–4 June
Troops use force to enter Beijing, killing civilians and take over Tiananmen Square.

5 June
US President George Bush announces the suspension of all government-to-government sales and commercial exports of weapons to China.

9 June
In a major speech, Deng Xiaoping justifies the repression.

23 June
The Central Committee meets to oust Zhao Ziyang from his positions (although he retains his party membership). Jiang Zemin, Mayor of Shanghai, is named General Secretary of the Party.

July
Secret visit to China by US National Security Adviser Brent Scowcroft.

October
For the first time in a decade, industrial output falls on a month-to-month basis (by 2.1 per cent).

6–9 November
Fifth Plenum of the Thirteenth Central Committee. Yang Shang-kun is promoted to first Vice-Chairman of the Military Affairs

Commission with Deng Xiaoping resigning from his last official party post as Chair of the Commission. He is replaced by Jiang Zemin. A final communiqué issued confirms the party's intention to proceed with the economic austerity programme.

9–10 December
Visit to China by US National Security Adviser Brent Scowcroft.

26 December
Yao Yilin is removed from his State Council post as Minister-in-charge of the State Planning Commission. He is replaced by Zou Jiahua, the Minister of Machine Building and Electronics Industry.

28 December
Beijing Municipal People's Congress passes regulations banning gatherings, rallies and demonstrations in Tiananmen without prior permission.

1990

10 January
Premier Li Peng announces that Martial Law will be lifted in Beijing.

28 February
The *Liberation Army Daily* calls for a tightening of political work in the PLA to ensure that 'guns are in the hands of the politically reliable'.

February
Li Peng visits Shenzhen Special Economic Zone and announces that the further opening of coastal areas and establishment of SEZs were still major components of the reforms.

9–12 March
Sixth Plenum of the Thirteenth Central Committee adopts a resolution calling on the party to develop closer ties with the 'masses'. This stresses the need to solve problems that concern them.

20 March–4 April
Third Session of the Seventh NPC opens in Beijing. It accepts Deng Xiaoping's resignation as Chair of the State Military

Affairs Commission and his replacement by Jiang Zemin. The session passes the 'Basic Law of the Hong Kong Special Administrative Region'. Despite reaffirming commitment to the austerity programme, there are clear signs that it is being relaxed.

15 April
The *People's Daily* publishes a Chen Yun speech from 17 July 1987 calling on leaders to listen to different views within the party.

23 April
Premier Li Peng arrives in Moscow, the first such visit for twenty-six years. No joint communiqué is issued.

1 May
Martial law is lifted in Lhasa.